100 JEWISH BRIDES

100 JEWISH BRIDES

Stories from Around the World

Edited by Barbara Vinick and Shulamit Reinharz

INDIANA UNIVERSITY PRESS

This book is a publication of

Indiana University Press
Office of Scholarly Publishing
Herman B Wells Library 350
1320 East 10th Street
Bloomington, Indiana 47405 USA

iupress.org

Manufactured in the United States of America

First Printing 2024

Cataloging information is available from the Library of Congress.

ISBN 978-0-253-06836-1 (hardback)
ISBN 978-0-253-06838-5 (ebook)

Cover image: *Upper left*, Cynthia Castro Cohen-Henriquez and Rabbi David Cohen-Henriquez, Panama. *Upper middle*, Noreen Daniel and Rabbi Romiel Daniel, India. *Upper right*, brides with gifts, Madagascar. *Lower left*, Rut Wangeci and attendants, Kenya. *Lower right*, Mushka Kantor Kaltmann, Chabad, Thailand.

With appreciation to Kulanu and Hadassah-Brandeis Institute

CONTENTS

ACKNOWLEDGMENTS

We are extremely grateful to the authors who generously expended time and effort to share their stories with us, either writing the stories themselves and graciously accepting our edits or making their contributions as patient and forthcoming interviewees online or in person. This is your book!

We are also grateful to the people whom we contacted to ask for referrals to potential authors. The following people provided information that often resulted in a story from a country we wanted to include in the collection, as well as those who gave us other information. Our sincere thanks for your efforts. We couldn't have obtained stories from eighty-three countries without you.

Sara Bauminger
Nina Ben-Ami
Joseph Benatov
Karen Bermudez
Rita Blitt
Harriet Bograd
Ayelet Cohen
Paula Dolinsky
Michael Durbin
Roslyn Eschelbacher
Lisa Fishbayn Joffe
Harriett Fox
Beverly Frankel
Titti Frankel

Ali Freedman
Julia Freedson
Kaj Fried
Beverly Friend
Rachel Garrity
Desiree Gil
Rita Gomel
Eliana Gurfinkiel
Rita Hanin
Charlotte Ikels
Shamira Joshua
Ieshia Karasik
Irina Karasik
Ruth Katz

Judi Kloper
Hadassa Kubat
Molly Levine
Roberta Leviton
Janet Levy
Nina Lichtenstein
Devorah Lynn
Erica Lyons
Sharon Oran
David Orenstein
Alvah Parker
Rabbi Peretz Chein
Amy Powell
Rabbi Michael Ragozin

Judy Remis
Shep Remis
Katka Reszke
Tania Reytan-
   Marincheshka
Sarah Rosehill
Amy Rotenberg
Myra Schiff
Annika Schildt
Bea Schutz
Marilyn Segal

Noam Sender
Edward Serotta
Riki Shapira
Marjorie Siegel
Richard Siegel
Monica Sisay
Carole Skowronski
Marian Sofaer
Lucy Steinitz
Ana Stella Schwartz
Bonita Sussman

Anne Vinick Garrity
Emily Vinick
Ezra Vogel
Shep Wahnon
Felicia Waldman
Jani Wase Vinick
Debs Weinberg
Ruth Weinstein
Martin Weinstein
Sarah Winer
Anita Zwick

We are grateful to the staff of Hadassah-Brandeis Institute, especially Lisa Fishbayn Joffe, Sylvia Fishman, Nancy Leonard, Debby Olins, and Amy Powell.

Barbara thanks the board of Kulanu for opportunities to meet people from the far corners of the globe.

Shula thanks her husband, Jehuda, for traveling with her to many of the countries represented here.

100 JEWISH BRIDES

INTRODUCTION

SEVERAL YEARS AGO, Brandeis University sociologists and friends Barbara Vinick and Shulamit Reinharz decided to explore the variation of Jewish customs around the globe, drawing on Jewish women's reports that we would gather. Are Jewish customs fixed and uniform, immune from change? We knew that not all Jews lived according to the rules of Jewish law. How do Jews around the world actually live their lives? How do Jewish customs reflect the cultures in which the participants live? For our first project, we asked if Purim—the springtime holiday celebrating Queen Esther's courage in saving the Jews, which is described in the Scroll of Esther—was celebrated the same way everywhere. What we found startled us. In some communities, Purim was the most important Jewish holiday of the year and was celebrated extensively, in contrast to other communities where it was a minor occasion.[1]

We were able to undertake the Purim project because each of us had extensive contacts among Jews in a variety of countries. Barbara is a devoted board member of Kulanu (Hebrew for "all of us"), an organization that supports isolated, emerging, and returning Jewish communities in Africa, Asia, Latin America, and elsewhere around the world.[2] In 1997, Shulamit created a new research center at Brandeis University, Hadassah-Brandeis Institute (HBI), whose purpose is to develop new ideas about Jews and gender worldwide.[3] In doing so, she had a large network of Jewish scholars, rabbis, and activists from around the globe. When we finished gathering our stories, they were assembled in a softcover illustrated volume, replete with photographs, in an internal publication supported by National Hadassah and HBI. Copies of *Esther's Legacy: Celebrating Purim around the World* quickly ran out after it was used as a learning tool in many Jewish groups.

1

Intrigued by what we learned, we embarked on our next project. This time our focus was on bat mitzvah, the Jewish girl's coming of age at twelve or thirteen, when she assumes adult responsibilities. Our questions were straightforward: Are b'not mitzvah (plural of bat mitzvah) recognized and celebrated throughout the world? When and where was the first such celebration held? Are the customs around bat mitzvah varied or basically uniform? Once again, the material we discovered astonished us. We learned that the first recognition of girls' coming of age took place in Italy and was then imitated in the United States. We learned that some ceremonies involved a single girl while others involved a whole group. And we learned that there was a wide range of expectations: some girls engaged in extensive learning of Jewish and Hebrew materials beforehand, while others put on a musical-theatrical performance, typically organized by their mothers and involving elaborate costumes and set designs. Our collection of photographs and stories about b'not mitzvah was so large that we turned to Indiana University Press to publish our book, *Today I Am a Woman: Stories of Bat Mitzvah around the World* (2012). Once again, our work generated interest and was nominated for and won awards, and the two of us—either together or separately—were invited to make presentations throughout the country.

You can probably guess what happened next. We embarked on our third cultural project—Jewish weddings from the bride's point of view. Do Jewish weddings vary in diverse international communities? Are particular features always present? As was the case in our previous projects, we found enormous variation in every aspect of the Jewish marriage ritual, from a brief ceremony in a home or rabbi's study to weeklong rituals and elaborate shindigs.

It turns out that the topic of weddings was much more complex than that of Purim or bat mitzvah. The stories in our book on Purim were arranged alphabetically by country; we arranged the material about Jewish girls' coming of age by the continent of the country where the bat mitzvah ceremony took place. In the case of our stories about weddings, we have arranged our material in two ways: by stages of the wedding process and by special topics. The "stage" structure we developed derived from what the women (or their surrogates, including their mothers and daughters) told us about the process of Jewish marriages. Our book—and many of the stories we collected—starts with how Jewish brides met their partners. Next, we highlight courtship and engagement or betrothal. Stories that concern brides' conversion to Judaism before marriage come next. Subsequent chapters deal with invitations to the wedding ceremony, how the bride or others selected the venue for the wedding, special activities that occurred before the ceremony, and the ketubah (wedding contract). The ceremony itself played a large role in most of the stories, but we chose some of the most fascinating examples for that chapter. Our final chapter within the "stages" framework deals with customs that took place shortly after the wedding.

As you will see, these testimonies are not devoted exclusively to one stage of the journey to the bimah and beyond; we could have placed many stories in multiple chapters. Our decisions were based on elements that were unique, interesting, or particularly relevant to that story.

Because our Jewish brides' stories come from all over the world and from previous eras, we decided to create separate chapters for special topics, particularly circumstances that varied significantly from the norm, such as arranged marriages and Jewish weddings that occurred during or shortly after the Holocaust. We also decided to create a separate chapter for stories of weddings in Israel because Israeli weddings are currently the subject of intense and even acrimonious debate and policymaking. Because Jewish intermarriage is pervasive around the world,[4] except for in Israel, and steadily increasing, we have two chapters on the topic that focus on prenuptial conversion and intermarriage, respectively.

It is our hope that readers of this book will enjoy learning about how Jews marry—and used to marry—around the world and may get some ideas about how they want to celebrate their own marriage. Readers may not be aware of the existence of all of these Jewish communities. Simply learning about them is eye opening. Focusing on marriage shows us that Jewish life is always in flux over time and space. Weddings now reflect the tastes and interests of the couple as much as they do Jewish law and customs.

Barbara solicited stories from women around the globe who came from diverse Jewish communities, some well known and others unfamiliar to mainstream Jews, and gave them few instructions: include the place and date of the wedding, attach a photograph, and limit the story to about one thousand words. (She interviewed in person or remotely a few women who declined to write their stories but wanted to have them included.) When we received the stories, she edited them as lightly as possible and sent them back to the authors for approval. Then the two of us sat down to analyze and organize what had been sent to us.

As it turned out, women did not limit their stories to the wedding ceremonies but rather placed their marriages within the context of a larger narrative of their lives. Most included how they met their partner and how their lives have evolved since they married. We also discovered that many women wanted to write the stories that had come down to them of their mother's or grandmother's wedding—some in amazing detail. When they did not find their own wedding particularly interesting, they wrote about someone else's—as long as a Jew was involved—such as a cousin's or a congregant's. People wanted to write a story that had an interesting twist. Some wrote about why they rejected old customs with which they no longer identified, and others wrote about why they chose to perpetuate these customs, some of which had been adopted through the ages from their non-Jewish neighbors. All in all, the stories are reflections of the way people understand Jewish weddings, with their joys, strains, and variations. This is not a complete compendium of wedding customs—that would probably require an encyclopedia. Rather it is a glimpse into the stories that brides tell about one hundred Jewish weddings from eighty-three countries in many historical eras. In summary, this collection represents a larger project of learning about how Jewish life was and is actually lived around the world by hearing about women's activities and listening to their voices.

ONE

—ᘓᘏᘉ—

MEETING

THE MEETING OF THE BRIDE and groom is always the first step in an eventual marriage, whether the couple were childhood playmates or had first laid eyes on each other the week before. Meeting the spouse is a universally vivid memory for those involved and often a milestone event in family lore.

"Meeting stories" are as old as the Bible. Although we do not know how Sarah met Abraham, we do know how their son Isaac met his wife, Rebecca, a story told in detail in Genesis 24. Abraham's emissary, Eliezer, found the virtuous Rebecca at a well. Similarly, a generation later, Isaac's son Jacob saw his future wife, Rachel, at a well. Rachel's father, Laban, then tricked Jacob into marrying his older daughter, Leah.

In these ancient stories, the father had a major role in the couples' meeting and deciding whether they could marry. To this day, among some groups of ultra-Orthodox Jews, the parents (or just the father) still have this role not so much by Jewish law but by custom. *Shtisel*, an Israeli television series now popular in the United States, shows the prerogative assumed by a father, with the help of a shadchan (matchmaker), to find an appropriate wife for his son in a contemporary ultra-Orthodox Jerusalem community.

This type of "arranged" marriage was commonplace in Mizrahi (Middle Eastern) Jewish communities in generations past. Chapter 11, "Arranged and Forced Marriages," tells some of these stories. For the most part, however, Jewish women have been free to choose on their own. This does not mean that parental and community influences have been lacking. Many Jewish women remember mothers and other interested relatives and friends urging them to meet a Jewish man, even going so far as to fix up a couple on a blind date. This chapter's story from Zimbabwe illustrates what the writer calls an "assisted" introduction, as does the story from Scotland.

Similarly, Jewish institutions—synagogues and community centers—encourage endogamy (marriage within one's own group) by supporting youth groups, social clubs, and singles groups. Hillel chapters, social action groups, and other organizations where Jews gather provide fertile ground at institutions of higher learning. Several of the brides in this chapter—from Australia, Ireland, and Russia—met their spouses at these venues.

Meetings that lead to Jewish inmarriage (a marriage between two Jews) may be accidental or intentional. The most intentional meetings nowadays are those aided by online dating sites such as JDate. A recent study indicated that in 2017 close to 40 percent of couples in the United States met online,[1] a method that has surpassed introduction by a friend or relative. An intentional relic of the past was the mail-order bride, a stranger brought from afar by a single man with the intention to marry. The unusual story from Syria documents such a situation. While several stories in this collection describe "love at first sight" on the part of people initially attracted to their mates, this one begins with revulsion.

"Accidental" meetings are not uncommon, however. The story from Belgium memorializes an unplanned meeting during a voyage on board a ship. But the workplace has been and continues to be the most significant site for couples to meet accidentally. The entrance of large numbers of women into the labor force since the 1960s has provided financial independence for women, accompanied by later marriage and greater choice of marital partners, including partners who are not Jewish. Chapter 12, "Intermarriage and Interethnic Jewish Marriage," and accounts in other chapters record the stories of brides who met their husbands through work.

AUSTRALIA

Peta Pellach

Peta's story illustrates how meetings, weddings, and the circumstances that surround them change from generation to generation. Nowadays, the marriage of a twenty-year-old Jewish bride and a twenty-one-year-old groom would be more unusual than it was when Peta's parents married in a traditional synagogue ceremony in the early 1950s. Her own wedding in her parents' garden, rushed because both spouses, who met while folk dancing, were students thousands of miles away, was emblematic of the times. Peta's daughter's wedding was also a sign of the times, planned and financed by the bride and groom themselves. Of course, not every family includes grandparents who divorced after forty-seven years and a divorced mother in her eighties, unable to remarry (due to a rabbinical stricture) and living with her partner.

In 1950s Melbourne, if a Jewish girl wanted to meet and marry a Jewish boy, she would go to a synagogue dance. Mizrachi Shul in Melbourne was—and still is—Orthodox as were all except one of Melbourne's synagogues in those days. Perhaps surprisingly, holding dances for young adults, where boys met girls to dance to the latest music, was considered acceptable and even advisable. There, in 1951, my parents met and, after a brief courtship, decided to get married.

My father was not yet twenty-one, and his father thought it was too early for him to marry. So my parents waited until my father was twenty-one when they no longer required parental permission. My mother had just turned twenty. As they walked down the aisle of Melbourne Hebrew Congregation, her father whispered to her, "You don't have to do this, you know."

Except for this comment, everything was traditional—a synagogue service on a Sunday afternoon, a white dress, bridesmaids, a wedding reception at a city hotel with lots of speeches and mediocre kosher catering, followed by a honeymoon at a nearby resort for a few days.

The marriage lasted forty-seven years. Then my mother decided that her father had been right. My father had another wedding. My mother, now in her eighties, lives in Israel with her partner. As she is a divorcée and he is a *kohen* (a descendent of the Jewish priestly class), they cannot marry under Orthodox law. But one wedding was enough for her!

My husband and I also met at a dance—Israeli folk dancing at Columbia University in New York, where I was a graduate student. He drove me home and, miraculously in Manhattan, found parking near my apartment. We had coffee and I taught him to play Scrabble that first night. Our courtship was brief. When Aharon rang my parents to ask for permission to marry me, they had no idea who he was. I explained to them that we were on a summer break and if we were to marry in Australia, everything had to be arranged very quickly.

I had always dreamed of getting married in our garden. By giving them such short notice, I realized my dream. The wedding was held at my parents' home, which was large enough to accommodate fifty guests inside and many more in the back garden for the ceremony. It took place in perfect late winter weather on a Sunday morning. All of my childhood friends were there. They had some light refreshments, danced in the garden, and then they went home. We continued inside with the wedding breakfast for close family members and a few VIP guests.

I should have admitted earlier that broken marriages are something of a family tradition. My paternal grandparents were divorced in an acrimonious breakup. At the breakfast, they refused to be in the same room. So we had some guests in the large study with Gramps, some guests in the lounge with Nana, and the bridal table for immediate family in the dining room between them. Luckily, the family all behaved, the caterers managed well, and by late afternoon we were done. Two days later, we went back to New York to continue our studies.

Our eldest daughter was born eleven months later. That daughter's wedding typifies her generation much as ours did and my parents did theirs. Meirav and Yair met at a party in Tel Aviv, knowing immediately that they were right for each other. Older than their parents had been and financially independent, they did not expect us to arrange the wedding for them. We flew in as guests.

Meirav and Yair chose Friday morning for their ceremony, a day and time that has become quite trendy in Israel. The wedding feast had to be vegan—otherwise, the groom would not have eaten! The venue had to be beautiful, so a rooftop in Jaffa was chosen. But some things were traditional. Yair went to the chuppah first, accompanied by his parents. Little girls threw rose petals ahead of Meirav's entry. Aharon and I walked the last steps to the chuppah with her. There were speeches at the wedding breakfast, something quite unusual in Israel. The couple addressed each other, Yair explaining that he had waited so long to get married because he had not yet met Meirav, and Meirav expressing her love by singing to Yair.

After more musical entertainment by family members and dancing to recorded music, people gradually filtered out to prepare for Shabbat. That night, I hosted our family and Yair's for a Friday night dinner in our rented apartment in Tel Aviv. On Sunday, we all went hiking. The couple went on a honeymoon a couple of weeks later, after Aharon and I had returned to Australia.

We have since made aliyah to Israel. Another of our children has married in a typical Israeli wedding, held in a wedding hall with over four hundred guests. Whether my two unmarried daughters choose the model of my parents, us, or either of their siblings, it will be fine with us.

Postscript: Aharon and I have no plans to continue the family tradition of divorce.

BELGIUM

Suzanne Vromen

*Some memories are indelible, including the smallest details. Suzanne's recollections
of meeting her husband and their courtship may be more out-of-the-ordinary than
most, but their vividness is not unusual concerning milestone events. Suzanne's
family was among the lucky Belgians who were able to flee when Nazi Germany
invaded at the onset of World War II. They escaped to the Belgian Congo where her
father had business contacts. She remembers boarding a train with paper money
secreted around the handle of the tennis racket she carried. Suzanne is cofounder of
the women's studies program at Bard College and professor emeritus of sociology.*

On a sunny late afternoon in 1952, the Artzah, an Israeli ship owned by the
Zim shipping company, let out a sharp whistle and slowly edged out of Haifa
Bay. I had been working in Jerusalem at the Israeli Ministry of Labor, and now
I was heading home to Brussels. I waved to my boyfriend Martin who was seeing me off, turned away from the deck when a gong announced mealtime, and
went in search of the dining room. In 1952, food was scarce in Israel. *Tzenah* this
scarcity was called. It meant very little meat and fish, severely rationed, and few
fresh vegetables or fruit. Bread and cakes were available but hardly anything
else. Once the boat had left territorial waters, real meals could be served. The
purser seated me at a large round table next to a good-looking young man with
abundant salt-and-pepper hair and wearing an old-fashioned brown suit. We
were soon served a delicious meal. A platter of large schnitzels was especially
remarkable. I had not seen a schnitzel for ages and had nearly forgotten its taste.
We did not talk much as we were too busy enjoying the plentiful food. Everyone
was stuffed. "Who would like the extra schnitzel?" asked our waiter, pointing
to the lonely piece of meat on the large platter. My neighbor volunteered. "He
has a healthy appetite," I thought to myself.

As we were finishing our meal, my neighbor, who introduced himself as
Ben, turned toward me and said, "Would you like to meet Lena Horne? I have
a letter of introduction to her." Lena Horne had just finished a rousing series of
performances in Israel and was on our ship, traveling in first class. Of course I
wanted to meet Lena Horne! Off we went to meet a most charming and beautiful woman who would dance with the corpulent captain every evening for
our shipmates' entertainment. She wore the most beautiful outfits, pale green
or mauve with matching shoes. In her arms, the captain became as light as
a feather. When we met her that evening, we chatted for a while about Ben's

friends who had given him the letter of introduction and whom Lena Horne knew very well. She wanted to know about the Weizmann Institute, where Ben and his friends worked at the time, and she invited us to come and chat with her every day around noon time. Obviously, she liked us and we gladly accepted her invitation.

Ben and I spent much time together, with and without Lena Horne. I learned that he had grown up in the Netherlands and left the country for Palestine less than two months before it was invaded in 1940. He had earned a PhD in inorganic chemistry from the Hebrew University and was on his way to a post-doctoral fellowship at MIT. I soon realized that he was not a narrowly educated scientist. When Ben recited by heart a French poem by Arthur Rimbaud, my favorite poet, I was really smitten. One afternoon, as we were visiting Lena Horne, she said to me, "Won't you be lonely in Brussels while your husband is at MIT?" I gasped and exclaimed, "My husband? But we just met!" And Ben, in the background, uttered, "Not a bad idea!" We laughed and went on to other matters. When the boat stopped in Naples, we went ashore to visit Pompeii. As we were visiting the ruins, we came to a room where the entrance was blocked by a guard. The guard turned to Ben and asked, "Do you allow your wife to enter?" "Yes," Ben responded. There must have been something in our demeanor, in our ease with each other, that triggered people's perception of us as a couple. So we entered the pornographic room. I don't remember what we saw; it was probably way beyond what I understood at the time.

When the boat docked in Marseille, we took the train to Paris, where we explored some museums. Then Ben went on to Le Havre to catch his boat to the United States while I went home to Brussels. We promised to write to each other. Did we kiss goodbye? I don't remember. Ben sent me a photo of himself sprawled on the lawn at Tanglewood, the famed summer home of the Boston Symphony. Meanwhile, I was working part time as a temporary secretary in a few different offices in Brussels. I particularly remember an employer who dealt in armaments with Czechoslovakia and also sold toilet seats around the world. I also took economics courses at the Free University of Brussels, where I had previously received my degree in social sciences.

After a few months, Ben wrote that he would like to see me on his way back to Israel. On the appointed day, the doorbell rang. There he stood, in a dilapidated coat so long that it nearly reached the ground and carrying a guitar. Our cook, who opened the door, took one look at him, went back to the kitchen, and declared to my mother, "This is not for our Suske!" by which she meant me. As I later learned, the coat had been given to him by his Dutch aunt; it had belonged to his late uncle. It was cold in Holland when he stopped off there, and, as an Israeli, Ben had not bothered to acquire a coat of his own. As for the guitar, no, it was not his; he was bringing it for a friend. Our cook was soon mollified when Ben praised the dishes she had prepared. I had bought tickets to Carmen at the opera house. They were high up in what was called "The Paradise" at the old Theatre de la Monnaie. We were sitting so high and the curtain hung so low over the stage that we mostly saw the legs of the singers. But the music was divine. Later, I took him to one of my favorite nightclubs, but he did not care for the smoking and drinking. Nevertheless, we decided that I would come to see him in Israel.

At the end of the academic year, I took my oral exam in economics with a bushy professor, a White Russian who was a family friend. After marking his satisfaction with my performance, he asked, "And now what are you going to do?" I looked straight at him and replied, "Now I am going to get married!" He jumped up with a big smile, "Congratulations, congratulations!"

I had saved the money from my part-time work, which I used for my ticket to Israel to join Ben in Rehovot, where he had rented an apartment. We wed in December 1953. By coincidence, the waiter who had placed us next to each other on the ship served at our wedding reception. Born of a shipboard romance, our marriage lasted sixty-one years. Ben died in 2015 at age ninety-three.

IRELAND

Anne Lapedus Brest

When Anne's parents married in 1943, the Jewish community of Ireland was reaching its peak of about fifty-five hundred. The majority, like Juliet and Stanley, were children and grandchildren of migrants from Lithuania and Latvia. The area of central Dublin where they married in the now-closed Adelaide Street Shul was known as "Little Jerusalem." In decline after World War II, the Jewish community is making a comeback with an influx of employees to high-tech companies. Anne, a writer, photographer, and genealogist, presents a detailed account that attests to the central roles that family members play in the lives of young brides and grooms.

My mother, Juliet Maureen Marcus, was born in 1920 in Dublin. Both of her parents were born in Ireland. Like the majority of Irish Jews, her mother's family was originally from Latvia and her father's family from Lithuania. Her father, Ellie Marcus, was an optician. One of five children, Julie went to

Anne's Ma and Da on their honeymoon

St. Catherine's School for Girls and later to Wesley College High School in Dublin. A member of the Dublin Jewish Girl Guides, she was known as a kind, gentle, and soft-spoken young girl.

The Marcus family lived in the South Circular Road area (the SCR), a Jewish area from the time that Lithuanian and Latvian immigrants arrived in Ireland in the mid-1880s. Julie's cousins lived there too; they were like sisters all of her life. By the time they were teenagers, her family and her cousins' families had moved to the more fashionable Terenure area, which became a locus of Jewish life as well.

My father, Stanley Lapedus, was born in 1915 in Dublin to parents from Lithuania. His father came from a family of cigarette makers. One of three brothers, Stanley graduated from Dublin High School and became an optician. He was a talented swimmer, an excellent bridge player, and a good dancer who enjoyed music and had a great sense of humor. Like Julie, Stanley grew up in the SCR. In 1935, his family moved to Rathfarnham, a beautiful district close to Terenure. When a bomb landed in the Lapeduses' back garden during World War II, Stanley's father sold the house in five minutes and moved back to the SCR, much to my grandmother's distress.

Julie and Stanley met at "the hops," a dance hall in town where young people would go to dance and socialize. Many years later, my mother told me that she had spotted a handsome, simply marvelous dancer on the floor. When he came up to ask her for a dance, she almost froze on the spot. After dating for three months, Julie brought him home to meet her parents. It was quite a coincidence that Stanley was an optician like her father. My grandparents were thrilled on sight; Stanley was charming, dashing, funny, and he helped the younger children with their homework. As was the norm in those days, he asked Julie's parents for her hand in marriage, and they became engaged in 1942.

On March 16, 1943, Juliet and Stanley married at Adelaide Road Shul, Dublin. Simon Lapedus, the father of the groom, and Ellie Marcus, the father of the bride, walked the handsome *chossen* (groom in Yiddish) to the chuppah. Stanley was debonair in his black evening suit with a white shirt and bow tie. As he walked down the aisle with white silk gloves in his left hand and a white carnation in his lapel, there wasn't a person in the shul who didn't think he looked like a prince. Then Ellie came back down the aisle to collect his beautiful daughter, the bride. As he walked her proudly down the aisle on his arm, his piercing blue eyes became misty. He was so proud of her on this very special day!

Julie, the young *kalleh* (bride in Yiddish), was wearing a classical wedding dress in the style of the day with a long veil that flowed softly and gently as she walked toward the chuppah to her chossen and toward her new life. Ellie held

Julie's arm closely as they walked up the three steps to the chuppah. As Julie and Stanley stood together under the chuppah, their parents, Ellie and Bertha Marcus and Simon and Rosie Lapedus, were *kvelling* (overflowing with happiness and joy).

Bertha first and then Rosie lifted Julie's veil so that she could sip the wine. Then Simon and Ellie give Stanley the wine *becher* (cup) to drink from. Doley Freilich, Julie's cousin and the *chazan* (cantor) at Adelaide Road Shul, sang splendidly, as did the choir. Rabbi Alony officiated as Stanley handed Julie the ketubah and, as tradition dictated, placed the wedding ring on her forefinger, later to be transferred to her ring finger. He oversaw benevolently as Stanley solemnly intoned his marriage vows: *Ha'ahray at mekudeshet li betaba'at zu, kedat Moshe v'Yisroel* (Behold you are consecrated to me by means of this ring, according to the laws of Moses and Israel).

Julie, classical and elegant, and Stanley, tall and handsome, smiled as they stood together, their eyes bright and their lives ahead of them. Finally, Stanley broke the glass, signifying that no matter how happy a *simcha*, Jewish couples always remember the destruction of both of the temples in biblical days. Mazel tov! Mazel tov!

They went on their honeymoon to the west of Ireland where they spent time on country walks, visiting farms, and meeting the country folk of Ireland. In 1946, their daughter, Anne, was born and in 1949, their son, Robert.

A branch of my father's family had moved to South Africa in 1922. They made it their life's mission to encourage my parents to move there as they believed it would be an easier life for us than in Ireland in the 1950s. My mother had gone for a look-see in 1955 and loved it. Both my parents hated the cold weather in Ireland, and South Africa seemed like a paradise.

So in 1961, my father got a job as an optician in Johannesburg, and away we went to the land of sunshine and golden opportunity. Sadly, after just two years in South Africa, my father passed away at age forty-seven. My mother lived until 2016, age ninety-five. She had five grandchildren (my two children and my brother's three) and five great-grandchildren.

RUSSIA

Luba Ioffe

What was the lure that encouraged people like Luba, ignorant of Jewish observance and the child of parents who denigrated it, to learn and return to Jewish practice and identity? She does not tell us in her story, but hers is one that shows the resilience

Luba and Rudolf on a summer
hike ten years after their
marriage

of Judaism that has allowed its survival for millennia, sometimes against all odds. Luba did not marry in a Jewish ceremony, but who can doubt that she was a Jewish bride? Of the hundreds of thousands of Jews who remain in Russia after the mass exodus to Israel, Europe, and the United States that began in the 1970s, people like Luba are reclaiming their heritage for themselves and their children, renewing public and private Jewish life where formerly it was prohibited and disparaged.

My parents were one hundred percent Communists. They sincerely believed that ethnic and cultural backgrounds were of no importance for the "brave new world"—the ideal society they were building all of their lives. Religion was out of the question: it was considered a concern of the elderly and uneducated. My knowledge of Judaism was close to zero.

The late 1980s was the time of Perestroika, the restructuring of the Soviet political and economic system. Societies representing different ethnic groups sprang up everywhere in Russia, especially in Moscow, where I lived. Someone told me about a Jewish Culture and Education Society founded by a retired army colonel, Yuri Sokol, located in his two-room apartment in the central part of the city. By that time, my interest in everything related to Judaism had grown. I went there to find out what the society was about. When I entered, I was thrilled to see a large collection of books in several languages on Jewish history and tradition as well as life in Israel. They were mainly gifts from foreign guests who by that time were allowed to come to the Soviet Union and to bring such literature openly. The society organized all kinds of seminars, lectures, and workshops devoted to various aspects of Jewish life and history.

Soon I started coming there regularly not only as a guest but also as a volunteer, offering my services as an English/Russian translator and interpreter. I helped with translating letters and documents and with welcoming English-speaking guests. Visitors from abroad understood that masses of Russian Jews were devoid of their past—their traditions and their history—and they came to help us restore the losses.

In 1989, the society organized a one-day conference on the problems of antisemitism. We rented a big auditorium and prominent public figures were invited. The conference started with the screening of a documentary by the Simon Wiesenthal Center followed by a number of reports and a discussion. The film was in English and my responsibility was to translate it into Russian and to read the translation during the screening. After the film, there was a short break during which I had some time to rest. Suddenly, a middle-aged man came up to me with the silliest question one could imagine: "Do you really know English that well?" It was Rudolf Brodetsky, one of the participants in the conference and active in the same Jewish society. As I guessed later, it was his way of getting acquainted with me.

We spoke for a while and soon discovered that we had something in common besides being Jewish: both of us were hiking and trekking fans. So the next Sunday, instead of taking me to the movies, or an art exhibit, or a restaurant, Rudolf invited me to join his group for a thirty-two-kilometer one-day hike (almost twenty miles!) in the vicinity of Moscow. I accepted the invitation and, after several more hikes during the next couple of months, he proposed to me. As you can see, our courtship was very brief.

We did not have a traditional Jewish wedding. Strange as it may sound, we did not have any wedding at all—we simply registered our marriage at the local registration office. Both of us hated pompous ceremonies, and at that time, neither of us was very advanced in our knowledge of Jewish tradition. In all probability, we were subconsciously reluctant to do it the Soviet way and were not yet ready for the Jewish way. We do not have even one picture of that period of our lives.

Actually, that was the start of our long journey to Jewish observance, a life-long journey of Jewish learning. Our daughter, Emma, was born in 1990. We became part of the Jewish community, celebrating Jewish holidays, attending seminars on Jewish topics, and vacationing at Jewish family camps in the summer. In 2000, we had our first Passover seder in our home and in December 2002, we celebrated Emma's bat mitzvah at the Congregation for Progressive Judaism in Moscow. The three of us continued to enjoy hiking in the woods in summer and winter.

I am sad to say that my husband passed away in 2011. Emma represents a new generation of Russian Jews, who from their earliest childhood know what it means to be Jewish. The Moscow Jewish community plays an important part in her life; she has worked as a counselor at youth and family camps since the age of fifteen. I am waiting and praying that one of these days she will be a Jewish bride with a good Jewish husband.

SCOTLAND

Lina Zatzman

The life of Lina's mother, Hilda, could be the plot of a romance novel: an orphan caring for her ill sister while trying to eke out a living in a poor section of Glasgow meets her daring cousin against the backdrop of World War II, weds in an atmosphere of anxiety and grief, and finds ultimate prosperity in Canada. Lina does not tell us the location of her parents' wedding ceremony, but there are currently seven synagogues in Glasgow, where the majority of Scotland's six thousand Jews reside. The great-great-nephew of the owner of Geneen's, the now legendary restaurant where the wedding reception took place, still operates a kosher deli in Glasgow. Lina is a retired speech and language pathologist who lives near Toronto.

My mother, Hilda Samson, was born in Glasgow in 1917, the youngest of seven children. Her mother, Lina, contracted tuberculosis and died in a sanatorium when Hilda was three. Her observant father, Elias, had studied architecture but made his living as the owner of a small tobacco store. The family rented a cold-water flat in the tenements of the Gorbals, a gritty area populated mainly by poor Jews, where Elias established a small yeshiva. By age thirteen, Hilda was an orphan. Her older siblings had left Glasgow to seek better lives in Australia and the United States. So she and her beloved sixteen-year-old tubercular sister Hannah moved into a small room in a nearby tenement. Working in a jewelry store, Hilda became the sole breadwinner for her sister and herself, often forced to move to smaller and cheaper rooms.

Hilda and Sol Gilis

Hilda had left school at thirteen, but she was a voracious reader and continued her self-education at the library. She was very pretty, loved to dance, and was never without a partner at the dance halls and Jewish clubs where young people gathered to mingle and flirt. Despite the hardship in her circumstances, she was resilient and fun-loving.

In the summer of 1939, Hilda heard that her first cousin, her mother's brother's son, Shliomas (Sol) Gilis, had left Lithuania to make the journey to Leeds, England. Sol's uncle owned a textile factory there, and Sol and his brother, Nehemiah, were able to obtain visas to leave the country to learn about a new machine. Sol traveled through Germany and made it to England; Nehemiah took a different track and never made it, presumably shot en route. One of Hilda's cousins met Sol in England and raved about her handsome cousin from Lithuania.

On Sunday, September 3, 1939, Hilda took the train from Glasgow to Leeds to meet her cousin. It was a significant day in several respects. By the time Hilda reached Leeds, Britain had formally declared war on Germany. And Sol fell in love with her the minute he laid eyes on her. When he proposed that day, her response was, "Court me." They spent the day together until Sol reluctantly escorted Hilda to the train station. The trains were full of young soldiers, and Hilda had to fight her way onto a late train. Sitting on her suitcase in the aisle, she joined in the songs being sung by excited young men who did not know what lay before them.

Hilda and Sol's courtship consisted of letters and Sol's visits to Glasgow. Sol sent money whenever he could, and Hilda helped him with his English. At that time, Hilda's sister Hannah became too ill to stay at home and was admitted to a sanatorium.

Hilda and Sol married in Glasgow on September 1, 1940, a year after they met. With Sol's help, Hilda bought a beautiful long white satin wedding gown—wholesale, of course. (When her friend Rose married soon after, she wore the gown, as did a number of young women who came knocking at her door throughout the war.) The wedding was small, attended by a few of Hilda's cousins and friends. The reception was held at Geneen's, a kosher restaurant owned by a family friend. My mother described her wedding as a sad affair, with her parents dead, her beloved sister dying, her other siblings scattered around the globe, and the fate of Sol's family in Lithuania unknown. Tragically, as Hilda and Sol were returning to Glasgow from their honeymoon, Hannah died.

Almost a decade later, in 1949, Hilda and Sol and their two young daughters, Lina and Ruth, moved from Glasgow to Yarmouth, Nova Scotia, where Sol opened a knitting factory with the aid of government grants. The family prospered, and in 1990 my sister and I and our families hosted a surprise fiftieth-anniversary party for them. In contrast to their wedding, it was a joyous affair.

Hilda and Sol died in 2006 within six weeks of each other.

SYRIA

Sara Gerson

Sara is a successful Mexican children's book author whose parents emigrated from Ukraine in the 1920s. She heard this unusual story when doing research for her 1993 adult book Nueva Casa (New Home), histories of Jews who fled their countries and found a homeland in Mexico, including a large community from Aleppo and Damascus. Mail-order bride Latife/Leticia, an assertive and bold woman, may be more typical of her time than we think. After riots in 1947 and the horrors of a civil war that has ravished the country, only a handful of Jews are left in Syria, a

*former hub of Jewish life since biblical times. Organizations and individuals in the
United States, Canada, and Israel have worked for decades to bring Jews to safety
by whatever means possible.*

Abdo Mizrahi lived in Sham, another name for Damascus. He was called
to the Torah by the name Ovadia. In 1921, he emigrated to Mexico. On arrival,
he became Adolfo Mizrahi and was known by this name the rest of his life. In
those days, the Jewish community was small. Few families had arrived, and the
Syrian Jewish community was composed mostly of young men seeking a better
future. Life was not easy for the newly arrived. Like many others, Adolfo started
out as a peddler, selling handkerchiefs, shoelaces, socks, ties, razor blades, and
all sorts of trinkets that he could carry in his box.

After a few years of hard work, he established himself as the owner of a small
store in the Lagunilla market of Mexico City, a popular low-income, commercial neighborhood. In 1926, with a feeling of economic stability, as well as letters
of encouragement from his mother back in Damascus, he wrote home asking
his relatives to help him find a bride. There were not many single young women
among the immigrants to Mexico City.

Adolfo's descendants don't know how many pictures he received, but there
was one in particular that caught his attention: a beautiful face of lovely proportion with enormous light-colored eyes bordered by dark eyelashes. Her name
was Latife. Adolfo wrote her a letter (or several) and asked her to marry him, to
leave her family behind and travel halfway around the world to build a family
with this besotted stranger. Latife and her family accepted. All the particulars
were carefully detailed and settled on by mail.

Several months later, Adolfo traveled to the port of Veracruz to welcome
his soon-to-be bride. He was accompanied by an older Shami (as Jews from
Damascus are known) woman who was to serve as Latife's chaperone until the
day of the wedding. The groom-to-be was nervous and eager, deeply in love with
the owner of the most beautiful eyes he had ever seen, and about to meet her in
person. Dressed in a light-colored three-piece suit, he stood on the pier under
a tree, nervously holding in his hand a brand-new Panama hat, waiting for the
passengers to descend from the ship.

When Latife came down the gangplank, he immediately recognized the
striking face, the one he knew so well from the picture that he fervently con-
templated during the day and dreamed of in his sleep—the light eyes, the
dark eyelashes. As she approached, he also saw that his beloved beauty was the
owner of a body that weighed at least 170 pounds and was barely five feet tall.

Adolfo was stunned. He put on his precious hat and arranged for the voluminous luggage to be transferred. Then he hired a car to take him, Latife, and the chaperone to the hotel. Staring through the windshield, he saw the palm trees go by and did not utter a single word. When they arrived at the hotel, Adolfo ordered the porters not to unload the luggage. He helped Latife out of the car. To escape the humidity and heat, he led her into the hotel lobby. There, he took her aside. When he was certain that no one could hear him, he told her that the marriage was off, that she was not the person he expected to see. Therefore, she had to go back to Damascus. He explained that she had to take advantage of the fact that the ship was leaving in a few hours, for he was not going to marry her.

In the assertive manner that characterized her all her life, Latife looked him steadily in the eye. With a calm and firm voice, she told him that she was not going back to Damascus and that she was not going to be shamed by him. She reminded him of his promise, of the fact that he had sent word that he was looking for a bride, that he had asked for a picture, and that he had made the proposal. He, therefore, had an obligation to her and her family.

Adolfo was flabbergasted, unable speak.

Adolfo and Latife married a few weeks later in Mexico City. It is needless to say who had the last word in that household. They formed a solid family, lived according to Jewish practice, and became prominent members of the Shami community. They had seven children.

In the Syrian tradition, grandchildren are named after their grandparents, even while they are still alive. Latife and Adolfo saw fourteen grandchildren who bear their names, a girl and a boy from each of their children—Adolfo for the boys and Leticia, changed from Latife, for the girls. Today, there are more than two hundred descendants of Adolfo and Latife. Most of them live in Mexico City and some in different parts of the United States. Their ancestry is evident: many of them share Latife's beautiful eyes.

ZIMBABWE

Modreck Maeresera

Modreck's delightful story of his cousin Tapiwa's marriage to Primrose comes from a community that maintains indigenous African traditions with underlying Jewish ones. The fifty thousand Lemba, who live in central Zimbabwe and the north of South Africa, have an oral tradition that they are the descendants of ancient Jews. They observe cultural customs that include avoiding pork, ritual slaughter,

Primrose grinding millet using mortar and pestle, gifts at her wedding

and practicing circumcision in an area where it is not common. DNA testing has validated the belief that the Lemba have Jewish roots: members of their priestly clan have the "Cohen" genetic haplotype in the same proportion as other Jewish groups around the world. Modreck is the leader of a community of a few hundred Lemba who are committed to returning to their ancestral religious practice of Judaism, learning and attending a synagogue and cultural center he established in Harare, the capital. Under his leadership, Modreck has spurred successful innovative agricultural projects to benefit his community.

Just like my grandmother always said, Lemba marry at a ripe age. True to that tradition, my cousin Tapiwa married at the ripe age of thirty-three, and his was a typical Lemba marriage. Although Lemba marriages are not arranged, they are somewhere in the gray area between being arranged and . . . not arranged. The word that comes into my mind is *facilitated*: they are facilitated marriages. So my cousin Tapiwa's marriage was a facilitated one, just like his parents' marriage was facilitated, just like my parents' marriage was facilitated. You see, Tapiwa is my cousin because his father is my father's brother, and his mother is my mother's sister. When my parents got married, the elders agreed that my mom came from a good traditional Lemba family. So pleased were the elders with my cultured, hardworking, and intelligent mother that they wished Uncle Solomon, my father's youngest brother, to marry someone from my mother's family.

That is why Aunt Elsie, my mother's youngest sister, always came to my village to visit during school holidays, especially whenever Uncle Solomon was around on leave from work in Harare, the capital city. As it turned out, although they were not forced on each other, Auntie Elsie and Uncle Solomon got married after a brief courtship. That was a typical Lemba marriage: two Lemba families being joined together.

At the age of thirty-three, Tapiwa was very shy and self-conscious but still a young man by Lemba standards. He belonged to a generation of young Lemba who moved to the city because of the need to look for employment or to be educated there. In Tapiwa's case, his parents had moved to Harare soon after their wedding. In Harare, they moved into a municipal house. Aunt Elsie, Tapiwa's mother, would alternate between living in the village and the city. Uncle Solomon's income was not sufficient for the young family, so Aunt Elsie supplemented her husband's meager income by growing cash crops in the village during the agricultural season. During the dry season, she would then move back to the city to be with her husband. My cousins grew up and went to school in the village, visiting their father in Harare during school holidays. So Tapiwa experienced both village and city life, but he later moved permanently to the city to get a college education. He was part of a new generation of city Lemba who lived away from the villages of their origin. Always exposed to influences for assimilation, most of these city Lemba ended up marrying non-Lemba wives, and some abandoned Lemba culture altogether.

So my cousin Tapiwa became part of the elders' headache when he decided to settle in the city permanently. As a sophisticated young man with a master's degree in English, there was always a chance that he might end up not conforming with Lemba cultural norms and expectations. My Aunt Elsie especially hated the idea of Tapiwa marrying a city girl. So the elders decided to facilitate a marriage for Tapiwa.

When my cousin Caisy's mother passed away in the village at age eighty-seven, all of us city Lemba traveled back to the village for the funeral. Cousin Caisy had taken as a wife a young woman from a village close to our own, and Caisy's wife had a beautiful young sister who had just finished high school. Everybody agreed that cousin Caisy's sister-in-law would make a good wife for

Tapiwa. As Tapiwa was driving to the village for the funeral in his new Mazda sedan, Auntie Elsie called to tell him to pick up Primrose, Caisy's sister-in-law, who was stranded at a shopping center seven kilometers away from our village. Tapiwa was told Primrose was having a difficult time finding transportation. Primrose, on the other hand, was told to wait for Tapiwa "who didn't know his way to the village" so she could show him the easiest road. So Tapiwa picked up Primrose thinking he was helping a stranded young lady, and Primrose thought she was helping her brother-in-law's cousin who had become too sophisticated to know his way back to the village.

After three weeks, Primrose and Tapiwa were madly in love, and Tapiwa was traveling to the village every other week to see Primrose. Six months later, they were married in a simple traditional Lemba wedding. We all traveled to the village for the wedding on a sunny, warm, and beautiful Sunday morning in June 2014.

The wedding took place in the groom's village where a feast was prepared. Two cows and several sheep were slaughtered, and traditional beer was brewed. The bridal party arrived toward noon, with the bride and a group of aunts at the head of the procession. In Lemba culture, aunts (father's sisters or cousins) are responsible for the girl child's cultural education and have the responsibility of handing the girl over to her husband during a wedding. So the bride was accompanied by her aunts when they arrived in our village. When they arrived at the edge of Tapiwa's family homestead, the aunts and the veiled bride stopped. It is Lemba custom that the bride be given a gift before she can enter the groom's homestead. Primrose was given the customary winnowing basket and a broom. After receiving the gifts, the bridal party went into the compound amid ululation, dancing, and a lot of celebration. They were led to the hut that was reserved for the bride and groom and the bride's attendants. When they got to the entrance of the hut, they waited again for a gift—a clay pot—that was due to them before going into the hut.

My cousin Tapiwa, elegantly dressed in a new suit, was then accompanied by two of our uncles, our mothers' brothers, for the unveiling ceremony. The unveiling would complete the wedding formalities, and the couple would be considered duly married under Lemba law. A traditional unveiling gift was given by the groom and his family—a mortar and pestle. Then my cousin Tapiwa lifted Primrose's veil. After confirming that it was indeed his fiancée under the veil, the veil was torn in half. One-half was given to Tapiwa's uncle and the other to Primrose's aunt as proof that the couple were married under Lemba law. Then it was time to eat and drink and celebrate.

TWO

—⟋⟍⟍—

COURTSHIP

IN THE PREVIOUS CHAPTER, we learned of one man who proposed on the day he met his wife-to-be. That is quite unusual. Typically, couples have some time between meeting and deciding to marry once they get to know each other. This period used to be called courtship (traditionally a time for the man to court his potential bride) but is now more commonly called dating. Ideally, it is the time when couples fall in love.

This chapter has stories of Jewish courtship from Belarus, Egypt, Italy, Poland, Sudan, and Thailand. Besides those in Italy, these communities are small, fragile, or no longer exist. As is true for all the stories in this book, each has more than one theme. We selected these to illustrate the varieties of courtship within the larger context of brides' marriage stories, some filled with drama and danger.

The period of courtship can be short or long, depending on a variety of factors. In traditional communities of the past and even today, couples may be brought together for the stated purpose of marriage (the *shidduch* in Yiddish), so courtship may be brief or nonexistent. But this does not mean that brides have no say. (Stories in chapter 11 highlight arranged marriages and some unusual and unfortunate situations of coerced brides.) An article by the Orthodox Chabad organization affirms the Talmudic mandate that couples give their full consent to the match and that women must be mature enough to make an intelligent decision.[1] The stories from Thailand and Poland, while far apart in time and place, attest to the power of potential brides in traditional communities to make decisions about their future mates.

These authors remember heightened emotions that often accompany court-ship—joy, tears, drama, and sometimes turbulence. Internal factors such as the reluctance of the groom's family to approve the match (Poland) or external world events (Italy) make for dramatic stories. All of these stories, however, demonstrate the influence of families at this stage of the bride's journey to marriage, whether encouraging the potential match (Belarus) or intervening for the suitor (Egypt).

Preserving the bride's chastity used to be a priority for families, who would provide a chaperone, often a young relative, before formal betrothal (Sudan). Liberal branches of Judaism, while acknowledging the ideal of sex within mar-riage, recognize societal changes that condone more flexible attitudes toward premarital sex, especially as brides are older these days and more couples live together before marriage. Parental permission and supervision of courtship may largely be a thing of the past, but parents' approval of the boyfriend is still beneficial to potential brides, and the support of parents still makes life easier.

BELARUS

Raisa Baskin

While not exactly an arranged marriage, Raisa's union demonstrates the influence that families exerted in past generations—and perhaps still do, to a lesser extent—on young women's decisions to marry, even in countries where such arrangements are not the cultural norm. Often, they ended happily. Raisa's evocative memories of daily life in Belarus, where milk came from the family cow, a school uniform was made to last for ten years, and Jewish couples married in a government office, il-lustrate the profound changes that the wave of immigrants from the former Soviet Union experienced beginning in the 1970s when the doors opened and they left to seek better lives in Israel and the United States.

I grew up in Gomel, the second-largest city in Belarus, about a day's train ride from Minsk. I've known my husband, Gregory, most of my life. When I was a little girl, I was very skinny. The doctor said that I should have fresh milk every day to build me up. We had a cow, but it gave less and less milk, and then it died. (When we had bought the cow, the woman who had sold it to us had started to cry. After our cow died, my mother always said never to buy anything that is sold with remorse!) Gregory's family, our neighbors, had a cow that gave a lot of milk. Every day I went to his house for a glass of warm, foamy, unpasteurized milk straight from the cow. I hated it!

Raisa and Gregory at their grandson's bar mitzvah, 2016

People in our neighborhood were not rich. When you entered elementary school, you bought your uniform. This uniform lasted for ten years. You could take off the white collar and cuffs to wash or change them. As a child grew, the uniform was lengthened. It had a kind of apron in front, black on most days and white on holidays. The first thing you did when you came home from school was to take off your uniform. You never wanted to get it dirty. Out of similar frugality, my mother once made me a bathing suit from old clothes. I also learned how to sew. Everybody was like that. We didn't know then it was recycling.

When I was seventeen, I went to a university in Moscow to study fashion technology. At that time, Gregory was in the army. He got out a year later when I was in my second year of study. To tell the truth, my mother didn't put much stock in my education; she was more interested in my personal life. When she encountered Gregory, she would play up what a good girl I was. My sister, too, encouraged me to get together with him. So when I came home in June after my exams, we met. He was twenty-three, and I was eighteen. I hadn't seen him in several years. He was surprised that I had become a young woman while he was in the army.

It took him only three days to ask me to marry him. I told him I wasn't ready, but he told me he was. I said OK. We didn't fall in love—our parents were directing us. As the years went by, we learned to love each other.

The year was 1969. Everyone lived with their parents. I had a curfew of eleven o'clock and received a good-night kiss on the cheek from my future husband. We signed a marriage application at the town hall. Then you had to wait a month until the marriage became legal. During that month, you took a blood test and attended marriage classes, men and women separately. The future grooms would be given a certificate to buy a wedding ring, just a plain gold band—diamonds were unheard of. The rings all looked the same.

In those days, no one had a traditional Jewish wedding under a chuppah. On our wedding day, we came with our parents and friends to the registrar's office. I was wearing a little knee-length wedding dress that I bought in the market. (Later on, I made it over as a dress for my little daughter.) We signed the papers; then everyone walked to the central square monument of the unknown soldier, where we laid flowers in front of the statue and took pictures. From there, we walked home. That evening we had a party in a restaurant. Everything had to be economical, as I was the second of four girls in my family. We received pots and pans and towels with big flowers. I particularly remember a little electric fan. The relatives got together and bought us a wardrobe for clothes. That was our one piece of real furniture.

I became pregnant after a few months. Life was hard. My father helped me find a job in a tailor shop, where I became a dressmaker. I studied on my own in the library and went to Moscow every three months for exams. Gregory found a job in construction and took college courses until eleven o'clock at night.

Finally, we both finished college. I was in charge of technology for a big factory that made women's clothes; then I taught in a school for kids with mental disabilities. Gregory taught construction methods. We were comfortable. But in 1979, everyone was talking about emigrating. Our daughter, Natasha, was nine, and our son, Dmitri, was three when we left Belarus for the United States. When you're young, you think you can do anything!

We came to Providence, Rhode Island, where we had relatives. I found a job doing alterations in a women's clothing shop, and Gregory did home reconstruction projects. When a better construction job became available in Miami, we moved there. I studied and became an EKG technician in the cardiology department of a hospital, where I worked for twenty-three years.

I've had a fulfilling life. My husband and I were taught good basic principles by our families. We have five grandchildren, whose lives are completely different from ours when we were their ages. But this is what we planned and expected.

EGYPT

Racheline Abécassis Barda

Author of The Egyptian-Jewish Emigrés in Australia, *based on her PhD disser-tation, Racheline is well acquainted with Egyptian Jewish history, both from her research and from her own and her family's personal experience. Arriving in Aus-tralia with her husband, Joe, as a refugee from Alexandria in 1958, Racheline settled in Sydney, where she lectures in the Jewish Studies department of the University of Sydney and volunteers as a guide at the Sydney Jewish Museum. She and Joe have three children and seven grandchildren. Her story is impressive in describing the details of her parents' courtship and wedding, down to the lining of the shoes in her estimable mother's trousseau!*

My mother, Esther Lévy, was born in Alexandria, Egypt, in 1909. Her par-ents had moved to Egypt from Aleppo, Syria, via Palestine in the early 1900s in search of better economic conditions. With the boom of the cotton industry, the opening of the Suez Canal in 1869 linking the Red Sea to the Mediterra-nean, and the subsequent collapse of the overland trade routes known as the legendary Silk Road, Egypt had become a land of opportunity. It attracted migrants from all over the Mediterranean basin and the Ottoman Empire, particularly Jewish migrants.

My grandfather died at the age of thirty-two when my mother, the eldest of three siblings, was about six years old. Her mother was left virtually penniless. Acutely aware of her obligation to support her family, my mother went to work as a telephone operator at the tender age of thirteen, pretending she was fifteen, and then worked for a dry cleaner.

My mother had an entrepreneurial and independent spirit, rare for a woman so young, particularly in a patriarchal society such as Egypt's. She taught her-self to sew by going to department stores, creating patterns of the dresses on display. Her first clients were overseas dancers and singers performing at the local Casino Alhambra and other nightclubs in Alexandria. She also made a variety of costumes to wear to dress-up balls (*bals masqués*) that were popular at the time. Apparently, her costumes always won first prize. I still have her legendary peacock costume covered with multicolored sequins sewn by hand in geometrical shapes.

My mother was in her early twenties when she met my father, Léon Abécas-sis, a dashing young man who looked like the famous actor Rudolph Valentino, the heartthrob of women all over the world at the time. His parents came to Egypt from Morocco at the beginning of the twentieth century and moved

Racheline's parents, Esther and Léon Abécassis

to Alexandria in the late 1920s. My mother first met my father's cousin, who encouraged her to leave the dry cleaner shop for a receptionist job in a French Jewish firm, La Société d'Avances Commerciales. My father worked there as a bookkeeper. Léon fell madly in love with her but had to compete with another employee of the firm for her affection. The dispute came to blows when both men threw cardboard folders at each other.

My mother, on the other hand, was not keen on marrying anybody. Being the only breadwinner in her family, she felt her first responsibility was to them. Both her sister and her brother were still at school. She supplemented her office wages of four pounds per month with her earnings as a seamstress, whereas my father only earned three pounds. His own family tried to reason with him, pointing out that he couldn't afford to get married. But my father would not be swayed. He was so smitten that he had my mother followed by one of his many cousins. Nevertheless, she still turned down his proposal. He grew so desperate that he threatened to kill himself. His mother, who had just lost a younger son from acute peritonitis, came to my grandmother's place along with his three older sisters to plead his case, begging her to convince her daughter to marry him. My mother finally agreed.

According to Jewish custom in Egypt, the bride was responsible for her trousseau and the bed furnishings. The payment of a dowry was also an integral part of the marriage contract. But in my mother's case, there was no dowry, and she paid all the wedding expenses, including my father's clothing because his family could not afford it. She embroidered all her lingerie and bed sheets; she made her own wedding dress in silk satin as well as her mother's and sister's outfits and bought her brother a suit. She even lined her shoes with the same fabric as her dress. But on the wedding day, she developed a blister on her foot and could not wear closed shoes. Instead, she wore white slippers adorned with flowers. My father always teased her about the fact that she got married in slippers.

The wedding was held at Eliyahu Hanavi, the beautiful Great Synagogue of Alexandria, on September 23, 1934. The synagogue, one of the largest in the Middle East, was built around 1836 on the site of an older synagogue that was destroyed by Napoleon's army at the end of the eighteenth century. Right before the wedding, the young couple, the Chief Rabbi of Alexandria, and their witnesses had signed a "single status affidavit" (proof of celibacy). This document ultimately found its way to archives in Jerusalem and, amazingly, was found more than sixty years later by a colleague who was researching official documents of the Alexandria *beth din* (rabbinical court).

It was customary in Egypt to offer wedding guests a bonbonnière (favor) filled with dragées (sugared almonds), which my mother personally prepared. There were about forty other couples getting married on that day because the festival of Sukkot was imminent. In the ensuing crowd and confusion, she was never sure if her precious bonbonnières were actually given to her guests. Afterward, a modest wedding reception for both families was held at her mother's place. It consisted of a delicious buffet of Sephardi and Syrian delicacies, such as *borekas, baklawa, maamoul,* and *konafa,* all homemade by my grandmother and other women of the family. There was no paid entertainment. The guests themselves, who told jokes, shared personal anecdotes, and sang popular songs, provided the entertainment.

My parents went to Cairo for a short honeymoon, paying the customary visit to the Sphinx and the pyramids. Upon returning to Alexandria, they first moved in with my grandmother. My mother went back to her job as a receptionist for another three years until the birth of my elder brother, Nelson. Sadly, their firstborn, Simon, had died of meningitis when he was eleven months old. Gradually, my parents' financial situation improved, and they were able to rent their own apartment. I came along just two months before World War II started, followed in 1942 by twins, Jacques and Jacqueline. I vaguely remember the war years, the British soldiers who used to visit us at home, and running to shelters in the dark whenever the Italians dropped bombs on Alexandria.

My parents worked hard to give us the best care and the best education in private schools. But in 1957, in the wake of the Suez War, we were forced out of Egypt. Like other Jewish communities from Arab lands, we undertook a "second exodus." Our family experienced extreme dislocation, as my brother went to study medicine in France and remained there, I married and settled in Australia, and my parents settled in Canada with my two younger siblings.

My parents were married for forty-five years when my father passed away suddenly in 1979 in Sydney, where they had finally joined me. My mother lived to be a great-grandmother and a centenarian. To her delight, she received the usual letter of congratulation from Queen Elizabeth. She died peacefully nine months later on December 9, 2009. A few hours before her death, I had been able to give her the wonderful news that my eldest daughter, who lived in Paris at the time, was finally pregnant. She acknowledged my words with her sweet smile, as she was too weak to talk. I believe that the joy she took with her eased her passage from this world to the next, and that thought brought great comfort to me.

ITALY

Racheline Barda

Racheline's story vividly illustrates how individual lives are affected by large-scale events such as the war between Egypt and Israel. Racheline's parents must have been desperate for her to reach safety when they allowed her to leave her home for the first time at age seventeen, travel to a faraway place, and marry a man she had known for only a few months. And Racheline, with the optimism of youth, must have been a very plucky young woman.

I met my husband, Giusy (also known as Joe), in Alexandria, Egypt, in 1956. I had just turned seventeen. School was out, and I was looking forward to a long, wonderful summer of parties, movies, and lazy days at the beach with my friends. One Saturday night, a group of us went to the Jewish Sports Club's annual fair. It was always a very lively event with music, dancing, game booths, and good food. I remember that my mother made me a beautiful dress for the occasion, light blue with polka dots, tight bodice, voluminous skirt, and starched petticoat—the latest fashion in those days.

As I walked around, I approached the horse race booth. The young man who was running it called out to me, insisting that I put a bet on a horse. I wasn't interested and started to walk away. Suddenly, I saw him leave his cubicle, jumping athletically over its little gate, to follow me. He introduced himself and asked me for a dance. He was extremely attentive, and I felt flattered that an older boy (he was all of twenty-two) was paying so much attention to me. He claimed that he had spotted me a couple of years before and decided that I would be the one!

Over the next two months, Giusy and I became boyfriend and girlfriend, totally oblivious to the deteriorating political climate following the nationalization of the Suez Canal and the dire consequences it set in motion for the Jewish community. At the beginning of September, my boyfriend suddenly announced that he was leaving Alexandria for university studies in Rome. I was devastated. What I didn't know at the time was that Giusy's father had been advised through a friend in the Egyptian secret police that, in case of war, his son was going to be arrested for an alleged connection with a group of Zionist spies. It was essential to send him away as soon as possible without revealing the real reason.

Racheline and her husband's family outside the Great Synagogue, Rome

On the eve of his departure, Giusy told me that we should break up and that he didn't know when or if he would come back. My distress was unbearable. Then, just before his ship sailed the next day, I received a call. He somehow managed to ring me on the ship's phone—no small feat in those days. He asked me to forget what he said the night before; he wanted me to wait for him and promised to come back for me. I was in seventh heaven!

In early October, I went back to school for my final year. We were exchanging letters and postcards, but the mail was very slow, and the constant waiting was frustrating. On weekends, I went to the movies or the occasional party with my friends, but I felt in a kind of limbo.

Suddenly, the world as I knew it collapsed. On October 29, 1956, hostilities broke out between Israel and Egypt, and we were at war. The security of Egyptian Jewry was severely compromised. The wealthy Jews—such as my boyfriend's family—suffered sequestration of their businesses and freezing of their assets. Hundreds of Jews were picked up, imprisoned, and then expelled or held under house arrest. The schools were closed. A climate of panic and hysteria spread throughout the Jewish community. People were selling whatever they could to secure a place on a ship or a plane, leaving in droves for different destinations—Israel, Europe, the Americas, and even faraway Australia.

By December, Giusy's parents, totally dispossessed, were issued an expulsion order and left the country for Italy. Unable to continue his university studies, Giusy found a job with El Al Airlines in Rome. He was sending me frantic telegrams, asking me to join him there and get married. In February, on behalf of Guisy's parents, his aunt paid a visit to my parents to ask for my hand in marriage. I was jumping for joy!

At that stage, my parents could not leave the country. Reluctantly, they agreed that I should go anyway, probably to get me out of harm's way. My mother worked tirelessly on my trousseau, even making my wedding dress. By bribing the proper officials, my father obtained a traveling document for me, a laissez-passer, which was stamped with a one-way exit visa and a three-month visa to Italy. Since I was under eighteen, I needed my parents' written authorization to get married, as well as a birth certificate, a certificate of celibacy, and a certificate of good conduct. On the eve of my departure, we had a family dinner. I tried on my wedding dress, and everybody clapped and shouted *mabrouk, mabrouk*, the equivalent of *mazel tov*. My mother bravely hid her tears.

The next day, my parents accompanied me to the port of Alexandria but were forced to leave before I went through security. By then, the seriousness of my situation finally hit me. The reality was that I had never traveled farther than Cairo. Here I was, alone, leaving my family behind to travel to a country I had never seen, to marry a guy I had known for barely two months! I could not believe my parents had agreed to let me go. I was terrified, and tears streamed down my face.

Neither my tears nor my youth softened the heart of the Egyptian security people. They inspected every one of my suitcases, handling my wedding dress and making lewd remarks. They threw away my schoolbooks, confiscated one of my gold bracelets, and turned back a trunk that contained linens. The final indignity was to be strip searched before being allowed aboard the ship.

After four days at sea, I arrived in Naples where my fiancé was waiting for me. Like a breath of fresh air, my doubts dissipated as we drove back to Rome. We arrived at the apartment where he was living with his parents and two siblings, as well as his uncle and aunt and their two young children. My future mother-in-law welcomed me and showed me my bedroom. In fact, it was Giusy's bedroom. He was elated and couldn't believe his luck. His elation was short-lived, however, as his mother promptly told him to pack a little bag because he was going to sleep at the local *pensione* until our wedding day! Since my mother had entrusted me to her, she would treat me as her own daughter and make sure that all the traditions were respected.

Prior to the wedding day, I went to the mikveh accompanied by my mother-in-law. On April 14, 1957, we got married at the Great Synagogue of Rome.

Apparently, we were the first refugees from Egypt to get married there. We had few guests, about eight or ten of Giusy's relatives and a few friends. My brother, a medical student in Montpellier, was the sole representative of my family. The religious ceremony was simple but emotional. My father-in-law walked me down the aisle in lieu of my father. After the synagogue, we all went to a local restaurant called Piperno, known for its Roman Jewish cuisine. A few years ago, we visited Rome and went looking for that restaurant. It was standing in the same spot, and we had a lovely romantic dinner.

After a brief honeymoon in the outskirts of Rome, we needed to have our religious marriage formally registered. Much to our dismay, we discovered that the Egyptian documents I had brought with me were not acceptable. As my three-month visa was coming to an end, I could be forced to leave the country. Finally, we went to the Red Cross, where an employee told us of a shortcut—a civil marriage in the Republic of San Marino. All we needed was a certificate signed by ten witnesses attesting to my identity as an unmarried person of good conduct. We found our witnesses there, hanging around the office.

With that certificate in hand, we took the train to San Marino, a tiny principality on the Adriatic coast, and presented ourselves at the mayor's office, which was also the local bakery. As soon as we said we wanted to get married, the mayor put on his formal attire, asked one of his employees to act as a witness, and took us upstairs to conduct the civil ceremony. It took a few minutes. Back in Rome, to our great relief, we were finally able to legalize my situation, and we were officially married.

Eighteen months later, with the help of HIAS (Hebrew Immigrant Aid Society), we boarded a ship bound for Sydney, Australia, where some of Giusy's extended family had migrated. We landed in Sydney with the sum of fifty Australian pounds. This is where we made a good life for ourselves and where we raised three beautiful children, Daniella, David, and Monique. I feel blessed and thankful.

POLAND

Miriam Sivan

Miriam is the retired head of elder services in Petah Tikvah, Israel. At a time when girls were expected to stay at home until the family arranged a marriage and then to live close by or in the family home, Miriam's mother, Dora, must have been particularly brave (and desperate to escape poverty) to leave her village for work in another town. Following her beloved to Warsaw, where they married, also took a large measure of daring and resilience. These were qualities she shared with her husband, Izik, and must have passed on to Miriam. They enabled the family to survive. One of Miriam's little cousins, now a grandmother, rightly credits Miriam with saving her life.

My mother, Dora, was brought up in a poor family headed by a single mother, as her father had died when she was eight months old. Dora was an intelligent young woman. She excelled in her studies, and at age seventeen, she determined that she had to leave home to earn her living. She soon found a job at a primary school in a small village near Bialystok, about thirty kilometers from her home. There, she taught Hebrew, Jewish history, and traditions to the Jewish students while their Catholic schoolmates had different religious instruction. Among her Jewish pupils were two sisters of the well-known Ryba family.

In a small village, it was inevitable that Dora would meet the sisters' older brother, Izik, a religious young man who fell head over heels for the tall, pretty teacher. They wanted to marry, but Izik's family did not approve. Not only did she come from a poor family, but she had also left home before her marriage, which was improper. Moreover, she was a member of a local theater group and had a lot of male admirers.

When Izik asked his parents if they would bless his marriage to Dora, they refused. So what could they do? Izik ran away to Warsaw, a few hours from the village, where he got a job in a carpentry shop (and, according to his family, lost his religion along the way). Soon after, my mother left her teaching job to join Izik in Warsaw. They found a rabbi, and in 1931, in the presence of two friends, they married in a simple ceremony. When the rabbi asked where their families were, they replied that they didn't have any. I was born the next year.

Starting from practically nothing, my father built a successful business making wooden cases for radios. We had a good life in Warsaw. After several years, my father's family finally accepted my mother, and when I was four years old, I met my grandfather for the first time. Then, in 1939, the Germans savagely beat my father on the street. My parents and I had to make our escape from Warsaw. All I remember is walking through the dark forest at night on our way to my mother's home village. It was on the side of Poland that the Russians controlled and at that time was safer.

You had to get permission to live and work in the Russian territory. We were sent to a settlement in the north near Siberia, where conditions were terrible. We stayed there for two years. When I was eight years old, thanks to my father's resourcefulness and a series of events too lengthy to be told here, my family, along with two of my father's sisters, the husband of one of them, and two little girl cousins, managed to evade liquidation in the Minsk ghetto. We survived by sheltering in the factory where my father and my uncle worked as slave laborers producing radios for the German air force and my mother and my aunts worked as launderers, kitchen hands, and cleaners. I was ignored and in hiding with my little cousins—one a toddler and one a baby—who were under my care and whose lives were dependent on me. My mother became the unofficial manager of our family group.

After the war, each of the families went to live in Israel. My twin brother and sister were born there when I was fifteen, four years after we arrived. My quick-witted and capable father passed away at age seventy-eight. My clever and resilient mother lived to age ninety.

SUDAN

Daisy Abboudi

Four of Daisy's grandparents come from the little-known Jewish community of Sudan. To preserve the memories of her grandparents and their generation, Daisy, a Londoner in her thirties with an MA in history, created a website (talesofjewishsudan.com) that includes interviews with former residents, recipes with delicious-looking photos, and a brief history of the community like the one she includes in her story. She is currently working on a book about the community, which hosted the wedding of her great-aunt and great-uncle in the capital Khartoum in 1963, one of the last before every Jew left the country.

In 1898, after a brief period of independence, Sudan became a territory of both Britain and Egypt, an arrangement called a "condominium," when two countries share power jointly. Under this agreement, Sudan's economy began to grow. A railway was built connecting Cairo, Egypt, and Khartoum, the capital of Sudan. This allowed Jews, and other communities, from all over the Middle East and North Africa who were seeking economic opportunity to immigrate.

At its peak between 1930 and 1950, the Jewish community of Sudan consisted of roughly two hundred fifty families, based mainly in the Nile cities of Khartoum and Omdurman. This small, tight-knit community of Jews lived peacefully alongside their Muslim and Christian neighbors. Its members grew to be well-off economically, primarily as merchants of textiles, silks, and gum arabic, building a synagogue with a resident rabbi (who was also a *shohet* and *mohel*) and a bustling Jewish Recreation Club that served the entire community.

The Jewish community of Sudan, while not particularly observant, was very traditional. Gender roles were clearly defined, and strict rules around dating and marriage were enforced. Socializing between unmarried men and women was frowned upon, and "dating" happened only in the presence of a chaperone after an engagement had been arranged. This chaperone was often a younger member of the family who would tag along, happy to go to the cinema late at night or on picnicking day trips.

The engagement process was instigated in one of two ways—via a match-maker or by the couple themselves. The matchmaker was often an older female member of either family who spotted an opportunity for a match and made introductions. The latter route was more common, especially from the mid-1940s onward. A boy would ask his mother or aunt to approach the mother of the girl he had set his mind on, often someone he had known from childhood or someone he had seen in synagogue. The girl's parents would then in turn ask (or in earlier years tell) her about the proposed match. After the girl gave her approval, word would be sent back to the aspiring groom, and he would ask the girl's father for his permission to court and then marry her.

After this, a wedding would take place within months. Men typically married in their early to midtwenties, once they had become independent and financially stable. In the earlier years of the community, girls were married as young as fourteen. From the latter half of the 1940s, brides were typically between sixteen and eighteen years old. Marriage between first or second cousins was not uncommon.

The Jewish communities of Sudan and Egypt were close, with almost every family in Sudan having some sort of relation in the Egyptian community. As a result of this, as well as the shortage of eligible young men in Sudan, a fair number of marriages took place uniting the communities. Wealthier families of Sudan often sent daughters of marriageable age to visit family in Egypt, where they happened to find a relative to marry, or sent for an eligible male relative to come and work with them.

According to synagogue records, as collated by Nahem Ilan, 109 *ketubot* were signed over fifty-eight years of Jewish life in Sudan. A very small handful of these were carried out after one partner completed a conversion process, done in strict accordance with Jewish law. Before the wedding, the bride would visit the mikveh. This was first situated in the rabbi's house and then on the synagogue grounds. The ceremony was typically short, lasting no more than ten to fifteen minutes. It would be conducted in the Khartoum synagogue by the resident rabbi or a visiting rabbi sent from Egypt. The ketubah, often stating the financial terms of the marriage, would be signed on the bimah/tebah. Family members would hold up a tallit as a chuppah. The whole community would be invited to the ceremony and the synagogue was often exceptionally full. Brides wore Western-style white dresses, all handmade by a professional seamstress or by the bride and her female relatives themselves.

The wedding ceremony would be followed by a quick trip to a photography studio (if it were within budget) and then a party, the scale of which varied greatly according to the wealth of the couple and their families. In the community's early days, wedding celebrations were traditional in style. The whole community would gather at the bride's house, where the bride and groom would sit on two large, throne-like chairs. The yard would be decorated with multicolored light bulbs, strung out like fairy lights. There would be dancing, lemonade, homemade finger foods, and, of course, ice cream.

By the 1950s, far more individualized celebrations were in fashion. While couples of more modest means would still have a small, self-catered party at home or at the Club, wealthier couples could splurge on a larger party at the Grand Hotel in Khartoum. Full sit-down meals were catered, guests were invited, and singers were often hired. All of these parties—at home, at the Club, or at a hotel—would be held outside in the warm desert air. Ladies would be given bonbonnieres (small boxes or lace pouches filled with sugared almonds) to take home with them.

My great-aunt and uncle married in Khartoum in 1963. They met when my uncle saw my aunt coming out of a friend's house opposite the synagogue where he was praying on Rosh Hashanah. My great-uncle came from a moderately wealthy family, and he had opened his own shop in Khartoum. My aunt was a student at the University of Khartoum and lived in Omdurman, so although he recognized her, he didn't know who she was. After setting eyes on her, my uncle immediately asked his mother about her. She, together with my aunt's mother, arranged a joint family trip to the countryside where the two young people could get to know each other.

After this trip, they became engaged. My uncle would borrow his father's car every evening to meet his fiancée at the university where she was studying, spend some time with her, and drive her home to Omdurman, about twelve kilometers away on the opposite bank of the Nile. Of course, with a little sibling or friend in tow. They were married at the synagogue in Khartoum by Rabbi Elbaz. Guests included the remaining members of the Jewish community, as well as their Sudanese neighbors, my great-aunt's friends from university, her lecturers, and my great-uncle's business partners. They had a party at the synagogue for all of their guests, went home for a short rest, and finally went to dinner with their close family members at the Grand Hotel. The next day, they left for Asmara in Eritrea, then a province of Ethiopia, on their honeymoon—a beautiful city and a middle-class destination somewhere between a trip within Sudan and a more expensive holiday to Europe.

My great-aunt and great-uncle's wedding was one of the last Jewish weddings in Sudan. After Sudan gained independence in 1956, hostility against Jews began to grow and many families left for Israel and other European countries. After the Six-Day War in 1967, life became unbearably hostile for the remaining Jewish families, and a few years later almost every Jew had left the country.

THAILAND

Mushka Kantor Kaltmann

We are grateful to Mushka for providing an intimate glimpse into Hasidic traditions and customs, from the bride's and groom's first meeting to the wedding celebrations. And in such an unexpected place! Chabad families are emissaries to Jewish communities everywhere in the world. The experiences Mushka relates are a wonderful mélange of time-honored and modern traditions. Some revolve around the late Rabbi Menachem Schneerson (1902–1994). Each year, thousands of people make their way to the Rebbe's and the Rebbeitzen's graves (the Ohel) in Queens, New York. They also send letters and emails to the site asking for the Rebbe's intervention, as Mushka's mother did. Mushka and her husband, Gabi, now parents of five, serve as Rabbi and Rebbitzen of ARK Centre, a synagogue in Melbourne, Australia.

In 1993, as a tiny baby, I moved to Bangkok, where my father was the rabbi of the Jewish community. At that time, there were no big shopping malls, sidewalks, or automatic traffic lights. There were no kosher restaurants, Hebrew schools, or steady prayer services. Yet the small Jewish community of Thailand had a strong, diverse, and committed core of members, Ashkenazic and Sephardic, dedicated to preserving Jewish life. These members became the family I cherished and loved.

In 2014, I was lucky to have the first large Hasidic wedding in Southeast Asia. Needless to say, everyone was invited! When you grow up in a place that feels far from a typical Jewish community, every Jew you encounter feels like family. Relatives and friends came from all over the world. It was held at the Shangri-La Hotel in Bangkok, and there were over five hundred guests.

I am often asked how Gabi and I met. I joke that it was thanks to Mark Zuckerberg. A friend of mine, who saw photos of Gabi on Facebook, was convinced

Mushka joyfully dances with women guests at her wedding

that we would be suited for each other. I saw that he came from a similar religious background and, like my dad, his family is also from Australia. He was
working in the United States at the time, and I suggested to the matchmaker
(who was a family friend) that we first meet virtually to see if there was any potential. However, Gabi insisted that we meet only in person, as he didn't think
he would give a good impression over Skype. (There was no Zoom back then!)

My maternal grandparents live in Los Angeles, so I flew to LA to see them
and to meet Gabi. When I arrived late at night, my phone wasn't working, and
I didn't want to bother my grandparents. Luckily, someone at the airport was
kind enough to let me borrow a phone, and I called Gabi. He was so relaxed,
and even though I was supposed to meet him at a formal date the next night, he
came right over and drove me to my grandparents' house. I can't fully explain
it, but something about him felt different from other dates. Yes, he was very
good-looking with a charming personality. But something felt different—a
strong and wholesome feeling, a completion.

Marriage is a big decision, and as they say, you can never be one hundred
percent sure. We had a week and a half before Gabi was leading a Birthright
trip to Israel and I had to get back to my job in Bangkok. We saw each other
every day and had many meaningful conversations at different spots, including
my favorite at Venice Beach. We kept in touch after I left LA. It seemed that we

were compatible; our priorities and the characteristics we had been searching for in a mate were the same, and our chemistry was palpable. But we were both nervous about taking the big leap. I remember Gabi telling me that marriage is like constructing a building: it does not happen overnight. You need to start from the foundation and then slowly build up brick by brick, every day being a work in progress.

Four weeks later, we met in New York for our formal engagement. By that time, I knew Gabi was my soul mate; we had a venue booked for our engagement party. However, my father insisted that there had to be a formal proposal. So two days before our engagement party, Gabi proposed to me at a Starbucks with a candy ring and coffee cups that said, "Will you marry me? xx."

On the sixteenth of Tammuz, July 14, 2014, we went to the Lubavitcher Rebbe's resting place in Queens. We said prayers there, and Gabi and I left a letter asking for a blessing for our engagement. In keeping with Chabad tradition, it was only at that point that our engagement was formalized, and in keeping with Gabi's active social media presence, we took a selfie to be posted right then and there on Facebook. After that, Gabi left to watch a World Cup match with his friends, and I went to have my hair and makeup done and to get dressed.

We had a party in Crown Heights for 150 people that night, which didn't end until two o'clock in the morning. Gabi walked me to a friend's house where I was staying. It was late, and I was locked out. I was tired after a long day and starting to feel helpless. But then I remembered that it wasn't just about *me* anymore. It was about *us*; we were in this together! It was a magical night as we wandered the streets of Brooklyn and dozed on (separate) park benches until the morning.

We got married six weeks later in Bangkok. The date was set without a confirmed venue for the wedding. It was hard to find a place that could accommodate so many people with an appropriate place for a chuppah on such short notice. My mother was getting really worried. So three weeks before the wedding, she faxed a letter to the Rebbe's resting place in Queens. She asked for a blessing to be able to hold the wedding as scheduled in the best possible manner. The next day, the Shangri-La Hotel called. They had a cancellation, and we could have the wedding there!

Gabi and I didn't speak or see each other for a week before the ceremony. The bride and groom must always be accompanied wherever they go during that week. They are considered VIPs who are never to walk around alone. I went to the mikveh two days before the wedding. It was very emotional for me and an auspicious time to pray. When I was under the water, I felt a spiritual sense of rebirth, humbled by the thought of connecting to thousands of Jewish women before me. It was private, restoring, and very special.

I spent the next day with friends and met Gabi's three sisters and four brothers and my future mother-in-law for the first time. Then it was my wedding day. As is customary, that day I read *tehillim* (psalms) whenever I had a chance. It is also the custom to put coins in the charity boxes of the house. It was especially emotional having both sets of grandparents, who flew in from America, at my side. My four sisters (ages eighteen, sixteen, fourteen, and eleven) helped me dress. They and my three brothers (ages twenty, nine, and six) had been excited about my wedding for years!

The women and men were in separate rooms. Gabi came to my room to put on my veil. It is the custom for both the bride and groom to wear something under the chuppah that belonged to a holy and righteous person. The lining of my veil, therefore, came from a garment that belonged to the Rebbe. Under his jacket, Gabi wore a shirt that belonged to the Rebbe. After my father, my father-in-law, and my grandparents gave me their blessings, my mother and Gabi's mother supported me as we walked to the chuppah outside on the bank of the Chao Phraya River. It was gorgeous and very hot—luckily, everyone had water bottles.

Gabi and I had fasted that day. I walked around him seven times. My dad explained that the souls of our departed loved ones were present at the chuppah. Men close to the family were honored with reading the *Sheva Brochot* (seven blessings). The women, including my grandmothers, held candles under the chuppah. The Israeli ambassador to Thailand came and stood under the chuppah while Gabi broke the glass. Everyone shouted Mazel Tov.

Gabi and I then went to the *yichud* (seclusion) room for about ten minutes. We hadn't seen each other for a week and had no physical contact during our dating period. Being in a room with only Gabi, having a few moments to ourselves before the big party, reminded us that marriage isn't about what you will do or achieve but about the commitment you have to one another. It starts with those few minutes of giving each other undivided attention in that sacred space. It was also a chance to hydrate after our fast. When we came out, it was the most heartwarming and exciting moment, seeing the community and so many family members and friends who flew in from abroad to come and celebrate with us. Then the dancing started—men with men and women with women, separated by a *mechitsa* (barrier) made of gorgeous flowers that my mother specially designed. It went on until one o'clock in the morning—truly a night to remember!

THREE

—⟋⟍—

BETROTHAL

BETROTHAL IS AN OLD-FASHIONED English word that means "engagement." In liberal branches of Judaism today, the usual symbol of engagement is a ring the future spouse gives to the intended bride following a proposal of marriage. Usually private, sometimes creatively planned far in advance, proposals in the United States are occasionally public spectacles, witnessed by strangers at sporting and other events. With the receipt of a ring, the intended spouse becomes the bride's fiancé (from the old French, meaning "a promise"). The engagement might spark a variety of celebrations—parties attended by both women and men as well as a series of women-only bridal showers featuring gifts, food, and games hosted by family members and friends, or even bachelorette trips or hen dos to far-off destinations, popular among women in the United States and Britain, respectively, who are able to manage the cost.

In days past and in traditional Jewish circles, betrothal was and is signified by more than ring-giving. The stories in this chapter describe a variety of customs and ceremonies directed by the future brides' and grooms' families that mark the beginning of the betrothal phase before the wedding.

Whereas a Jewish non-Orthodox engagement can be broken—and people are likely to think that it is better to break up before marriage than to divorce later—historically, a Jewish engagement was binding and still is to some extent among the ultra-Orthodox.[1] The ancient legal ceremony of betrothal is called *erusin* or kiddushin (sanctification), aptly labeled in this chapter by the author from Burma as the "half wedding" of her thirteen-year-old mother. Typically, the erusin took place a few months before the wedding ceremony (called *nisuin*) but no longer than one year prior.

45

Traditionally, the erusin ceremony contained elements that, starting in the Middle Ages, were combined with the nisuin ceremony to form today's wedding ceremony under the chuppah. The erusin involved two blessings over wine and the reading of the *tenaim*, a declaration of the couple's intention to be married, as well as the financial conditions of the marriage, agreed upon by the families of the bride and groom. This often included the terms of the dowry given by the bride's family. An ancient component of the ceremony is sometimes referred to as *kinyan* ("acquisition" of the bride) by giving her a ring or another object of some value accompanied by a formal declaration of betrothal. (The ritual of a single ring from the groom to the bride during the modern wedding ceremony has been rejected by many, if not most, brides, who exchange rings with the groom. This may be interpreted as a sign of egalitarian union rather than the "purchase" of the bride.) The betrothal ceremony ended with the breaking of crockery by family members, prefiguring breaking the glass at the end of modern wedding ceremonies.

Aspects of erusin rituals have come down to modern times. In this chapter, two sisters from Chile describe their mother's brief engagement ceremony when the couple held a white handkerchief between them, said a blessing, and then the bride accepted a ring in front of the assembled guests. (A similar ceremony is described in a Moroccan enclave of Spain in chapter 10.)

In Turkey, following a meeting of the two fathers, the families gathered at the bride's parents' home where, as custom dictated, the future groom's family brought a silver bowl (a bonbonier) destined to become the bride's heirloom, filled with chocolates and sugared almonds.

Several stories in this collection mention the dowry, a gift of money or property given to the bride by her family for use in her new marriage. As a symbol of social status in the community, the dowry was of importance until the recent past and the subject of intricate Jewish law and discussion.[2] Birth order might determine which of several sisters in a family would have a large dowry and a more luxurious wedding, as the story from 1920s Romania illustrates. The custom of *spander ashugar* (hanging the dowry), adopted from the larger Bulgarian culture, is no longer practiced as it was in the story from the 1930s, when family members had to fund the garments for a poor bride. In contrast, the well-to-do bride from Lebanon spent months before her wedding being fitted for a trousseau (the clothing she would bring to her marriage), but she refused to let her father offer a dowry.

Stories from Jewish communities in Africa describe little-known betrothal ceremonies, rituals grounded in the indigenous cultures of the areas where the communities are located. Among the Abayudaya of Uganda, who adopted

Judaism a century ago, the *kwanjula* introduction ceremony is practiced as a precursor to a mainstream Jewish wedding. In Nigeria, the betrothal ceremony, observed after formal negotiations between the families and led by the *onye mbe* (middleman), follows a series of proscribed rituals more elaborate than the wedding itself. Interestingly, a bride price is paid at the betrothal and comes from the family of the groom rather than the bride's family.

Each of the diverse stories in this chapter is personal and unique, but they have something in common: the involvement of the family in the betrothal of the couple after the decision to marry. Formal or informal negotiations between the parents of potential brides and grooms ensured that the parents approved the union and that preparations, including celebrations, could commence. Of all the procedures that betrothal entailed, almost everyone remembered one set of details—the regional mouth-watering delicacies that were served to guests at celebratory gatherings.

BULGARIA

Luiza Kario

Translated by Leon Benatov

After Nazi occupation, Bulgarian Jews were saved from deportation to death camps thanks to intervention by Parliament, the king, the clergy, and ordinary citizens. Nevertheless, Jews number only about five thousand due to immigration to Israel and other countries after World War II. In October 2017, Barbara Vinick met with members of the Ladino Club of Sofia in the beautiful Central Synagogue, one of the largest Sephardic synagogues in Europe. Members get together monthly to speak and preserve Ladino, the fading language of Sephardic Jews based on Spanish. The following story appeared in Para Ke No Se Olvide (In Order Not to Be Forgotten*), a book with stories in Bulgarian and Ladino by members of the club. It is used with permission of the club and the author's family.*

In 1933, my sister, Victoria, was eighteen years old. At that time, movies and popular songs were filled with love and romance. My sister fell in love with Albert Perez, a young man of twenty who had not yet done his military service. They wanted to get married. They had lost all common sense.

Mama, Papa, and all the relatives tried to tell them that they were young, had time, could wait. But the young people didn't want to listen, saying that if they were not permitted to marry, they would commit suicide.

Central Synagogue, Sofia

At that time, people did such things. What to do! The relatives on both sides gathered. They gave in. Albert's family wanted a dowry and wanted to have a look at the dowry. We had no money, and my father was depressed about it. So our relatives promised that everyone would help.

My mother, Rachel, only thirty-four at the time, made marzipan and placed it on a beautiful tray with mother of pearl and foil leaf. My brother, Isaac, and I took it to the relatives-in-law. Then we started to collect a dowry. We had to supply fabric for clothes and underwear and everything that the bride and groom needed. Each of our relatives bought many things—lingerie for the bride, linens for the household, fabric that Mama brought to one of our neighbors to sew dresses, as well as a hat, bag, coat, and shoes, all of which were bought according to the fashion of the day.

We did the traditional spander ashugar (hanging the dowry) in our house. We lived in one room with a kitchenette. We put some of the clothes on the bed, with dresses hanging on hangers on the windowsill. Some things were hung on the curtains with pins.

We invited the women from both families. When the guests came, they started looking around, running fingers over the clothes, and praising the good things. Then the women sat down and Mama, Victoria, and I started to serve the treats. Mama had made delicious *kezadikas* (a kind of cheese-filled muffin), *chukuros* (a rolled pastry), and other kinds of pastries. Finally, we served coffee.

The women began to sing wedding songs with tambourine accompaniment and to dance.

> *You are giving a bit, my in-law,*
> *you are giving a bit to your daughter,*
> *your beloved daughter.*
> *I will give her seven dresses, one for every day,*
> *seven jackets, seven camisoles.*

Finally, the song ends:

> *I will give her a golden necklace,*
> *her fiancé to enjoy.*

There wasn't a mikveh then, so my sister did the prewedding bathing in the public bath. Again, the women from both sides came. Mama brought treats for the relatives and the women who worked there.

The wedding was at Central Synagogue. I remember that the rabbi was dressed gorgeously, all in white, his robe decorated with spangles, all shining. He sang magnificently. The newlyweds were very beautiful. I was dressed in a lovely pink dress and hat. I was nine years old. I remember this wedding from the past with great love and respect.

BURMA

Sally Joseph

Arriving in the mid-eighteenth century, mainly as businesspeople from Iraq, the Jewish population of Burma lived well, as Sally reports, and at one point reached

Sally (far right) and her family,
1957. Her father died the next
week.

*about two thousand. In 2015 there were approximately twenty Jews left in Burma. As
Sally's story documents, her mother and father were among a small number of Jews
(about two hundred) who returned to Burma, also called Myanmar, after World
War II. The synagogue where Sally's parents married is a prime tourist destination.
The kiddushin (betrothal) phase of marriage that Sally's mother experienced is an
ancient Torah-mandated practice that has been merged with the nisuin (marriage)
phase in modern-day wedding ceremonies around the world.*

My mother and father are both descendants of the Joseph family who came
from Baghdad to Rangoon (now known as Yangon), the capital of Burma, in
the 1800s. My mother, Florence Shamash, was the second eldest of seven children from a wealthy family, well known in the Jewish community. My father,
Abraham (Abie) Ezra Joseph, was twenty years older than my mother, and
they were first cousins. My mother was kiddushin (betrothed) at age thirteen,
at which time she left her family and went to live with her mother-in-law until
the marriage. This was the traditional, religiously sanctioned "half wedding"
that could be broken only by a *get*, a Jewish divorce. I am sure that family background played a big part in the decision. (My paternal grandmother appeared

to have an encyclopedic knowledge of the background of most of the families in Rangoon who were originally from Baghdad. Until her death, she didn't hesitate to voice her disapproval if my sisters and I were friendly with descendants of "unsuitable" families.)

A dramatic series of events had occurred before the engagement. During World War II, in anticipation of the Japanese invasion of Burma, both families had to flee and leave everything behind. The women and children were able to leave for India on a British ship. But when the British suspended evacuation operations, the men had to walk out of Burma into India. My father was among those who made the month-long trek from Burma through the Hukong Valley. Few people survived. He arrived at Assam, India, with a very high temperature that the doctors treated as malaria.

My mother spent several years in India, first in Pune and then in Mumbai, where her father passed away when she was twelve, leaving her mother a young widow. In 1947 when the war was over, both my mother's and my father's families returned to Rangoon. There, Florence and Abie had the first postwar Jewish wedding. It took place at the beautiful Musmeah Yeshuah synagogue. My mother was sixteen. Already an accomplished seamstress and homemaker, Florence sewed her own wedding dress and made her own bouquet. Because it was so soon after the end of the war, no electricity was available and the wedding was held by candlelight. I was born the next year.

There were twenty-five hundred Jews in Rangoon before the Japanese invasion, but after the war, many had left for Australia, England, or the United States. My parents, my two younger sisters, and I lived very well in Rangoon. Everything was done for us. We had a servant who cooked and took care of us children and another who only cleaned the bathrooms and emptied the trash. Tragically, my father's fever returned, the result of an unidentified tropical virus, and he was not able to recover. He died at the age of forty-six in 1957.

After my father died, the Jewish population went down to almost nothing. My mother worked hard to run my father's business, no mean feat in those days. But in 1960, after the government required foreign nationals (we were considered British) to relinquish their nationality and become Burmese nationals or leave, we left for London. My mother was the only wage earner, and it was tough to make a pound go far. My mother used to buy fruit once a week, and I remember her saying, "Girls, you can eat this all at once, or save some for the rest of the week." Without servants, we learned to do everything for ourselves.

In 1969, after ten years in London, Florence fulfilled her intention to live in the United States, an objective begun when Abie was alive and aborted when he died on the cusp of proceeding with their emigration. She made a good life in Los Angeles, where she was joined by her three daughters, and in 1980 she married Maurice Shamash from a well-known Iraqi family in Rangoon. It was a happy marriage, ending with Maurice's death fifteen years later.

My mother is well known in the Sephardic community of Los Angeles, where she and I live together. Soon after she arrived, she got together a group of women from India, Indonesia, Singapore, and Rangoon, who had formerly kept to themselves, to form a sisterhood at our synagogue, Kahal Joseph Congregation. She also helped to start a Sephardic Jewish day school. Florence's strength and will to succeed have made her an inspiration to friends and family. The word *can't* does not appear in her dictionary.

CHILE

Ronit Behar and Ruthy Benoliel

Ronit and Ruthy, sisters who now live in Miami, are active members of the Jewish community. Ruthy is the national vice president of WIZO (the Women's International Zionist Organization), and Ronit divides her time working as a real estate agent and volunteering for charitable organizations. They describe an age-old engagement ceremony called tenaim (literally "conditions"). Traditionally, it included signing a document specifying financial arrangements by representatives of the bride's and groom's families. Ronit and Ruthy do not mention a formal document, but they do note a part of the ceremony called kinyan in which a handkerchief or kerchief is held by the engaged couple, signifying their intention to be wed, and the bride is given a ring or something else of value. The ceremony often included the breaking of a plate or other crockery, similar to the breaking of the glass at the end of the wedding ceremony.

Our mother, Catalina Leonor (Caty) Gateno, was born in 1939 in Santiago, the capital of Chile. She was the first child of our grandmother, Esther Gateno, whose parents had emigrated to Chile from Izmir, Turkey, and our grandfather, Moises Gateno, whose family had moved to Chile from Izmir when he was twelve years old.

Life was comfortable in the small Jewish community of Santiago. There were no Jewish day schools, so Caty attended public school. Her family attended La Sinagoga Sefaradi located on Santa Isabel Street. There, her Uncle Alejandro performed marriage ceremonies and bar mitzvahs, led everyday prayers, and was also a *mashgiah* (kosher slaughterer).

Caty arrives at La Sinagoga Sefaradi, Santiago

Every Saturday Caty attended Maccabi, an international Jewish sports and culture organization, where she learned to love the State of Israel and socialized with Jewish kids in the area. She remembers some episodes of antisemitism at age twelve, when a few members of the large German community in Santiago would throw rocks at Jewish homes and once pushed her brother, Jacques, from his bike. Partially in response to such behavior, the *Estadio Israelita*, a club with a restaurant, swimming pool, and sports complex, was founded in 1958 and became the meeting place of Jewish youth. (It is still functioning, bigger and better than before.)

After high school, Caty attended the University of Chile where she studied physical therapy and rehabilitation. During that time, her family moved to Arica, a city in northern Chile near the Peruvian border. She remained in Santiago, living with her grandmother, Alejandrina, where she learned to cook amazing Turkish dishes.

In 1963, when Caty was twenty-four, she went to visit her family in Arica. While walking with her sister, they ran into Ovadia Shrem, whose brother was married to her sister's friend. Ovadia, who was twelve years older than Caty, was born in Turkey to a well-to-do family. When he was a young boy, his family moved to Aleppo, Syria, after losing much of their fortune. At age fourteen, Ovadia left Aleppo and, after a harrowing journey walking across the mountains, arrived in what was then Palestine. There, he made a living selling eggs in the streets, cleaning windows, doing carpentry work, and when there was a lot of rain, carrying people from one side of the street to the other. After his army service and jobs in New York and Brazil, and with his family finally established in Israel, Ovadia was living in Arica where he had three stores, successfully importing clothing from Europe.

Caty and Ovadia's first date took place at El Pinguino (Penguin) ice cream shop. The time from the day they met until the day they married was only twenty-one days! The engagement was celebrated in Arica at the home of Ovadia's brother whom he had brought from Israel to help with his business. It was a small affair since most of Caty's family and friends lived in Santiago. The engagement ceremony was performed by her beloved Uncle Alejandro Gateno. As customary, Caty and Ovadia held a white handkerchief between them, did a blessing, and then she was given a ring.

They were married in Santiago at La Sinagoga Sefaradi in a ceremony conducted by Rabbi Sibony and Uncle Alejandro. This was a big affair with 150 guests. After the ceremony, they celebrated in a party hall where they danced until two o'clock in the morning. Their honeymoon, which lasted seven months, began in Miami, continued in Los Angeles, and ended in Mexico where they spent five months traveling around the country. This trip was very special for Caty because it was the first time she ever traveled outside of Chile.

In 1965, back in Chile, they had their first daughter, Ruthy Miriam. A year later they moved to Lima, Peru, where their other three children—Marco,

Moris, and Ronit—were born. In 1971 they moved to Panama, where Caty still resides. Ovadia passed away in September 2014 at age eighty-six. He and our mother Caty were married for fifty-one years. Caty continues to travel to visit her daughters in Miami where they live and spends time in Israel where they have second homes.

LEBANON

Batia Shems

Batia's story describes age-old marital customs and rituals in a community where, in the 1960s, some women benefited from fresh outlooks. Women like Batia made their own decisions about whom to marry, and some successfully rebelled against the dowry process controlled by men of the family. Yet, tradition reigned in other aspects of betrothal and marriage, most notably in the necessity to supply proof of the bride's virginity. Today, like Batia's family who left after the murder of her father, hardly any Jews remain in a once thriving community.

The Jewish community of Beirut included about six thousand families. We all lived in the same neighborhood, Wadi Abu Jamil, and knew each other well. The dating scene began when we were teenagers. It was common for us to meet at the youth club in our neighborhood. Once we were university age, however, our parents were stricter about dating. While we did interact with non-Jews, we rarely dated them. Some marriages were arranged and often involved matches from abroad.

My courtship was unusual and took everyone by surprise. I met my husband, Moise, on a Friday afternoon in April 1966. He was in Beirut visiting his parents and was about to go back to the United States to resume his medical residency. We went out for a short date that day before Shabbat. He asked me to go out again the next evening after Shabbat. On Sunday night, while on our third date, he proposed. We got married in August of that same year.

Once a couple decided to get engaged, the process fell into the hands of their families. The groom was required to formally ask for the bride's hand in marriage from her father. Then the elders of the families would meet with both fathers to discuss the conditions of the marriage. Notice that only the males in the family met for these important decisions!

As in the time of our ancestors, the bride was required to bring a dowry to the union. We're not talking about a herd of sheep or a couple of chickens. A monetary dowry would be offered to the groom, revealing what a family was

able to contribute based on their financial situation. Tradition usually pre-
vailed, and agreements were usually reached.

My case was different, however. As my father was heading out to meet with
my future father-in-law, my fiancé, and his closest relatives, I firmly reminded
my father that I was not to be sold! If a dowry came up for discussion, I instructed him to walk out. My father was very torn since refusing to give a dowry
would appear that he was of limited means. As luck would have it, my in-laws
and fiancé respected my previously stated position and didn't insist on a dowry.

Next, the fun began. The first engagement party was typically held at the
future bride's home. My parents hosted an elaborate, catered dinner party. As
customary, my future husband and his family were present when he gave the
engagement ring to me.

A day later, as custom dictated, the groom's family invited me and my family
and friends to their house for a party. The bride would bring a gift of her own to
present to the groom, and in my case, it was a Swiss watch. With both families
formally welcomed, the wedding planning began. In general, the bride and
groom were not involved in the wedding plans. Our parents were in charge.

Like all brides, I began to prepare my trousseau, which included clothing
and jewelry. We hired a seamstress who came for weeks to measure and sew
custom outfits, including my wedding dress. Then we had a traditional party
before the wedding to show off the trousseau. Friends and family came for a
fun-filled afternoon.

On the eve of the wedding, I was taken to the mikveh. As usual, it was a
family affair. My mother, grandmothers, elderly aunts, and future mother-in-
law and her family were present. My mother-in-law gave me an elaborate spa
set that included a nice bathrobe, plush towels, perfumes, and a gold bracelet,
as well as a *hamsa* made of baked dough, the symbol to protect against the evil
eye. All were beautifully arranged in a basket.

My wedding was held at the synagogue in the mountain town of Bhamdoun,
a resort fifteen miles from Beirut. The guest list was in the hundreds, with
friends and family and also business acquaintances included. Both families
formed a receiving line at the entrance of the synagogue to greet the guests.
The whole place was filled with flower arrangements and baskets that had been
sent by guests. Meanwhile, I waited at home for my father to bring me to the
ceremony once all of the guests had arrived and the ketubah was signed.

I made my entrance on the arm of my father and headed to the bimah where I
was met by my future husband. The chuppa was crowded with members of both
families and our parents. Two rabbis officiated and blessed us, all in Hebrew.

After the glass was broken and the wishes and hugs shared all around, we headed to my in-law's home for a cocktail reception. When exiting the synagogue, guests were handed a pretty bonbonnière, a mini candy dish filled with sugared almonds wrapped in tulle and ribbons.

We spent our honeymoon night close to home since the next morning my mother was expected to stop by to retrieve a proof of virginity! A pretty lace handkerchief was discreetly slipped into her purse, and it was up to her to show it to the new mother-in-law. Lots of stories have been told about this custom and the various ways couples complied.

On the Shabbat following the wedding, my husband was called to the Torah for an aliyah in the presence of both families and me. While on the bimah, he was showered with candies. This was followed by an elaborate luncheon at his parents' home.

It was usual for couples to set up residence in the vicinity of both parents. Our situation was different, as we had plans to move to the United States so that my husband could complete his medical residency. During all the prewedding preparations, my mother was very emotional, knowing that I would be leaving home and living so far away.

Although we had planned to live in the United States for only a few years, we ended up settling there permanently because of the political situation. The wars in the Middle East and the civil war in Beirut destroyed our homes. The synagogues in Beirut and Bhamdoun are now in ruins. As for my own family, in February 1970, my father was murdered by Palestinian extremists while in his office. In the aftermath of this tragedy, my mother and the rest of our family left Lebanon and are now scattered around the world in Israel, Canada, and the United States.

More than fifty years after my marriage, I can hardly believe all those years have slipped by. We are now surrounded by our three grown children and their families and seven precious grandkids.

NIGERIA

Remy Ilona

Remy practiced law in Nigeria for many years before devoting himself to expounding the links between the thirty-two million Igbos in Nigeria, often described as the "Jews of Africa" and the people of ancient Israel. Author of The Igbos and Israel: An Inter-cultural Study of the Largest Jewish Diaspora *and other books and articles on the subject, Remy received his degree in religious studies in 2016 from Florida International University. His story of meeting Irene and their betrothal and wedding celebrations is filled with descriptions of rituals little-known in the West.*

Irene (Ifeyinwa) Malizu and I got married in 2008. A few things happened before we found each other. When I was a toddler, my parents and Irene's parents lived in the same compound in Lagos. After a few years as neighbors, Irene's parents relocated to England for a few years while my future father-in-law pursued his university education. Although both families came from the same clan, they lost contact.

Five years later, my mother was walking through the maternity ward of the hospital in Ozubulu, the city in Anambra State where we lived. There, she came upon her former neighbor, Monica Malizu, who told her that she had delivered a baby girl the day before. My mother congratulated the new mother, lifted up the baby, prayed for her, and, as tradition dictated, gave the mother some money for the infant before she took her leave.

My mother was not ordinary; she could *see* when she was alive. We have no way of knowing if she saw anything that made her go to the Ozubulu Joint Hospital that day because she is no longer with us. But the role that G-d caused that infant to play in my life is certainly remarkable.

In 2008, I opened my eyes and began to search for a wife. As a traditional Igbo, I wanted to marry a woman from home, that is, from my clan or from a very close clan. If these were not possible, then I wanted to marry another Igbo. In *omenana* (laws or things that must be done, kept, and observed), the ideal permissible marriage is the one between Igbos who are not close blood relatives, but whose families know each other well, to the extent that they can vouch for the characters of everybody in the families.

When I spotted the yearbook of the microbiology department of the University of Maiduguri for the year 2008, I began leafing through its pages. One slim darkish damsel, with a name that people from my clan usually bear, caught my eye. Checking her profile closely, I confirmed that she was from my clan, and I became interested.

In older times, I would have asked members of my family to begin investigations and negotiations before getting in touch with her. But as we have dispersed from home and have tech now, I dialed her telephone number, introduced myself as an Ozubulu lawyer and writer, and I told her that I would like to see her for "serious business." She responded that if the business was really serious, I should come to the city of Port Harcourt, where her parents lived, go to their house, and discuss the business with her and her parents.

A week later, I made my way to Port Harcourt. At the airport, I was happy to see that Irene was beautiful and felt that if all went well, the match would be an ideal one. We proceeded to her home, where, to cut the story short, we were asked if we felt that we could live together as man and wife. We said yes.

After I left Port Harcourt I called my younger sister, my eldest brother, and my mother's kinsman to inform them of this development. Since our family knew Irene's family well, we didn't need to do much investigation. Her grandfather was the oldest man in Ozubulu. He was over 115 when he passed on. Known to be a sincere and honest man, he lived all his life as a traditional Hebrew. My family is also an open book in my community. As a leading family of Ozubulu, the *obi* (personal place of worship) of the Egbema clan is on our land.

My sister and brother visited the Malizu family and told them in special language that "there is a fruit on a tree in their compound that the Ilonas are interested in plucking." The Malizu family responded that they would inquire from the fruit if it wanted to go with the Ilonas. Both families seemed to be on the same page, so my sister and brother informed the wider Ilona family, who agreed that the Ilonas could intermarry with the Malizus, who were of good stock and did not have any traceable blood relationship with them.

The Ilonas nominated Luke Orji, my mother's kinsman, as the *onye mbe* (middleman). His job was to relay information between the families and to serve as a guide to the husband and wife if the marriage were to take place. When the families met again, my family formally repeated the request, and the Malizus gave the go-ahead. My side heaved a sigh of relief. A date was set for the betrothal (*ime ego*), which, among the Igbo, is as strong as the marriage. That day the bride gives her consent publicly (or rejects the proposal publicly) and the bride price is paid.

But before the betrothal, Irene had to come to the Ilona homestead to spend some time, to appraise the family that she would be joining, and to let the members of the family appraise her too. Irene came to our house, spent one week, and returned to her home. Her family informed mine that the betrothal could proceed.

From very early in the morning on the day appointed for the betrothal, my family began to send jars of palm wine, cartons of beer, and crates of mineral water to the Malizu family. At the Malizu compound, serious cooking began. Youths cut palm fronds to set up the *okpukpu* (canopy) inside the Malizu obi. Toward evening my family and friends began to come. As the Ilonas and their friends arrived, they were shown to a corner of the obi prepared for them. I took my seat inside the canopy. When enough guests had gathered, my bride's mother and a young cousin brought in platters of kola nuts and handed them to the elders of the Malizu family, who asked the youngest member of the family to carry the offering and show it to us. We thanked them and soon after, the oldest member of the Malizu family asked for water and an *oji* (kola nut). He washed his hands, after which he raised the kola nut and began to pray, basically pleading that the marriage would be successful, as we all crave for *omumu* (increase in our families).

Irene was given a cup of palm wine and told to give it to her husband-to-be. Middleman Luke Orji intoned, *Ngwa jee nye onye o ya adiri gi na ya mma* (Now, go and give this wine to the person that we pray, it will be well with you and him). Everybody watched and waited with bated breath. Genuflecting slightly, Irene handed the cup of palm wine to me. I took a deep draft of the wine, gave the remainder to Irene, and everybody rose in joy. She had given her consent formally and publicly. The marriage had begun. Although, typically, dances are not performed at this event, some happy people got up and did a few turns.

Next, accompanied by the middleman, I went over to where my father-in-law was sitting. I paid the bride price to him and a conclave of the oldest members of his family. This called for some secrecy because a bride must never know how much was paid. This money belongs to the father exclusively.

As it was getting dark, the oldest man from the Malizu side elected to pray and thank G-d for the successful marriage before the feasting began. Standing up, he thanked Chukwu (the Igbo name for G-d) for connecting both families, for making the event a success, and asked Him to make their daughter a source of pride to them. As he prayed, many intoned, "She will be as fruitful as our ancestors. She will give birth to many sons and daughters."

One by one, members of our party began to move to the area for the feast. There, eating, drinking palm wine, and jesting began. The Igbo people enjoy a joke (*njakiri*). Much of the jesting was bawdy and directed to me about palm wine and its properties as an aphrodisiac. The partying continued until dawn, when the oldest man in my family got up and sent word to my in-laws that we were set to go. They told us to wait awhile so that they could get my bride ready. After an hour or so, some young maidens ushered Irene out with singing, accompanying her to where I was waiting. I then drove home with my new wife.

Two years later, we decided to have the wedding party (*ima ogodo na igba nkwu*). In olden times, this celebration followed the betrothal. But our ancestors wisely made adjustments: After the betrothal, a couple could go and build their home, gradually raising the resources for this costly event involving a feast for the whole community. If they have children by the time of the wedding, the children are not allowed to attend and must not taste even a morsel of food served at the occasion.

With the support of my siblings, I acquired much food and wine for this event. Unlike the betrothal, the wedding has relatively few rituals. The event took place at my in-laws' compound, where the entire community gathered and was feted. On this occasion, the mother of the bride receives gifts from her son-in-law and the bride's community is wined and dined with the bride as ambassador. Music was in plentiful supply at the party. At one point, Irene and I got up from where we were sitting under the okpukpu and began to dance. As we danced, friends joined in, and then everybody was dancing, stopping only when the *idu uno*, the dowry ritual, began.

Among the Igbo, only sons get a portion of the land, so daughters are given their share of the family wealth as items they need for the home. These often include kitchen utensils, beds, and baby furnishings, sparking laughter by jokers who are assigned to make funny comments when they are displayed. Friends give gifts as well. Wise elders, both men and women, advise the couple to build a G-d fearing home. They counsel the man to view his wife as a sister/mother, to love the wife, and the wife to care for the man who is in some ways a son and a brother too.

ROMANIA

Pnina Abir-Am

Pnina's story of her vibrant aunt Deedee brings to life the years between the two World Wars in Jassy (also Iaşi or Yassy), a center of Jewish cultural and religious life before the decimation of its Jewish population in 1941. Her story reminds us of the lasting power of family lore in the minds of younger generations. One might think that Pnina herself had been present at Deedee's wedding and had seen the couple's horse-drawn carriage as it proceeded down the streets of the city. Pnina, a historian and resident scholar at the Women's Studies Research Center of Brandeis University, has focused her research on the history of women in science.

Deedee's wedding was a staple of our family lore. It signified a remote time in the interwar era when my maternal grandparents offered the magical experience of a fairy tale wedding to their firstborn daughter, Sarah-Dvora, known to me and everyone else as Deedee. The bride's romantic outlook (all knew she married for love), her elegant lace gown, and the groom's uncanny resemblance to Clark Gable, which included a cylinder hat, carved cane, white suit, and silk gloves (he was a seller of high-end fabrics, especially silk), guaranteed that their 1929 wedding would be long remembered. As for me, any time a family member happened to mention Deedee's wedding when I was a child, I would shout excitedly "white horses," which I was told led the newlyweds' carriage in dignified beauty and elegance.

At that time, custom dictated that the dowry of a firstborn daughter be guaranteed by her parents since her marriage prospects reflected on the family's place in the community. This custom also meant that she need not learn a profession. By contrast, Deedee's siblings, six sisters and two brothers, were encouraged to go to vocational schools to become self-sufficient and contribute to the cost of their own weddings. As a result, Deedee's life experience and eventual character became different from those of her siblings, who acquired a more practical outlook on life.

To become known as a potential bride on the Jewish marriage circuit of the late 1920s—a time of relative prosperity that preceded the 1929 stock market crash and its subsequent worldwide economic depression—Deedee spent her adolescence frequenting tea salons (hence her designation as a "young salon lady") and dressing according to the latest fashion. Her fur muffs, a fashionable combination of purse and glove, also became memorable in family lore. Had she lived in England, she might have become known as a flapper.

But Deedee lived her first four decades in Yassy, a provincial capital in northeast Romania, well remembered by my aunts as a culturally vibrant city. Though Romania endured hardship on the battlefield after it joined the Allies in the last two years of World War I, it did exceedingly well at the Versailles Treaty, doubling its territory with areas ceded by its neighboring Austro-Hungarian and Russian Empires. Long known as Europe's granary, Romania was well-off during the 1920s, the period leading to Deedee's wedding.

Deedee's father, Gdaliahu the Levite (or Halevi in Hebrew), was a better-off version of Tevye the milkman of *Fiddler on the Roof* fame since as a milk supplier to the largest local hospital, he had a steady income. Moreover, according to an uncle born two years after Deedee, who often accompanied their father on deliveries, their father was also involved in the more lucrative grain trade. Part of a generation that had already enjoyed urbanization prior to World War I, Deedee's father had help from peasant boys in taking care of cows and smaller farm animals, mostly chickens, ducks, and geese. Deedee's mother, Feiga, who became Zipporah once she arrived in Israel in 1950 at age seventy, preached the credo of family unity, symbolized by an unbreakable bunch of branches (as opposed to breakable single branches), to her nine children who spanned all the interwar Zionist movements from Hashomer Hatzair to Gordonia.

A persistent puzzle for me has remained as to whether there was a connection between Deedee's growing up with the confidence that she would have a great wedding and her later unusual kindness and generosity to me. Though all my aunts were very nice to their nieces and nephews, Deedee was unique. Her zest for life, free spirit, and understanding that a youth must be treated as free and welcome, not a captive target of utilitarian inculcation, offered great relief when I was growing up. She alone among her sisters gave me a key to her apartment in Haifa, letting me come and go as I pleased when I was a young woman. Her conviction, acquired as a young salon lady preparing for a good marriage, that life is dull without romance was instrumental in conferring on me a more relaxed attitude toward life and courage not to give up on finding and marrying Mr. Right at a time such notions were so discredited that it took a decade to seal the deal.

Deedee left Romania with her husband, son, and two younger sisters and their husbands in 1947, settling in Haifa, Israel, after an eventful year in a British camp for detained "illegal immigrants" in Cyprus. Eventually, some of my family also gravitated to Haifa so as to be near Deedee, even though a majority of our aunts lived in Tel Aviv. By then Deedee was over fifty years old, but her youthful spirit made her look ageless. Even when she was close to her death at age ninety, that spirit shone through. That spirit and the image of her in a carriage driven by white horses together with a Clark Gable look-alike will always stay with me. Perhaps, as part of her enduring legacy, my own wedding in Tel Aviv, though lacking in white horses, still featured a movie star look-alike groom, hinting at Paul Newman of *Exodus* fame. Or so Deedee remarked on arriving at our wedding, half a century after her own.

TURKEY

Eda Birol

Most of Turkey's fifteen thousand Jews have not left the country although, according to Israeli and US Jewish media, anxiety is on the rise and people are departing in increasing numbers in the face of Muslim authoritarianism and animus toward Israel. How sad if weddings like Eda's at Neve Shalom Synagogue become only loving memories for a dispersed community that has thrived since the Ottoman sultan welcomed Jews fleeing the Inquisition. In the last decade, Eda and her family moved from Turkey to the United States, where she works for a baby products company as director of logistics and operations.

On my wedding day, I woke up with serenity and peace of mind. I was ready to start on a new path. Like many Jewish brides, my wedding would take place

Eda and Ari's parents surround them with a tallit

in Neve Shalom Synagogue, the largest Sephardic synagogue in Istanbul and the most beautiful. Its elegant architecture and decoration, emotional hymns, and chazzan's prayers make this a dream place to get married, like being a princess in a fairy tale.

We had come a long way to this day. Ari and I had met two and a half years before at my friend's sister's wedding. I always knew that love can come at anytime, anywhere, and usually when you least expect it. But, as much as weddings are a good place to meet and connect with others, I wasn't anticipating meeting anyone I didn't already know. How was I to know that was exactly what was planned for me that night?

We had been together for a few months when Ari proposed to me at another friend's wedding party. He caught me totally off guard. It was a moment of surprise, happiness, excitement, amazement, and shock! After I said yes, we needed to bring the families together.

As tradition dictated, the fathers met first. This meeting was followed a few weeks later by an evening at my parents' house when my husband-to-be and his family came to meet my whole family—grandparents, aunts, uncles, and cousins. According to custom, the groom's family comes with a silver plate or bowl, a bonbonier, filled with chocolates and sugared almonds. (In divorces, the bonbonier is sent back to the groom's family.) My bonbonier is still decorating my living room.

After the bonbonier night came the engagement celebration. Some couples have a wedding-like engagement party. We chose to do a small, cozy house party with family only, where happiness, laughter, and joy were in the air. We decided to marry in a year, so wedding preparations began. Where would we get married, which date would be best, did we want a summer wedding or a winter wedding? So many details, and the closer we got to the wedding date, the more we felt that we would never have everything ready on time.

In Turkey, a civil ceremony is necessary under the law. Another reason to have a party! Our civil wedding took place in a beautiful restaurant one week before our Jewish wedding. We said "I do" in front of the mayor and our families and close friends. The ceremony was followed by music and dancing. As women are the backbones of marriages, I was given the marriage license to keep.

A few days before the wedding, we had a henna party—minus the henna. At this nontraditional party, women family members and my best friends gathered to dance, laugh, and have fun. The days after that passed in a blur.

Finally, it was the day of the wedding. My mom's extraordinary happiness and compassion, my father's love and excitement, and my young brother's admiration filled my soul. A few hours before the wedding, family and friends started to come to the house, excited and energetic, as a photographer captured them wearing their most beautiful clothing.

As I left my home, knowing that after the wedding I would have another home, I had a weird feeling. As the car approached the Neve Shalom Synagogue, those thoughts disappeared. I knew that my husband-to-be would be waiting for me. Like all grooms, he had gone to the synagogue before, walking down the aisle with his parents and having a seat on the *tevah* (pulpit) with them.

As I entered the synagogue, my friends and family were waiting for me at the door. Everyone came to my side; some straightened my gown, some whispered in my ear, some held my hand, some took pictures with me. This continued until everyone was called into the sanctuary. All the members of my family walked down the aisle before me. After my mom went in with my brother, my father and I stayed behind. As we came to the entrance of the sanctuary, everyone stood up. I walked down the aisle with my father to a touching Turkish-Jewish hymn recorded by the renowned group Los Pasharos Safaradis. With a divine feeling, I sat down on the chair that was prepared for me beside my parents on the tevah across from my soon-to-be husband and his parents. Then the ceremony began.

I was helped by both parents to stand up and face the guests while my husband was busy giving the ring to the rabbi. Then Ari came to stand beside me. Our parents covered us with a large tallit that our mothers held over our heads as our fathers held the *tzitzit* (fringes) on both sides. The ceremony continued as the chazzan sang, Ari placed the ring on my finger, we drank the wine, and my now-husband stepped on the glass.

I didn't want the last part of the ceremony to end. As we, along with our parents, faced the arc, the arc's doors were opened and we were blessed. Then everyone who had walked down the aisle—grandparents along with siblings and their families—joined us on the tevah. There, we welcomed all the guests and received their best wishes.

Finally, after we walked back down the aisle as husband and wife and the last pictures were taken, we left the synagogue to our future hand in hand. But first, the party to celebrate our union would begin in a few hours.

UGANDA

Rachel Namudosi Keki

Rachel is a prominent member of the Abayudaya ("People of Judah" in the local Luganda language) community of about two thousand people who live among their Christian and Muslim neighbors in a dozen villages in southeast Uganda. Adopting Judaism in 1919 when their leader chose to follow the Old Testament, the community went underground to preserve their religion during the repressive reign of Idi Amin in the 1970s. Starting in 2003, waves of community members have been formally converted by rabbis from the United States and Israel. Rabbi Gershom Sizomu, an indigenous member of the community who conducts Abayudaya weddings, graduated from the rabbinical school of the American Jewish University in Los Angeles and was ordained as a Conservative rabbi in 2008. Rachel's story shows that some African marriage traditions have not been discarded by a community that has deeply embraced Judaism for more than one hundred years.

Kwanjula means "to introduce" in Luganda, one of the local languages of Uganda. I have attended a number of kwanjula ceremonies of my coworkers. Some of them are members of our Abayudaya Jewish community and some are not. During this ceremony, the bride-to-be formally introduces her future husband and his people to her parents, relatives, and friends. Traditionally, kwanjula served the purpose of marriage. Today, however, it paves the way for the wedding ceremony.

The hopeful husband-to-be writes a letter to his future wife's parents expressing interest in their daughter and offering a date when he intends to come for the introduction. The kwanjula cannot happen without a positive reply from the parents. They present the letter to the elders of the clan who make the final decision.

Before kwanjula, the future husband and wife are prepared for marriage by their paternal uncle and auntie respectively. They teach the couple about their duties in the home and, above all, how to please each other sexually. In traditional Uganda, the wife-to-be would stay indoors three weeks before the day of introduction to work on her beauty. She would be smeared with ghee (clarified butter) and honey to smooth her skin and would bathe using local herbs—ebombo as a perfume and rweza for good luck and opportunities in marriage. Now, however, many opt to go to salons for beautification.

On the day of introduction, the husband-to-be and his delegation come with many gifts to present to his beloved's parents and relatives, including her father, uncle, elder brother, mother, auntie, elder sister, and grandparents. The gifts are intended to show appreciation to the parents for the good job they have done in bringing up the girl. Traditionally, they include kanzus, long white or cream-colored robes traditionally worn by men, and busutis, also called gomesis, long brightly colored dresses with a square neckline and short puffed sleeves, traditional attire for women. The elder brother receives a rooster, and the father receives omutwalo, a dowry that is usually composed of material items and not money. A locally brewed beer is shared from one pot as a sign of unity. Other gifts may include sugar, salt, and meat. The date for the wedding is then fixed.

Both families have a spokesperson, knowledgeable in old norms and traditions, who indulge in a battle of words, spirited questions, and answers that make kwanjula memorable and unique from any other ceremony. It ends with lots of eating, drinking, and dancing.

Of the many Abayudaya wedding ceremonies I have attended, the one I enjoyed most was for my friend Joseph Namusuka and his bride Rebecca Katurah. Abayudaya weddings begin with the two people announcing the date when their wedding will take place. The bride and the groom are always honored on Shabbat by giving a *D'var Torah* (a talk based on the weekly Torah portion) or carrying the Torah during the service. These make them feel special and are signs of assuming Jewish responsibilities.

My friend Joseph and his beautiful wife, Rebecca, chose to hold their wedding on the grounds of our main synagogue on Nabugoye Hill. On the eve of their wedding, after Rebecca's immersion in the mikveh, the bride and groom invited friends to entertain them separately to kill the stress of wedding preparations. I attended the gathering for Joseph. All of us acted like children and sang the songs of our childhood. Besides the fun, friends had a session with him to share their experiences in marriage.

Very early in the morning, we joined Joseph's family to prepare breakfast, as Joseph and his best man headed to the salon. Dressed in his new black suit, Joseph looked exactly the man of the day, wearing a big smile and an Abayudaya-made kippah. We accompanied him to the synagogue where we found many people waiting to celebrate, welcoming us with dancing and singing as we waited for the bride to arrive.

In my community, the chuppah is made of four sugarcane poles and a white tallit to signify a sweet marriage guided by the Torah. Rebecca and Joseph's chuppah was special because we painted the sugarcane poles in white and blue to make it shine like the flag of Israel, a flag we hold very dear to our hearts. When the bride arrived, the couple circled each other seven times. This was followed by sharing wine and then the rings. The ketubah (Jewish marriage contract) was then read aloud so that everyone could hear and bear witness. Finally, Joseph broke the glass, which was a signal that it was time for us to party.

Our rabbi, Gershom Sizomu, invited all the married people to open a dance with the bride and the groom, then everyone joined in. Lots of Ugandan food was served, including my favorite, a stew of smoked tilapia and groundnuts (peanuts) with mashed matooke (plantain). The couple was showered with many gifts, which included utensils and chickens. This marked the end of the party.

FOUR

—ᴍ—

CONVERSION BEFORE
MARRIAGE

GIVEN THE SMALL PERCENTAGE of Jews around the world in comparison
to the populations of their non-Jewish neighbors, it is not surprising that interfaith marriage has increased since the 1960s.[1] In the United States, for example,
about 44 percent of marriages are religiously mixed. Statistics are sparse, but
conversion of one of the partners to Judaism remains small.[2] Nevertheless,
conversion to Judaism, a key decision before marriage, figures prominently in
several of the stories we collected from the far corners of the world.

According to Maimonides (*Isurei Biah* 13:14), conversion to Judaism has
been accepted since the beginning of Jewish history. Jewish courts, however,
did not accept converts unless their motives were spiritual. Conversion to Judaism is supposed to be a matter of deep sincerity, not convenience. The Talmud, the rabbinic commentary on the Bible, discusses this matter of sincerity
explicitly and draws on the story of Ruth, the biblical character who famously
declared her desire to adopt the religion of her Jewish mother-in-law, Naomi.
The subsequent marriage of Ruth and Boaz is celebrated as particularly virtuous; so much so that their child, Obed, became the ancestor of King David.

Jewish tradition states that Jews are not supposed to proselytize among
non-Jews, and surely Jews should never force anyone to convert to Judaism.
The abhorrence of forced conversion is reinforced by the Jewish experience of
being forced to convert, most notably during the Spanish Inquisition that lasted
formally from 1478 to 1834. Actually, the opposite is true: Jews are supposed to
discourage others from converting to Judaism. The Talmud states that the rabbinic court that rules on each potential conversion must start the questioning
by asking, "Why should you wish to become a convert? Do you not know that

the people of Israel have been persecuted and oppressed, despised, harassed, and overcome by afflictions?" One of the stories later in this book (chapter 13) gives a vivid example of a rabbi saying "no" to an eager potential convert who wants to marry a Jewish woman. The practice of rejecting a potential convert three times is a custom, not a Jewish law.

With a few exceptions, all branches of Judaism today are open to sincere converts, although the rules for conversion vary among denominations. The basic elements of conversion, described in these stories, are instruction, submerging in a mikveh (ritual bath), questioning by rabbis of a *bet din* (rabbinic court), and circumcision or symbolic drawing of a drop of blood (*hatafat dam brit*) for men. The most liberal branch of Judaism (World Union for Progressive Judaism, Reform in the United States) allows rabbis discretion in what is required beyond a course of instruction on Jewish practices, history, and philosophy. The Conservative/Masorti branch requires each of the elements we've noted. Orthodox conversion may involve a long period of learning and testing before the bet din assents to the conversion, as well as the mikveh and circumcision. Most Orthodox authorities will not accept the conversions of other branches.

In the United States and elsewhere with high rates of intermarriage, why do some people convert to Judaism before marriage? Introduced to Judaism by the potential spouse and often taking part in family holiday celebrations, many converts fall in love with Judaism. A 2019 article distributed by the Jewish Telegraphic Agency was titled "Stop Saying Women Convert to Judaism Just for Marriage."[3] Several stories in this chapter support that demand. Authors wrote about how meaningful, emotionally satisfying, and significant the process was. In fact, research has shown that Jewish identity and practice after marriage are no different among women converts and those born Jewish.[4]

On the practical side of reasons for conversion, Orthodox and Conservative rabbis will not officiate at weddings of Jews and non-Jews. (Many Reform rabbis will, however.) Based on the principle of matrilineal descent, traditional branches mandate that a bride whose mother is not Jewish must convert before marriage. In this chapter, the bride from Latvia, married by a Progressive rabbi, hopes to convert in the future, as did older brides from Nicaragua and Suriname who had been married years before in civil ceremonies when Jewish conversions were unavailable.

Two of the stories in this chapter—from Algeria and Uruguay—involve Jewish brides whose husbands converted. Worldwide, conversion of grooms is more unusual than conversion of brides, which is described in stories from El Salvador, Israel, Nicaragua, Panama, Suriname, and the United States. Stories from Kenya, Portugal, and Madagascar describe joyous Jewish weddings following conversions of couples from small communities who are finally able to marry Jewishly after appearing before a bet din to convert them and rabbis available to marry them.

ALGERIA

Aline Livni

Algeria's Jews followed an unusual course when they left Algeria after its independence in 1963. While the Jewish citizens of most Arab countries left for Israel during those turbulent times, 90 percent of Algeria's Jews went to France, as did the bride featured in this story. Aline's story reflects the motivation of the majority of Algerian Jews to emigrate to France: they considered themselves French. Indeed, Algeria's Jews had been granted the privileges of French nationality since 1870. This explains why Aline and her sister resented the singing and dancing at her cousin's henna party, which they associated with a culture that was not theirs. There are now no Jews in Algeria.

I was raised in a suburb of Algiers, the capital of Algeria. Algeria had been a département (an administrative unit, like a province) of France since 1830, and we considered ourselves French; I grew up in a French country, not an Arab one. My father, who was in the military, was a Zionist. I had been in the Zionist youth movement, *Habonim*, since age twelve. So in 1961 at the end of the Algerian War that marked independence from France, when a million people left Algeria, my family made aliyah to Israel. My father had family members in Israel and my sister's boyfriend had already moved there.

My cousin Jeanine married in 1957 before we left. I was a young teenager. Jeanine was one of five daughters of my mother's sister. These cousins were all beautiful. Jeanine had blond hair and blue eyes. Her family had an apartment above a school that had been turned into a military barracks during the war. Soldiers from France were housed there, including Jean-Pierre, a handsome paratrooper. They met, dated for a few months with chaperones, and became engaged with her father's permission.

Because Jean-Pierre was not Jewish, he had to undergo circumcision as part of the conversion process. My father could not understand that necessity, as he saw him limping around, because Jeanine's family was not observant and ate nonkosher food at home. (My sister and I loved to go there for charcuterie.)

Like in France, couples would go to city hall for a civil ceremony, usually on a Thursday, attended by their immediate family. The religious ceremony would follow three days later. What I remember most was the henna party at Jeanine's home a day or two before the wedding. People played Arab instruments and sang in Hebrew, French, and Arabic, including Jeanine's mother, Yvonne, who had a nice voice. There was dancing and ululating (trilling with the tongue to show happiness). My sister and I didn't like this singing and dancing, as we didn't want to be connected with this non-French history that we did not understand. Henna was applied to everyone's palms with a ribbon on top that was taken off after it dried. That was the fun part. We ate incredible pastries including *makroude* made with dates and semolina in a diamond shape, *cigares*, pastry tubes with almond paste inside, and small tarts filled with almonds. I don't remember gifts, as the family wasn't rich; my uncle was a *gendarme* (military policeman). The guests received *drangées*, white sugared almonds in small cones made of tulle.

The wedding was on a Sunday afternoon at the Great Synagogue of Algiers, which was converted into a mosque a few years later. It was not a big wedding—forty or fifty guests of all religions. None of the groom's family attended. My cousin wore a white wedding gown. A reception followed at a café, where a nice meal was served, probably not kosher.

After living with Jeanine's parents for a while, Jeanine and Jean-Pierre moved to Marseille, where they raised four children. One of them became religiously observant.

EL SALVADOR

Cecilia Kahn

Jews in El Salvador, the smallest country in Central America, number around two hundred. Cecilia and her husband are active participants in this tiny community, which nevertheless supports a synagogue, a women's group, and a variety of activities for children and youth. Her father-in-law was among the few Jews who did not emigrate during the civil war that killed about seventy-five thousand people between 1980 and 1992. Brides like Cecilia might abstain from circling the groom during the ceremony if they perceive the custom as a symbol of unequal gender roles—the groom as the center of the bride's universe. A popular egalitarian reform has the bride and groom circling each other or taking turns circling, representing the protection and centrality of each for the other in their new world of marriage.

Cecilia and Alfredo

My husband, Alfredo, and I were born and raised in El Salvador. I went to the German school in San Salvador, the capital, and he went to the French school. My mother was brought up as a Catholic. My father, although he attended a Catholic school, did not practice any religion, always following the simple principle of respecting others. Alfredo's father was president of the Jewish community for approximately twenty years. During the long civil war throughout the 1980s, he refused to leave El Salvador when most of the Jews fled the country. The community almost disappeared. I hear they had to close the synagogue, although they somehow managed to have services elsewhere. During that time, I stayed in the country and studied psychology. Alfredo was a student at Northwestern University near Chicago, but he came back to El Salvador after graduation and the signing of the peace treaty.

My husband and I met at work at an airplane maintenance base around 1993. I was in the human resources department; he was in avionics, electrical systems for airplanes. We were friends, as we were both dating other people. After I left that job for another, Alfredo started calling. We dated for two years. Getting married was a giant decision, as I had a career. Alfredo would pick me up on Friday night after he went to the service at his synagogue. After we started to think about marriage, he said, "Why don't you come to synagogue?" So I started to go with him.

Rabbi Gustavo Kraselnik, a very smart rabbi from Argentina, was at the synagogue then. He asked me to come to a class, Introduction to Judaism. (I was lucky to arrive at that moment, as he was there for only a few years.) It didn't necessarily mean that I would convert. But I felt comfortable there; the people were engaged and welcoming. We learned about the Jewish way of life, not just prayers. I had always known religion as a lot of preaching without any discussion, and this was different. Besides, I had always thought that kids need a guiding religious light. My husband-to-be came with me to the classes. I went through the conversion process with a bet din of three rabbis from Argentina and a mikveh ceremony.

Alfredo and I married in 1998. I was twenty-nine, and he was twenty-eight. Our parents were happy. My mother has always been open-minded, and one of my father's best friends was Jewish. Alfredo's parents were also glad; both my mother and my mother-in-law helped a lot with planning. I had many bridal showers with people from different phases of my life. We had a brief civil ceremony, required in El Salvador, conducted by my friend, a lawyer, and followed by a dinner at my in-laws' home.

Our Jewish wedding took place a few weeks later. It was the first Jewish wedding in El Salvador in more than twenty-five years. In El Salvador, everyone is invited, so we had around 350 people in a huge room in a restaurant. We built a chuppah in another big room. It was a beautiful non-Orthodox wedding with a cantor we brought from Argentina. We did the traditional things—exchanged the rings, drank the wine, broke the glass—but I did not circle the groom. Afterward, we had a reception with kosher food and lots of dancing and music, including Israeli dancing, until two in the morning. We went to Alaska for our honeymoon.

I am very involved in our synagogue and the Jewish community. I believe that you always have to give back. I am on different boards of directors of nonprofit organizations. The local Jewish community does many tikkun olam projects. One of my favorite projects has been Con Textos, which establishes libraries throughout El Salvador and teaches children to be critical thinkers. El Salvador is not doing well economically, and we want to keep democracy. People are hardworking, but it is a difficult situation. Most of the kids go abroad for college and many don't return.

ISRAEL

Libby Nitzan

The kibbutz movement began in the early 1900s when pioneers from Eastern Europe established agricultural settlements based on ideas of equality and community. Children were raised communally, meals were eaten together, everyone worked on the kibbutz, and money was handled collectively. Young volunteers, Jews and non-Jews, were welcomed from around the globe. Who knows how many, like Libby, intended to stay for a few months or a year, fell in love, and stayed? Life on the kibbutz has changed, becoming more individualistic, but Libby, an English teacher, still lives in Kibbutz Grofit, where she married and raised four children. Her beloved husband, Efi, died in 2021. She is, she wrote, "extremely satisfied with the way my life has turned out."

I arrived in Israel from England as a volunteer, planning on spending a year away after finishing high school. I loved being on a kibbutz—the lifestyle, the weather, and the people. And I fell in love with Efi, a young Israeli man. We picked May as a good month for our wedding, as we knew it wouldn't be too hot. Our Kibbutz Grofit is near Eilat in the south of Israel, and the heat in the summer can be brutal. As with all great plans, reality often differs, and May 1988 turned out to be the hottest in ten years! My parents, my sister and her family, and an aunt and uncle came to the wedding from England. And, as a surprise, my best childhood friend, who had been traveling in Australia, turned up with her brother. The whole wedding event was new to my family and my friend, who are not Jewish.

I had completed an Orthodox conversion a few months before, a decision that I made with no pressure from Efi's family or the kibbutz. I think they preferred my conversion, but I never felt it was a deal-breaker. Initially, my decision came from a sense of wanting to belong, and at times I felt I was putting on an act and trying to fit into a mold. But as I learned about Jewish practice and the history of Judaism and Israel, my life was greatly enriched and I have never regretted it. My parents had no objection as long as I was safe, healthy, and happy.

In those days Kibbutz Grofit was still very traditional, exemplifying the slogan "each according to his ability, to each according to his needs." We arrived at the ceremony sitting in the scoop of a decorated tractor. Still to this day, I can remember the look on my father's face as he clutched his *kippah* (skull cap), the wind whipping up around us. I must have forgotten to tell him that this was kibbutz-style.

We were married outside the communal dining room. During the ceremony, a sand storm began, kicked up by the wind, along with flashes of lightning. It got so bad that they had to take down the chuppah. My husband held his *tallit* (prayer shawl) over us instead. A rabbi from Eilat officiated. (In later years, he performed the circumcision on two of my sons.) I had read as much as I could about Jewish weddings, but I must not have noticed that the bride doesn't say, "I do!" I remember waiting for it and being most bemused. I think I was so busy waiting that I can't remember much of the ceremony!

To their credit, as always, my family went with the flow. Although my wedding was a new experience, they had visited the kibbutz in the past and felt at home. They loved the breaking of the glass and the shouts of mazel tov, the part you see in *Fiddler on the Roof*.

After the ceremony, we went to the kibbutz clubhouse for a buffet of salads and meats. Kibbutz members put on a show with skits, dances, and speeches. My mother said that after our wedding on a hill in the Israeli desert, weddings in England seemed rather ordinary.

More than thirty years later, I have four children and still live in Kibbutz Grofit. When I see the complicated, expensive, and stressful weddings couples go through today, I am quite happy to remember our simple proceedings.

KENYA

Yehudah Kimani

Yehudah has emerged as a leader of one of the most isolated Jewish communities in the world. Located in the windblown highlands of Kenya, with a synagogue origi-nally built of boards and plastic sheeting, the twenty-five-year-old community was founded by his father and other former members of the Messianic church. Yehudah and some other Kasuku Jews have made the difficult journey to Uganda to study with Gershon Sizomu, the indigenous rabbi of the well-established Abayudaya Jewish community, where the wedding of Yehudah's parents took place. As in other remote locations, formal conversion to Judaism is often followed by weddings of couples who, now officially Jewish and with rabbis on hand, want to celebrate their union in a traditional ceremony under a chuppah. For Rut and Yosef and their family (who, as customary, do not share the same last name), this was the joyous culmination of years of sacrifice and perseverance.

Rut Wangeci and bridesmaids

The Kasuku Jewish community was formed more than twenty years ago when my father, Yosef Njogu, and some people from the village of Gathudia met members of the Nairobi Hebrew Congregation. The members of this white congregation gave them books on Judaism. As they learned about the Torah and Jewish observance, they decided after a few years to establish their own congregation near the town of Ol Kalou, about two hours from Nairobi in the Rift Valley.

Today, the Kasuku Jewish community, as we call ourselves, is growing strong, with more than sixty members. My father, as the traditional rabbi, has taught us how to be Jewish. I am proud to be a young leader of the community. We keep kosher, observe Shabbat and all Jewish holidays, and love Israel. Many of us know how to read and write Hebrew. My parents are small-scale farmers who have provided a large family with food, clothing, and school fees.

In 2014, my father, Yosef, and my mother, Rut Wangeci, along with their ten children, traveled to Uganda to the Abayudaya ("People of Judah" in the local language) community, a well-known African Jewish community founded in

1919. My brother Samson is studying at the yeshiva created by the Abayudaya rabbi, Gershom Sizomu. Rabbi Gershom had gathered together a bet din, a group of rabbis from many places around the world, to formally convert my family along with three others from my community.

It was a great and blessed day for my parents. Especially because later that afternoon Rabbi Gershom and the rabbis of the bet din conducted a Jewish wedding ceremony for Yosef and Rut under the chuppah in front of the main Abayudaya synagogue in the village of Nabagoya. Although not planned long before, it was a smiling day for them. Up on Nabugoye Hill, people appeared to celebrate the wedding of the couple from Kenya—the first Jewish wedding of the Kasuku community. There was music, dancing, and singing in Hebrew and Luganda. Everyone was full of happiness. It is so beautiful and joyous to be a Jew!

LATVIA

Diana Pershtein-Lapkis

In spite of Diana's deep investment and involvement with the Jewish community since she was a child, traditional branches of Judaism (Orthodox and Conservative) do not consider her Jewish. The rule of matrilineal descent asserts that only a child born of a Jewish mother is considered a Jew. Diana's mother comes from a religiously mixed family and does not qualify as officially Jewish, so neither does Diana. No doubt that is why Diana and her husband, Lev, were married by a rabbi of the Reform movement, the liberal branch of Judaism that is not so strict in its interpretation of who is a Jew. The ceremony she describes included the major traditional elements befitting a bride so committed to Jewish values and observance.

When I was thirteen, I moved with my mother from Riga, the capital of Latvia, to Israel. I went to high school there, did my time in the army, and then enrolled at Bar Ilan University near Tel Aviv. While I was a student, I worked for the Jewish Agency for Israel as a *madricha* (counselor) for youngsters at Jewish summer and holiday camps. The first summer I worked in Belarus, and other times I worked in Latvia, where I could translate among Hebrew, Latvian, Russian, and English.

I met my husband, Lev, in 2004 at a seaside camp in Jurmala, a resort near Riga. He was working for an electronics company in Riga and helping the camp with information technology. When I first saw him, he was lying on his back fixing a computer. We became a couple for the one month we were there. Then

Diana watches Lev perform the traditional breaking of the glass

he went back to Riga, and I returned to Israel. We emailed and Skyped almost every day.

That winter he was scheduled to go to a winter holiday camp in Riga. We were both hoping for an opening for me, but no placements were available. At the last minute, one of the counselors was unable to go, so I was able to fill in for her. We met for the second time and knew that we were meant to be together. But I was studying and traveling for the Jewish Agency, so it was not easy. When I spent a year working in Switzerland, we were together only once a month. Finally, in 2006 we decided to live together in Latvia for a year.

The first day I arrived in Riga, Lev proposed and gave me a ring. I was surprised that it happened so soon after my arrival, but of course, I said yes. We were married in 2007 at a beautiful hotel in Jurmala. It was a big wedding for Latvia—120 people, many of them friends from abroad. I was twenty-five, and Lev was twenty-four. We were married by a Reform rabbi from Moscow, as my family is mixed religiously and my mother is not officially Jewish. My friend Maya, who was instrumental in our meeting, helped us plan the wedding. Lev walked to the chuppah with his father and uncle, and I walked with my mother and my mother-in-law. My two grandmothers also walked down. Two little girls scattered flower petals. My Israeli friend Anna was my attendant. She sang a song in Hebrew and Lev's ninety-year-old uncle sang a song in Yiddish accompanied by a Latvian Jewish band. It was touching and beautiful; I was crying.

I circled the groom seven times, we prayed, exchanged rings, and Lev broke the glass. At one point in the ceremony, Lev presented my mother with our ketubah. He had signed it that morning with his brother and two friends as witnesses. Then we had a reception with music, dancing, and speeches. There were many surprises, including a slideshow of pictures from our childhoods and a video of our friends from everywhere wishing us well. We had given the DJ a list of songs to play, and everyone danced until three o'clock in the morning.

As is customary in Latvia, we had a celebration with our friends the next day. We went to Lev's family's summer house on a lake, where we had a barbecue and used the sauna—an important component of Latvian culture—situated in a little cabin near the house. A few months later we took a honeymoon trip to Tunisia.

MADAGASCAR

Ahava Havotramahavalisoa

In 2016, more than one hundred men, women, and children, natives of the faraway island off the southeast coast of Africa, converted to Judaism after interviews with a bet din (a court of three rabbis from abroad) and immersion in a river mikveh. Organized by Kulanu, a nonprofit that supports isolated and emerging Jewish communities worldwide, the conversions culminated years of Jewish learning by three congregations whose leaders studied via the internet and fervently wanted formal conversion for their members. As the secretary of Kulanu, Barbara Vinick was honored to witness the joyous wedding of Ahava and her husband, Eli, one of twelve couples who remarried Jewishly the day after converting.

I was born in Antananarivo, the capital of Madagascar. I grew up in a Catholic family with five brothers and four sisters. My father became a gendarme (military policeman) and was sent to another city a day away from the capital in the east. So when I was a young girl, my family moved there and stayed for thirteen years. When we came back to Antananarivo in 1999, my little sister and I changed our religion and became Seventh-day Adventists. Although my parents were strict Catholics, the necessary thing was to pray.

I met my husband, Eli, at church, where he played the piano and I sang in the chorus. We were both in university. I was studying law, and he was studying

Ahava and Eli under the chuppah

marketing. He was the teacher for a group who were learning English and asked me to join. We saw each other every week and became friends. When we started to go out in 2000, I introduced him to my parents, as I did all my friends. We were married in 2005. I have my law degree, but now that I have children, I have to wait on taking an exam to become a lawyer. Eli works for the Bank of Africa and sometimes travels to other African countries.

In 2013, my father-in-law told us about Judaism. He told us about the community and said it was the true way. He and my son, who was seven, went to pray with Ashrey (leader of one of three Jewish congregations). I learned that there is a prayer for everything. I asked if I could go with them to services along with my mother-in-law. We stayed outside for five weeks, then we learned some Hebrew and the order of the service. I became a member of the congregation with my family, including my son and my younger daughters.

At first, I never thought about (formally) converting. I didn't think we needed to do it. But our congregation's leader explained about conversion, the bet din, and the mikveh. Women do a monthly immersion at home, so we didn't feel scared or uncomfortable about the mikveh in the river.

When I saw a Jewish wedding on the internet, I felt delighted and excited, but I never thought I could do it. I was very happy to be able to marry in a Jewish ceremony. I chose a blue dress with a little white for the wedding. When we came here for the ceremony, I saw that everyone was wearing white. I told my mother-in-law, and we walked quickly to the market and bought a white dress and scarf. You may have noticed that I was wearing blue shoes! My children were surprised when they saw me in a different dress. My husband found a ring that morning too.

My husband and I thank Hashem for this ability to marry again and to be able to pray as Jews.

NICARAGUA

Veronica Preiss

Veronica married her late husband, Kurt, three times: the first in a civil ceremony, the second in a Jewish ceremony not recognized by religious law, and the third in conjunction with Jewish conversions organized by Kulanu, a nonprofit based in New York. Kulanu also organized the most recent conversions of 114 people and 22 Jewish weddings in 2017, almost doubling the number of Jews in the tiny Nicaraguan community, most of whom had left in previous decades during times of political unrest.

I met my husband, Kurt, in 2003 when I was thirty and he was fifty-seven. Like most girls in Nicaragua, I was educated in Catholic schools. I had a profound belief in God but did not observe any religion. As we became closer, we went often to Honduras to visit Kurt's mother. Seeing her light the Shabbat candles and going to synagogue with her in Honduras, I became interested in Judaism. Kurt never tried to impose it on me.

Veronica and Kurt signing the ketubah with Rabbi Sussman

Back in Nicaragua, I started to go to classes on Judaism taught by Carlos Peres, a knowledgeable converted Jew. We decided to form a study group that met every Sunday at his house, which he built to look like a synagogue, including a mikveh.

My mother-in-law passed away in August 2008. It was always her wish that Kurt and I remain together. So in October of that year, we registered as a married couple in a civil union. A few months later, I became a Jew through what was called a "community conversion." A week after that, we got married for the first time in a Jewish ceremony performed by Carlos Peres. I say "for the first time" because we knew that perhaps my conversion and our wedding were not 100 percent according to *halaja* (religious law). But surely it was better than nothing.

Therefore, in 2011, when my husband, Kurt, as president of *Congregacion Israelita de Nicaragua*, was asked by a visitor what we needed most, he replied that our priority was an opportunity for formal conversions. Soon after, Bonita Sussman and her husband, Rabbi Gerald Sussman, representatives of Kulanu, a US non-profit that helps emerging Jewish communities, arrived to assess our situation. They learned that our congregation of about forty people had been studying Judaism for several years.

A few months later the Sussmans arranged the first bet din (religious court of rabbis) to ever come to Nicaragua. We refurbished the existing mikveh, and the rabbis converted twelve people. They also married three couples, including my husband and myself. So we had our second marriage ceremony in the presence of not one, but three rabbis!

PANAMA

Cynthia Castro Cohen-Henriquez

The first Jews to settle in Panama were hidden Jews, conversos (sometimes called Marranos or Crypto-Jews), who arrived in the early nineteenth century when Panama was a part of Colombia. The synagogue where Cynthia and David married is the oldest in the country, established in 1876. Today, the Jewish community is the largest in Central America, with a substantial proportion who came from Syria in the 1930s. Some might say that Cynthia's conversion and fun-filled Jewish wedding were meant to be (bashert, in Yiddish) based on her written desire to be Jewish when she was nine years old. She is probably not the only bride to faint during the ceremony.

My husband, David, and I got married in 2012 at Gamboa Rainforest Resort, about forty minutes from Panama City, the capital of Panama. The resort was created from a former US military base in the Canal Zone, a former US territory, on the banks of Gatun Lake that feeds into the Panama Canal. The architecture is what Panamanians call "American." I wanted an outdoor wedding, but June is the rainy season in Panama, so the next best thing was to hold it indoors in the jungle environment of the resort.

Most Jewish weddings in Panama are at hotels, or at the beach during the dry season, or at the *Centro Cultural Hebreo*, the community center where many Jewish celebrations and meetings take place. In contrast to the rest of Latin America, the majority of Jews in Panama are Sephardic, mainly from Syria. But our families are not Sephardic, and we are "alternative" people. So our wedding had some unusual aspects.

We had about two hundred guests, small for a Jewish wedding in Panama. The chuppah was set up in the middle, with the guests surrounding it. David entered to "The Imperial March" from *Star Wars*, his favorite film. I entered to

Cynthia and David on the way to the wedding reception on a 1950s bicycle

"Edelweiss" from the *Sound of Music*, one of my favorites, following four young flower girls, two from each of our families. One held a sign that said, "Here Comes the Bride." I made the sign myself, along with the wedding program and other elements. Rabbi Gustavo Kraselnik from David's Masorti (Conservative) congregation, Kol Shearith Israel in Panama City, officiated.

Guests were given an unlit candle as they entered the hall. As the ceremony began, one candle was lit. Then each guest lit their candle from the one beside them in the circle until the last one was lit under the chuppah. The candles and the weather made the room quite hot. As we drank the wine, signed the ketubah under the chuppah, and family and friends read the *sheva brachot* (seven blessings), I felt dizzy and a bit nauseated. After we exchanged rings, David covered me with his tallit for a blessing. They told me David's grandmother's nurse shouted, "David, catch her!" before I fainted. The next thing I knew, my father was shaking me and David was saying, "I hadn't even kissed her yet!" They gave me some water, and I recovered. I had never fainted before and never have since.

After the ceremony, my mom brought my platform sneakers so that I could change out of my very high heels and we went outside for pictures taken by my dear friend Tito Herrera. When we returned for the reception, David was pedaling a 1950s bicycle I had rescued from a neighbor and that my dad restored. I was seated on the rack in the back. After speeches from our parents, we had our first dance to "Till There Was You." Then we did a funny dance routine from an episode of *Friends*, the TV show. And, of course, they raised us up on chairs as the band and a string quartet of my friends played and everyone clapped. I had to have that!

Everyone in Panama loves to party, and we continued to dance to merengue, salsa, rock, and even Frank Sinatra until two o'clock in the morning with crazy hats and boas and a photo booth that everyone loved. At one point, I surprised David with an Israeli dance I had taught to all my friends and family, even to my mom. As another surprise, I hired a mariachi band and sang *Si nos dejan* (If They Let Us) to their accompaniment. Then it was my turn to be surprised as David grabbed the mic and sang *Y yo sigo siendo el rey* (And I'm Still the King), a popular mariachi song. Of course, we ate and drank. Our wedding cake was topped by a bride and groom made of legos. Before we left to spend the night at the resort, I threw my bouquet, which fittingly was caught by the nurse who ordered David to catch me at the end of the ceremony!

David and I met on Facebook through his cousin, who was my only Jewish friend. My parents and their families are from Peru and moved to Panama, where I was born, in the 1970s. My parents weren't religious, but I took part in a First Communion ceremony because all my friends were doing it. My great-grandfather on my mother's side was Jewish from Germany, but no one knew it until his wedding to my great-grandmother. Their children, including my grandmother, were raised as Catholics after their divorce.

We never talked about Judaism in my house, but for some reason, I was always interested in it. When I was nine, I wrote in a to-do list in my diary, "become Jewish." As I grew up, I thought about converting, but I didn't think I could because I didn't have a clear idea of God. I believed in the forces of nature and finally came to realize that was my God. So in 2007, I went to David's cousin for advice. He urged me to contact David who was studying at Hebrew College in Boston.

David was coming to Panama and told me he'd get in touch. He never did, but he kept track of my posts on Facebook. Finally, two years later he graduated from Hebrew College and invited me to a party in his honor in Panama City. He gave an emotional sermon at his synagogue and kept looking at me. It made me cry. We started dating, and I would visit him in New Hampshire where he got his first job as a rabbi. It was a long-distance romance. I fell in love with New England and with David. When he left New Hampshire to become rabbi at Kol Shearith Israel next to Rabbi Gustavo back in Panama, it gave us the chance to be married. I never thought that I'd marry a rabbi! My friends were amazed; they thought I'd be covering my head and wearing long skirts.

In 2011, eight months before the wedding, I was converted by a bet din of David's colleagues from Hebrew College at Mayyim Hayyim (Living Waters), an innovative mikveh and education center near Boston. I was especially scared to tell my paternal grandmother, a practicing Catholic. But she was excited about it and asked me a lot of questions. Family members were careful to prepare foods that were kosher. David's parents were not so happy at first because I wasn't converted by an Orthodox bet din, which is more accepted in Panama. But as they got to know me, we fell in love with each other, and I started reading Torah every Shabbat at the synagogue.

PORTUGAL

Navah Harlow

From the twelfth century, when Portugal was founded, through the Golden Age of Discovery in the fourteenth century, Jews had prominent roles in the cultural and economic life of the country. When their security ended in expulsion, torture, and forced conversion, thousands of anousim ("coerced ones" in Hebrew, also called Marranos, conversos, and Crypto-Jews) fled to places around the world, retaining Jewish customs secretly while practicing Christianity publicly. Thanks to the support of teachers like Navah and her husband, Rabbi Jules, who have traveled to Lisbon from their home in New York more than forty times, some are reconnecting with their Jewish roots, converting in time-honored rituals, and then marrying according to Jewish law. Besides her work with anousim, Navah is a national leader on end-of-life issues.

On March 30, 2006, my husband and I had the *zechut* (privilege) to participate in a miracle. Almost two years had passed since we began teaching a group of *b'nei anousim* in Lisbon. This was a *kehillah* (congregation) of about twenty individuals joined together by a passion to return to Judaism, to be counted as legitimate members of the worldwide Jewish community. Most traced their ancestry back five hundred years to the time of the Inquisition when their ancestors were forcibly converted to Christianity. Among our students were Graca and Mario (not their real names to preserve their privacy), both in their late twenties. They had joined the group after studying other religions and deciding that Judaism was the religion that fulfilled their intellectual and spiritual needs.

Navah and Rabbi Jules, Lisbon 2008

Rabbi Jules, as they affectionately called my husband, had determined that after sufficient study and mastery of the materials, six members of the group were ready to come before the Masorti bet din (Conservative religious court) in London for conversion. This meant being examined by the three rabbis who comprised the bet din as to their knowledge and commitment to Judaism. Graca and Mario were among those six. Rabbi Jules was invited to serve as a member of this bet din.

When we assembled early that morning in London, the close-knit group from Lisbon was solemn; they were trembling with *kedushat ha-yom* (the sanctity of the day). We provided encouragement, support, and love. After each individual was interviewed by the bet din, he or she was escorted to the mikveh for ritual immersion, as is prescribed by Jewish law, with the appropriate prayers. This requirement in the conversion process brought tranquility and a sense of spirituality that was palpable. Next, when the Lisbon converts came before the open *Aron Kodesh* (Torah ark) and recited the *Shema* together for the first time as Jews, it was indeed, a holy moment. They were then presented with a certificate attesting to their conversion. As they each received their certificate, they were called by their Hebrew names for the very first time.

The day had been so full, yet there was more to come. Graca and Mario had been married several years earlier in a civil ceremony. Rabbi Jules had explained to them that they could not return to Lisbon as a married couple unless they had a Jewish wedding. They were thrilled by the prospect. And so, on a sunny afternoon after the conversion ceremony, we arranged to have a Jewish wedding ceremony for them at the host Masorti synagogue in North London.

Graca, a beautiful bride, wore a lovely wedding dress and veil, designed and sewn by her sister in Lisbon. Mario, handsome as always, wore a dark suit. I had the honor of accompanying Graca to the chuppah as a member of our group played *Erev Shel Shoshanim*, a Hebrew love song, on his violin. The four beautifully decorated poles of the chuppah were held by members of our Lisbon kehillah. Rabbi Jules, as the *mesader kiddushin* (wedding officiant), spoke in a beautiful and personal way to Graca and Mario. Rabbi Chaim Weiner, the rabbi who had presided over the bet din, read the ketubah. Mario broke the glass, and we shouted mazel tov. Then we began to dance together in a circle with members of the London congregation. Tears were streaming from our eyes. Yes, there are often tears at a wedding; but these were different: for the first time in their lives, our dear students were participating as Jews in a wedding ceremony. We knew that something special had occurred. A new chapter in the history of Portuguese Jewry had just begun—the first wedding ceremony of the first Masorti congregation in Portugal.

The London congregation, headed by Rabbi Jonathan Wittenberg, organized a lovely champagne reception. We presented the bride and groom with a silver mezuzah sent by some members of The Rabbinical Assembly, the international association of Conservative/Masorti rabbis who had heard about the wedding and conversions. They also sent silver kiddush cups to all of the new converts, inscribed with the Hebrew date, Rosh Chodesh Nissan, 5767.

On Shabbat morning, Mario was called to the Torah for the first time in his life. The congregation sang *Siman Tov u Mazel Tov* for Graca and Mario. Graca was called up to the bimah to stand by Mario as they recited together the *Shehe-cheyanu*, a prayer that expresses gratitude to God for having kept us alive to reach this day. Later in the afternoon, we reconvened for sheva brachot for Graca and Mario (a meal followed by the recitation of seven wedding blessings included in the traditional grace after meals) followed by Havdalah, the service that marks the end of Shabbat.

With a sense of exhaustion, relief, and euphoria, we took our beloved Lisbon students to celebrate at a kosher Israeli restaurant. For them, that was another first, since there are no kosher restaurants in Portugal. As always, parting from them was difficult. We promised to return to Lisbon as soon as possible.

SURINAME

Jacob Steinberg

Did you know that Suriname is in South America? It is the least populated country on the continent, blanketed by dense jungle with rare flora and fauna. A former colony of the Netherlands until its independence in 1975, it is the only nation outside Europe where Dutch is spoken by the majority. Jacob, a Canadian engineer called a "guardian angel" by a community leader, encountered the small struggling Jewish community on a business trip. With support he mobilized, the community restored a Jewish cemetery overtaken by jungle, leased the contents of an old unused synagogue to the Israel Museum in Jerusalem, sent teenagers on a Birthright trip to Israel, and encouraged the visit of the rabbi who conducted the Jewish wedding he describes.

My friends Betsy Marsan Duijm and Leendert Duijm married in 2009 in a Jewish ceremony under the chuppah. Betsy was sixty-six, and Leendert was seventy-seven. They had been together for almost fifty years. This was a second marriage for both of them. Their first was to each other. Let me explain.

Betsy and Leendert met in 1960 in Paramaribo, the capital of Suriname. Betsy was a babysitter for Leendert's little sister. Betsy's mother was born in Suriname and her father in Indonesia. Both of Leendert's parents were born in the small Jewish community of Suriname, his father related to the distinguished Abarbanel family that had originated in Spain in the Middle Ages.

A year after they met, Betsy and Leendert were married in a brief civil ceremony at the city hall in Paramaribo. Leendert remembers that he had to convince her family because of their age difference. There had not been a rabbi in Suriname for several years, and Betsy's mother was not Jewish, so they had no choice; a religious wedding was out of the question. Betsy was eighteen, and Leendert was twenty-nine. The families were poor and Leendert's father had recently died, so there may not have been a fancy celebration anyway. But immediately after the ceremony, Leendert went back to work at the Coca-Cola bottling factory where, he explained, production would have halted if he were not there. (Twenty-five years later, the same thing happened: Leendert left their anniversary party when a shipment of long-awaited sugar arrived at the bottling plant.)

Fast forward fifty years, six children, fourteen grandchildren, and five great-grandchildren later. American Rabbi Chaim Beliak, who specializes in the revival of out-of-the-way congregations, came to Paramaribo to teach religious classes and conduct services—the first time in more than five decades that a rabbi had resided in the community for more than a few days. This was the opportunity Betsy and Leendert had been waiting for. Betsy had formally converted when a bet din of rabbis came to Suriname from the Netherlands in 2004, but they did not stay to conduct Jewish weddings.

Under a chuppah in their backyard, witnessed by one hundred family members and friends, including the First Lady of Suriname, Betsy and Leendert Duijm were married by Rabbi Beliak in a Jewish ceremony. The chuppah was held by two of their sons, the community's self-taught cantor Jacques van Niel, and Shul Donk, the president of the community. This time there was a celebratory party in a local club, with food and drink and happy socializing.

Betsy and Leendert are core members of the Jewish community, attending services and events at the sandy-floored eighteenth-century Neve Shalom Synagogue in Paramaribo. Nowadays, Leendert is retired but stays active. As his father did before him, he conducts *levayot* (funeral services) at the two active cemeteries in Paramaribo. Both in use since the early to middle 1800s, one cemetery was established by those with Ashkenazic heritage and the other Sephardic. Betsy stayed at home to raise her children and remains the matriarch of their large family. Luckily, most of Betsy and Leendert's adult children continue to live in Suriname. But many members of younger generations have moved away from the small isolated Jewish community, lately emigrating to Israel, the Netherlands, and Australia.

URUGUAY

Gabriela Fraenkel

Many brides have described the feelings of peace and well-being they experienced when immersed in the mikveh in the days before their weddings. Gabriela must have felt special emotion as she looked forward to her Jewish wedding with Santi, whom she had not expected would convert. We could not find statistics for Uruguay, but it seems likely that they mirror those of the United States, where the majority of converts to Judaism are women (reported recently by the Jewish Telegraphic Agency).

Uruguay's twenty thousand Jews represent only half of their number in the 1970s, as assimilation and emigration have taken their toll. So Santi's addition to the Conservative Jewish community, heralding the creation of another Jewish family, was surely welcome.

My husband, Santiago, and I were married in October 2014. I am considered nervous and always in a rush, worried about everything. But as my wedding approached, I was very relaxed.

Santi and I met when we were sixteen. As is common in Uruguay, I went with my friend Daniela to offer support to her before her high school oral examination. Santi went too. A few months later, I was at Daniela's when Santi called. At that time, you went out with a group of friends—you would go to friends' houses, meet their parents, and vice versa. As we got to know each other, we began to get interested in each other and soon became a couple. Santi was Christian, but not a believer. After a while, he started to come with me to synagogue and Jewish holidays. He liked the life that Jewish young people live. Jewish kids in Uruguay join youth groups (*tnuot* in Hebrew) at age three or four and become leaders when they are teenagers, a system of socialization and education almost unique in the world.

We lived with our parents throughout my education in dentistry and his in telecommunications engineering. We worked and saved money and finally moved in together in 2013 when we were both twenty-five. We decided to get married the next year and went looking for a *salón de fiestas* (party hall). I never dreamed about having a chuppah, a Jewish ceremony, as Santi wasn't Jewish. I thought we would marry in a civil ceremony. But a few months later, Santi told me that he wanted to convert. He always knew that I was devoted to Judaism, and he wanted both of us to be exemplars for our future children. So he had a *Brit Milah* (circumcision) and studied with our rabbi for three months that year and seven months before our wedding, making up the year of study that is required for conversion. We went separately to the mikveh before the marriage, which for me was a very special moment.

Finally, after ten years of being together, the day of the wedding arrived and everything caught up with me. I started to shake, and the real meaning of the day came to me in a flash. I had tears in my eyes as I ran to the entrance of the wedding salon. I looked like a princess, but I said something out loud like, "Shit, I'm getting married!" Everyone who heard me began to laugh.

We had a traditional Masorti (Conservative) Jewish wedding, a celebration of our love. After his mother escorted Santi down the aisle, my mother and Santi's father came next, then eight bridesmaids dressed in violet and blue with the groomsmen. The ring bearer was the son of my nanny, the most important kid in my life. The flower girls were two small girls who knew my mother-in-law. Finally, I came down the aisle with my father. When we got to the chuppah, I could see the rabbi and *chazzan* (cantor) and only Santi's back. When he turned around, I could see that he was crying. My father gave him a brief message, which he did not finish because Santi was so anxious to begin the ceremony. He lowered the veil over my head, and we walked the few steps up to the chuppah. We put a tallit over us as our families looked on under the huge chuppah—a *glorieta* of flowers and greens.

We raised the ketubah three times together, then the rabbi read it. We were supposed to sign it during the ceremony, but we forgot. The chazzan, a friend of ours the same age, sang the sheva brachot (seven blessings). We drank the glasses of wine before our vows and after—white so it would not stain if it should spill. We exchanged rings and said our vows with a few extra sentiments about the steps we had taken and what we expected in the future. The rabbi spoke and the first thing he said was, "It was a long path" to this day. After Santi broke the glass, it was time for the fun party with our four hundred guests.

The ceremony began after eleven o'clock at night, as this was the only time available for the hall, so by this time it was past midnight. Our attendants entered, jumping to a choreographed dance. Santi and I were the last as we formed a circle and started the horas. Everyone danced energetically, had dinner, then more dancing. Santi and I love to dance, and we had taken lessons. Great entertainment came in the form of a huge robot on stilts arrayed with LED lights.

The party lasted until seven o'clock in the morning. That day was Election Day in Uruguay. For forty-eight hours before, a *veda politica* (political ban) had been in effect, a time when alcohol sales are prohibited. (Of course, that did not apply to private parties, as we informed people who asked.) We went straight from the party to our voting place. There, in our wedding attire, we were quite a sensation. Everyone wanted to take a picture with us, and we were interviewed on television. It was a special day!

FIVE

—ⱳ—

THE INVITATION

BEFORE JOHANNES GUTENBERG invented the printing press in 1440, weddings were usually announced in the synagogue. Starting in the 1600s, the wealthier classes were able to afford printed invitations. Today, the creation of wedding invitations is a big business in first-world countries, and Jews, like other groups, may go to great lengths to create something beautiful and distinctive. Formal invitations may be printed and mailed or less formally created electronically and emailed.

The story from Costa Rica in this chapter documents another means of conveying the wedding invitation, customary in some communities: personal delivery by the future bride and groom. Although thoughtful and pleasant in many ways, this method is not advisable, according to one Orthodox observer.[1] Citing the proper *halachic* (Jewish legal) sources, he writes, "It is a *mitzvah* (good deed which is commanded of Jews) for one who is invited to a [wedding] to attend; it is not proper to decline the invitation. It is, therefore, better not to extend a personal invitation to people who will not come." Presumably, if invitations are mailed, the pressure to attend is lessened.

Depending on how traditional the family is, the text may contain Hebrew as well as the language of the bride and groom's residence. In this chapter, the bride from Colombia describes creating an invitation printed in Spanish, Hebrew, and English after much deliberation. Besides providing the necessary logistical information, the invitation typically gives a hint of what the wedding and reception will be like, whether modest or fancy. In relatively small Jewish communities and in Israel, it is customary to issue invitations far and wide, sometimes to the whole community. Therefore, a number of stories in this volume feature weddings with hundreds of guests.

The invitation story from Germany is particularly poignant. A German pre-Holocaust wedding custom was to include a written-for-the-occasion poem in the invitation. Composed by a family member, the poem's words reflected on the couple and their hoped-for good fortune.

COLOMBIA

Ethel Schuster

Ethel, a college professor of computer science, seems destined for the role of family historian, keeper of family lore. As an addendum to her story, Ethel wrote that her daughter, Merav, married in a joyous four-day event in Israel in 2017. Ethel's long-married parents still live in Colombia, but many of the five thousand Jews in the country, about equally divided between Sephardim and Ashkenazim (descendants of people from the Iberian Peninsula and Eastern Europe, respectively) left for the United States in the 1990s in the wake of violence and kidnapping of well-to-do people, including Jews.

My maternal grandmother, Sara Cherkes Kisner, was born in Romania in 1910. She arrived in Barranquilla, Colombia with her mother and brother at the age of fifteen. My grandfather, Benjamin Schpilberg (a.k.a. "el Babo"), was born in Belarus in 1904, arriving in Barranquilla in 1927 via Brazil, Argentina, Chile, and Panama. His plan to go on to Australia was undermined when he fell ill with malaria and had to stay in Barranquilla to recuperate. When he met Sara, he decided to stay there and get married.

As was customary in those days in Colombia, Benjamin planned a serenade for Sara on the night before their wedding. He had befriended a group of musicians who played instruments to accompany silent movies at the Teatro Colombia, a local movie theater. He hired them to come to Sara's home after they finished their performance. The musicians arrived, but the piano, which had left the theater on its way to the bride's house in a *carro de mula* (a horse-drawn buggy), did not. After waiting for more than an hour, Benjamin and the musicians went to look for the piano. They found out its fate when they arrived at the local police station. The police thought that the buggy's driver had stolen the piano and arrested him. The wedding party affirmed his honesty, and the driver—with piano—was allowed to go to serenade the future bride.

On December 28, 1929, Sara and Benjamin had a civil wedding, with a friend serving as a witness. The following day, a Jewish wedding took place at the home of Mauricio Cherkes and Ethel Kisner, the bride's parents. One of the

Ethel and Haim with her parents Rina and Tole

guests said later that Benjamin drank so much at the wedding, he refused to loosen his grip on a lamppost because he was afraid of falling down.

My parents, Rina Schpilberg and Antonio ("Tole") Schuster, met in Barranquilla, where my mother was born. Tole, who was born in Poland, emigrated with his family to Colombia via Cuba when he was a year old. The family settled in Cartagena, about seventy miles from Barranquilla. Tole's sister, Olga, introduced him to Rina, and after two years of romance, they married in February 1952.

The wedding ceremony took place at the Shaare Tzedek Synagogue, followed by a reception at the Club Union, the Sephardic club next door. Rina's family lived close to the synagogue, so Tole went to her house to "lower the veil" (traditionally called *bedeken* in Yiddish). There were very few cars in those days, and my mother's family did not own one. At the end of the veil lowering, the groom, his parents, the bride's brother, and the bridesmaids got into the few cars that were there and left for the synagogue—leaving the bride and her parents behind with no way to get there. Eventually, somebody remembered and came to pick them up.

It was customary to invite everyone from the Jewish community, so three hundred people were invited to Rina and Tole's wedding. The celebration included dinner and dancing that lasted until the early hours of the morning.

In those days there were no catering services. Sara, the mother of the bride, prepared all the food for the wedding. The desserts were prepared by *el costurero* (literally, "the sewing kit"), a group of women who baked desserts for friends' parties. This tradition began when about twenty married women would get together once a week at somebody's house to sew or knit items for poor newborns' baskets. The hostess would prepare her specialties and serve them for tea. The women tried to outdo each other. They decided that they would start to make their goodies for parties—bar mitzvahs, weddings, brit milah, and other community celebrations. The tradition continues in Barranquilla to this day. The *costurero* women also collect money and donate it to a community charity at the end of the year.

Tole, who had studied baking in Minneapolis, baked the wedding cake, which had many layers. Their best friends, Yutta and Jaime, who had gotten married two weeks before, returned from their honeymoon to celebrate with their friends. Tole and Jaime had bought a Borsalino fedora hat together, which Jaime wore for his wedding. Two weeks later, Tole wore the same Borsalino. Subsequently, fourteen grooms wore this same hat—until it was lost.

Like my mother, I was born in Barranquilla. My husband, Haim, was born in Haifa, Israel. We met as graduate students at the University of Pennsylvania and were married two years later. Because Colombia has a *concordato* (an agreement between church and state, which recognizes only Catholic weddings), a Jewish wedding would not have been considered official. So, on May 7, 1984, we got married in a civil ceremony at the office of a Jewish judge in Philadelphia. That day was *Yom Ha'atzmaut* (Israel's Independence Day), so we decided to celebrate with friends by making and serving traditional Israeli delicacies. That began our yearly tradition of having a falafel party on *Yom Ha'atzmaut*.

Our Jewish wedding took place in Barranquilla a month later. The preparations began months ahead. My mother took care of most of the planning for 450 guests. Haim and I were in charge of a few details. One was the invitations. How could we send out invitations that could be read by Ethel's Spanish-speaking friends and family, Haim's Hebrew-speaking Israeli friends and family, and our friends in the country where we met, the United States? Well, our invitations had to be in all three languages. After much deliberation, we managed to have a relatively decent-sized invitation.

Then came the question of what we would wear for the wedding. Haim, as a typical Israeli, had never worn a suit and tie. My father and everyone else expected him to do so. After much back-and-forth, Haim agreed to wear a pair of white pants, a white shirt, and a jacket that belonged to my father—no tie! He did wear shoes, even though the myth in our community is that he wore sandals. Wrong! He did buy a pair of shoes that until today are called "the wedding shoes."

Our wedding was a memorable, happy occasion, with lots of dancing and celebrating. At 5:00 a.m., the party wound down, and we went home to change for our honeymoon trip to Brazil.

COSTA RICA

Carole Bourne

It must have taken a lot of effort to personally deliver wedding invitations for several hundred guests. Carole's description of the circling of the groom by everyone under the chuppah is a novel variation on the traditional custom of circling by the bride only. Latin American wedding celebrations surely are lively affairs!

My son Michael and his wife, Karen, married in 2003 in San Jose, the capital of Costa Rica. Karen is a chemical engineer who went to graduate school at MIT. (She is not like the typical Jewish girl from Costa Rica who lives at home until she marries at age twenty or twenty-one.) The couple met at a party in Boston after Michael's return from Japan, where he had lived for three years. I understand that he spotted her from across the room. They dated for a year, then after Karen worked for a while in California, they decided to get married and make their home in the Boston area.

As the ceremony would be a traditional Orthodox one, I had to prove in advance that I was Jewish, otherwise the rabbi in Costa Rica would not have officiated. Ordinarily, I would have sent a copy of my ketubah. But my husband, Rick, and I were married in a Conservative synagogue, and I do not recall that we had a ketubah. Fortunately, I was able to produce a copy of our marriage license, and our friend, the Chabad rabbi in our town, wrote a letter of support. So the wedding proceeded as planned.

Rick and I went to Costa Rica from Boston a few days before the wedding. Many of our friends and relatives went too. We quickly became good friends with Karen's parents, Mario and Rebeca. Mario's family came to Costa Rica from Poland when he was a child, and Rebeca was born and raised in Panama. The day before the wedding, Karen and Michael went to the city hall to sign the necessary civil marriage documents. A rehearsal dinner for about one hundred people followed that night. When Rick, who spent some time in the Peace Corps in Latin America, gave a brief speech in Spanish, everyone was surprised.

It is customary in Costa Rica to hand deliver wedding invitations. Most of the Jewish community in San Jose was invited, and 350 people came. The wedding took place at the Marriott Hotel, located on the grounds of a former coffee plantation. It was a beautiful ceremony held outside, with two rabbis in attendance. We accompanied Michael down the aisle to the chuppah in front of the bridesmaids, Karen's cousins, and her sister. Under the chuppah with Karen and her parents, we all circled Michael seven times as I held Karen's train. One of the rabbis sang throughout the ceremony in Spanish, English, and Hebrew. It was totally overwhelming and spiritual. Then at the end of the ceremony, after Michael broke the glass, it was time for the reception.

I had never seen such fancy dresses! The women were more dressed up than in the United States and were wearing tons of makeup—even Karen. The orchestra of twelve to fifteen musicians started with Jewish music and then went to salsa, which they played continuously throughout the night. Rick and I had taken salsa lessons at a dancing school in our town, so we joined in. By that time, it was late and everyone was starving. Rebeca is a kosher caterer who specializes in sweets, so when they put out the desserts before the meal, many of the guests—who kept telling us, "Wait until you see the desserts!"—went there first.

As the party went on, everyone was singing, dancing, and celebrating strenuously, wearing funny hats and leis, long into the night. We left at one o'clock in the morning. The party continued for at least another hour.

The next day, after a tour of some nearby tourist sites, out-of-town guests were invited to a cousin's home in the countryside, a farmhouse complete with chickens in the yard and spectacular views. Music, singing, and swimming were part of the fun, as well as the most delicious barbecue with rice and beans. This gave us a chance to enjoy the beauty of Costa Rica and to become better acquainted with the bride's family before, reluctantly, we had to leave for home.

GERMANY

Miriam Harel

Miriam, a retired plastic surgeon who sadly and unexpectedly passed away in 2021, compiled a family history for her English-speaking relatives. She shared some unusual information—the sumptuous menu and a poem—from the wedding of her father's brother Rudolph and his wife, Grete. Her translation of the wedding Tischlied has tragic resonance when we know that the bride and groom did not survive; they waited too long and then were unable to emigrate before they were transported to Auschwitz, where they were among more than 140,000 German Jews murdered in the Holocaust. Miriam's father did not attend his brother's wedding. Eight months before, he had left for Palestine where he met Miriam's mother, a refugee from Austria.

On December 25, 1934, my uncle Rudolf Kaiser married Grete Buchthal from Essen. The wedding took place, with all the bells and whistles, in Wittenberge, a town in northern Germany on the Elbe River. It is evident that despite the gathering clouds, the family celebrated with the usual flair befitting the occasion.

I have a copy of the invitation and the menu, which includes in order:

Truffle cup
Chicken soup with noodles
Blue stream trout with horse radish
Vegetable plate with tongue
Goose with Sicilian salad
Praline-maraschino parfait
Palm ice cream cake
Mocca
In the evening: A cold buffet

As was the custom in parties for life's milestones, there was always a ceremonial part. In the Kaiser family, as in many other German Jewish families, someone always wrote a poem with rhymes, sometimes to a popular tune, or someone gave a speech. The poems were called *Tischlied* (Table Songs). I have several examples of those, written by various members of the family for different occasions. (My father wrote a poem when I was born and gave a speech when I went over the hill at my fortieth birthday party.)

For this wedding, the poem was printed on a folio of good paper in an elegant font and sent to the guests, probably with the invitation. It would be too much to translate all eleven verses, eight lines each. Therefore, I chose the last, located on the back of the folio:

To its end arrives the song
It lost some of its force,
The tune is nice, though a bit long
The voice is getting hoarse.
To the couple a thunderous roar
For joy and luck in married chore
Bring forth the juice of vine
Let all the Buchthals live just fine.

SIX

—ᴍᴍ—

BEFORE THE WEDDING
Mikveh and Henna

IN THE UNITED STATES and other Western countries, brides typically experience prewedding activities according to their individual situations and tastes
rather than Jewish law. In other countries, and at other times, some prewedding
rituals were considered so important that it was inconceivable for a Jewish wedding to take place without them. Foremost among these practices is immersion
in the mikveh, the Jewish ritual bath, within four days before the wedding ceremony. According to Jewish law and tradition, immersion in the water must be
complete without any barriers—including clothing, jewelry, and makeup, even
nail polish among the most observant—and overseen by a woman attendant.

The mikveh still plays a very important role in Orthodox Judaism, somewhat less so in other branches, representing purification and the beginning
of a new life as a married woman. Throughout history, a Jewish community
was required to construct a mikveh even before building a synagogue. Jewish
communities had to take the extreme step of selling Torah scrolls, or even the
synagogue itself, if needed to fund construction of the mikveh. This is why
intact or remnants of mikva'ot (plural) can be found at the sites of long-gone
Jewish communities throughout the world.[1] Jewish marriage—and therefore
Jewish life—was dependent on the availability of a mikveh.

Contemporary stories from Mexico and Morocco, as well as others in this
book, describe women-only celebrations that take place in the mikveh after the
bride emerges from the water. Prewedding customs, such as the beautiful candle ceremony at the mikveh described by the author from Mexico, embed the
bride deeply into the circle of women in her life and in her Jewish community.

Celebrations usually include special sweet delicacies for the bride-to-be and her guests. The emphasis is first on ritual purification and prayers to God, followed by pampering and increasing the joy of the bride.

As we will discuss in a later chapter on Israeli Jewish weddings, permission to marry is granted by the Orthodox rabbinate, which requires that brides go to the mikveh before their marriage and obtain a certificate from the mikveh attendant that they have done so correctly.[2] The bride must present the certificate to the rabbi before he will conduct the ceremony. Some brides go to the mikveh enthusiastically and others reluctantly, some fearful of the cleanliness of the water—including the author of the story from Israel in this chapter—or the presence of people who will not respect her privacy.

Not all Jewish brides want to go to a mikveh or have one available. Some, like the Greek bride in this chapter, immerse in the sea, a river, or a lake. According to information provided by Mayyim Hayyim, a modern mikveh near Boston, some grooms have embraced the custom of immersing in the days prior to their weddings even though this is not a traditional or required practice for men.

Among Mizrahi Jews (those from the Middle East and North Africa, also labeled Sephardic), as well as Jews from India and Pakistan, the henna celebration in the days leading up to the wedding was—and often still is—as important and elaborate as the wedding itself. Traditions vary from community to community, but all involve the application of henna, a dye derived from a flowering plant, to the hands or the feet of the bride and sometimes the guests, as the author from Pakistan noted. Food is always a highlight, as well as bridal gifts. Yemenite henna celebrations are famous for elaborate headdresses and jewelry, often family heirlooms, worn by brides even today in Israel. And which community can top the henna party for five hundred guests in Marrakesh, Morocco that the author describes? The ritual in Mexico, when rosewater mixed with henna was poured over the feet of the bride, may have been imported from Turkey, the native country of the bride's grandparents.

Many prewedding rituals, including henna, involve modifying and beautifying the woman's body. In the 2008 Franco-Tunisian film *The Wedding Song*, the Jewish groom instructs his Tunisian bride to remove all her pubic hair before their wedding, as was the painful custom. Talmudic scholars have debated whether it is appropriate, forbidden, or even preferred for brides to retain or remove their pubic hair. In our Uzbekistan story, the writer focuses exclusively on the bride's mandatory removal of eyebrow hairs in the company of her female friends and relatives. In contemporary life, brides beautify themselves at hair salons and makeup studios, with or without others present, as the bride from Israel remembers in her story.

GREECE

Zanet Battinou

Zanet, director of the Jewish Museum of Greece in Athens, is one of a dwindling number of Romaniote Jews who date their ancestry back two millennia to the Roman Empire of northern Greece. Ioannina, where Zanet was raised, was the center of Romaniote life. It still is home to a small number of Jewish families like hers who survived the Holocaust. Through the decades, the majority of Romaniote survivors have assimilated into the larger Sephardic Greek communities of Athens and other cities. Their distinctive Judeo-Greek language and Torah chanting are vanishing. Zanet's joyful memoir of her wedding-while-pregnant is unique in this collection.

As I contemplate my wedding, the first thing that comes to mind was my deep sense of happiness. You see, I was five months pregnant with our daughter, Linda Sarah, a pregnancy that had not been achieved easily or quickly, and I was over the moon! I was also very much in love with my fiancé, Isidore Tiano, who had been instrumental in bringing about my happy state and could do no wrong in my eyes.

So, with an established pregnancy, we decided it was time to pledge our troth before our families and friends. We wanted a romantic evening wedding, so we chose a moonlit night in late June 2003 for good weather, practically guaranteed by the temperate climate of Athens, and an elegant outdoor venue. We calculated about three hundred guests, so it would be a medium-sized affair, with the ceremony taking place first, and a dinner dance following, all at the same lovely seaside garden.

Since I come from Ioannina in the northwest of Greece and most of my family perished in the Holocaust, my husband-to-be, who is a native of Athens and has an extensive family, accounted for the vast majority of the guests. Wanting to spare me any extra fatigue that the arrangements might cause, he very capably took everything on himself. He designed and wrote up a plan for the wedding ceremony in which everyone had their positions and each part was accompanied by the appropriate musical theme—Jewish, classical, Greek, and even themes from our favorite movies and musicals. I was given a single task: to find a pretty dress that would fit my growing tummy. This was accomplished easily, as the third gown in the first bridal collection I tried on seemed perfect.

It was champagne-colored, off-the-shoulder with a wide empire-style skirt, elegant and understated, comfortable and right up my street.

I also took care of our bonbonnieres, a Greek tradition of giving candied almonds to guests at the end of the ceremony. I wanted to revive an old custom of the Ioannina Jewish community, where every guest was offered some almonds in the palm of the hand from a cut glass bowl using a silver spoon. But in our hygiene-conscious times, this did not seem a viable idea. So I reached a compromise. I found champagne-colored, square linen hankies edged with lace, bought good quality candied almonds, and my dear colleagues at the Jewish Museum of Greece helped tie almost five hundred bonbonnieres with broad champagne silk ribbon. There were enough for the wedding guests and some to send and give to family and friends unable to attend.

My mikveh took place on the Thursday before the wedding. It turned out to be a most cherished experience. At first, I thought that maybe, because I was already pregnant, I would not be able to participate in the mikveh ritual. I was incorrect about that and was overjoyed. But because the Athens mikveh was undergoing restoration work, I decided to have my mikveh in the sea. It was a very special occasion, with my mother-in-law, now of blessed memory, my granny, my mom, and my closest friends in attendance, sitting on towels on the beach across the street from our apartment. My friends had brought sweet and savory delicacies to nibble on, and my mom-in-law had prepared the traditional basket of luxurious towels, perfume, and bathroom goodies that every bride receives. (I have kept the lovely towels for my daughter to use someday, please G-d.) My mikveh was full of love, meaning, and reverence for me. I will never forget it.

And then the big day came. I was grateful that my father, who was gravely ill at the time, had recovered enough to be able to give me away. We dressed and set out together from our apartment, with Isidore driving our car and me taking up the entire back seat with the voluminous skirt of my wedding gown spread out. Instead of bridesmaids, we had chosen two flower girls and eight couples of friends and relatives as our attendants. These special people had played a part in our meeting and in our early days together. They walked in front of me and my parents and flanked the chuppah, brought in from the Athens synagogue, four couples on each side. According to Isidore's planning, there was special music playing as the couples walked to the chuppah, which became different as the rabbis appeared, and changed as I walked down the aisle with my parents. The two officiating rabbis led a lovely ceremony that went without a hitch. Then, lots of photos with family and friends, as we had opted not to have a video, which we thought of as disruptive and intrusive.

By that time, a gentle night had fallen, and the dinner dance took place under the stars. Before the sit-down dinner was served, we said a blessing for the meal and cut our wedding cake. My new husband then decorated my face with a spoonful of it. After the meal and the cake were consumed, we opened the floor with the first slow dance. We partied until the early hours of the morning saw the end of our merriment. I must say that I enjoyed every minute of our big lovely Greek wedding!

Our daughter was born three and a half months later, turning our happiness to bliss. She was tickled pink to realize, as she got older, that she attended her parents' wedding from an unusual vantage point, and she tells the story proudly at every opportunity. She was followed, almost five years later, by twin brothers, Samuel and Joseph, who completed our family and demolished any hope of peace and quiet for the next ten to twelve years. But that, as they say, is another story.

ISRAEL

Sheba Grinhaus

Sheba describes the hoops through which she had to jump before being allowed to marry in Israel in 1973. The situation remains the same forty-five years later, in spite of activists working for the liberalization of laws governing marriage. (See the story under "Cyprus" in chapter 14 of this volume.) Like Sheba, the majority of brides accept the stringent rules, which she recounts in detail. Indeed, she remembers the compulsory meeting at the officiating rabbi's home as enjoyable. A year after their wedding, Sheba and her husband moved to Canada where she became a successful manufacturer in the bakery business, university graduate, mother, and grandmother.

The year is 1973, and I am an eighteen-year-old Canadian Jewish woman who has just graduated from a Toronto high school. I have been accepted to two Toronto universities but decide instead to study at the Hebrew University in Jerusalem. So off I go, to the chagrin of my parents who would rather I remain in my Canadian nest.

I am enamored with Israel and feel that this is my home. I am there four months later as the Yom Kippur War, which hits Israel by surprise on October 6, 1973, escalates. I cannot go home. I would feel like a deserter. I am part of this country now, and what I am experiencing is more than one can ever learn from books in school. The university is closed. The professors are called to the defense forces, and I take a job in the post office to fill a now vacant spot.

My boyfriend Haim, recently released from his compulsory Navy duty, is called up with all the other young reservists and ships off to the south where the war is being fought with Egypt. His older brother and his father are mobilized to the north, to face off with Syria.

I had met Haim two years earlier as a backpacking tourist. We had written letters for two years before I came here. I am not thinking of marriage. Thankfully, there is a cease-fire on October 25, and Haim comes back to my apartment in early November. He proposes marriage. I accept. War makes you think seriously about life's consequences. We hear of so many casualties in this war and of so many young brides-to-be left alone because their fiancés have been killed. The morale of the country is so low. Why wait any longer to marry?

I fly home to visit my family in Canada with my good news, and it is met with less than enthusiasm. I am too young, I am told. Who is this Haim, I am asked. How can I be sure Haim is on the up and up, my parents say? While marrying at an early age is acceptable at this time in Israel, it is much too early in Toronto, apparently! I get it, and although I want to marry Haim, I also want my parents' blessing. I assure them about Haim's character, his maturity, his work ethic, and how responsible and generous he is. I confirm that he is a mensch. My parents accept it. They trust me: that is so important for me to know.

The wedding will be in Israel, and I am quite happy to leave all the details to my mom. I know she will enjoy choosing the tablecloths, the menu, and making the arrangements. She informs me that she is bringing material to Israel to have my wedding dress handmade.

Here I am thinking that it's all just a question of hiring a hall, a band, and buying rings. But no—we are in Israel! Evidently, there are some prerequisites to a marriage in the Holy Land—a whole list, in fact. The rabbinical authorities must be satisfied or no wedding!

First, my parents have to find a rabbi in Toronto who will write a letter to the Rabbinate in Israel to confirm that I am a one hundred percent Jewish woman who has never been married. This is a particularly sticky point because my husband-to-be is a Cohen. *Cohenim* cannot marry divorcées. Who knew?

Next, I must go to a *rebbitzen* (rabbi's wife) in Jerusalem who will size me up, test me on my Jewish background, and most importantly, ask me when my last menstrual period was. This last point will make or break the wedding date. I will get a pass for the wedding date we chose if it falls on the date of my ovulation. Since we have booked the hall already, I am doing some furious backward counting of dates to make it work while on the bus to visit this woman. Who knew?

During these arrangements, Haim and I travel the country, delivering our printed invitations personally to our guests. It is considered a nicer gesture than mailing them. It is, in fact, a pleasure to visit all our prospective guests, for me particularly because I get to know everyone better before the wedding.

As the big day approaches, Haim and I are invited to a havdalah service at the home of the rabbi who will marry us. It is expected that we will attend. He lectures us on how to follow the faith and keep a kosher home. It is a moving and enjoyable experience, but there is yet one more religious hurdle to jump: I must go to the mikveh, the ritual bath. This is not optional because if I do not get the certificate from the mikveh that I have undergone this ritual immersion to present to the rabbi at the wedding, he can call the whole thing off and just leave the hall.

Haim's mother assures me that her friend will sit on the front steps to the mikveh early, before it opens, so that I am the first one in the pool with fresh water. The wedding is on a Tuesday, and Tuesday is a special day for weddings in Israel. So Monday night at the mikveh is busy with many brides. I am grateful that I can be the first in the pool and not have to go in after many others. Evidently, the water is not changed after each person!

Finally, the big day arrives, and I'm off to the hairdresser. What a show! Thirty-five other brides are there on the same day, and the salon is like a factory. Everyone gets the star treatment but in assembly-line fashion. We get the manicure, the pedicure, the schnitzel lunch with little cakes and coffees, as we sit in rows, heads full of curlers, under huge jet engine-sized hair dryers. My hair is done, and I am herded upstairs for makeup. The makeup artist looks bored, and everyone is getting made up the same way no matter what they look like. Yikes! I do my own makeup. We all get dressed at the salon, and as I look around at the other dresses, I appreciate my mother's insistence on a seamstress-made dress more when I see my reflection in the long mirror.

Haim picks me up from the salon, and after photography, we are off to the hall. We have to be the first ones there, with our parents, in order to greet the guests. I am seated on a white throne on a raised floor, and each guest comes down the long aisle to congratulate me while Haim sits with our fathers and the rabbi and signs the ketubah. He soon joins me at the throne.

We are married on the dance floor under a portable chuppah held by four close friends. The service is not long. I like that everyone in the room comes to stand around the chuppah during the ceremony instead of being seated formally, as we do in Canada. Once Haim steps on the glass, the chuppah is quickly folded up, the band begins playing a hora, and everyone dances.

We are married on August 6, 1974, and ours is one of the first weddings since the war that is truly joyful and lively. Weddings in the months immediately following the war's breakout were very low-key because the entire country was in mourning for those we lost. Our friends and cousins make up three-quarters of the crowd, so it's a young group. My best friends come from Canada for the event, and many of Haim's friends take leave from the army and arrive in uniform. We remember those who have missed out on joyous occasions like this, as so many lives have been cut short. We are truly blessed.

MEXICO

Gabriela Mekler

The series of prebridal and wedding events that Gabriela describes would be exhausting if not for the exhilaration that such happy proceedings provide. Gabriela documents certain lovely Sephardic customs: pouring sugar water as well as henna on the feet of the bride-to-be and circling her with blessings as candles are lit one by one. The rosca tradition that she describes, when a cake is broken over the head of the bride, is similar to one described in the story about Afghanistan in chapter 10 of this book.

I was born and raised in Mexico City. My grandparents on my mother's side are from Turkey and on my father's side, from Russia. So I am half Sephardic and half Ashkenazic. My husband Ilan and I met in Miami. He had come there as a teen when his family moved from Israel. I was teaching at a Jewish preschool and getting my master's degree in guidance counseling.

My family was anxious for me to meet a Jewish man, and one of my uncles had a friend in common with Ilan's mom. She had three single sons and kept calling me to come for Shabbat dinner. I was always busy with my job and school, so I couldn't come. Finally, one day Ilan, the oldest son, called me. I was on a break from school, and I needed friends. We started to go out casually. Slowly, we fell in love.

My family had a vacation house in Cuernavaca, about fifty minutes south of Mexico City, where my dad had a little farm. Cuernavaca is known for its spring-like weather all year round and its butterflies. My dad passed away when I was thirteen. I have always associated his memory and that place with

Gabriela and Ilan

butterflies and had always wanted to get married there. Ilan proposed to me in Seville, Spain, six months after we started dating. When room service brought our breakfast one morning, there was a little box inside one of the domes. It wasn't a ring—just a little butterfly with a question mark.

A few months later, we were married in Cuernavaca. The wedding invitation had a butterfly on it. The day before the wedding, the most beautiful ceremony took place. The mikveh is an important part of weddings in Mexico. Every synagogue has one, and they are very luxurious. I went with fifty of my closest female relatives and friends. I dipped seven times and said a prayer. For me, it was like a rebirth. I felt absolutely pure. It was a precious experience—magical.

When I came out, my mother gave me a gorgeous robe to put on. According to Sephardic tradition, each woman came up to me with a special message and poured henna on my feet for fertility and sugar water for a sweet life.

Then we went into another room for chocolates and light refreshments. My closest relatives, including my mother, my sisters, and my grandmother, made a circle around me and held candles. As each candle was lit by the one before, each beloved person said a blessing. It was so emotional and beautiful—everyone had tears in their eyes. The candles are given to the bride-to-be to use on Shabbat after her marriage. This Sephardic ceremony is so lovely that the Ashkenazic community has adopted it, as well.

Another tradition has to do with *rosca*, a kind of bread or cookie, made in the shape of a *Magen David* (Jewish star). The two triangles that compose it represent the woman and man who were two and are about to become one. My mother and mother-in-law broke a big one over my head. This may symbolize the destruction of the temple, like the breaking of the glass at the wedding. Everyone said mazel tov and ate small versions of the *rosca*. I made a speech and told the women how important they are to me, with a special mention of my dad's mother, who was too ill to be at the wedding.

After that, everyone went to brunch in a tent in my aunt's garden, where more guests were waiting. There were gorgeous calla lilies everywhere. We had delicious Mexican foods—*nopales* (cactus) salad, chicken in *mole* (sauce), tortillas made on a big *comal* (a flat griddle), and quesadillas. Then we drove to Cuernavaca to the hotel to relax and go to the spa before the wedding.

As I was on my way to my wedding at 8:30 p.m. the next evening, the men were signing the ketubah. (Only men sign.) I arrived when everyone was seated in the tent on the grounds of the hotel. The rabbi and cantor were good friends from Bet El, a large synagogue in Mexico City where my family have been members since the beginning. In the United States, it would be called Conservative, but in Mexico it is Reform. My only attendants were eleven little girls—nieces and cousins' children—who scattered petals. Ilan was waiting for me under the chuppah. I hadn't seen him for three days. We wrote our own vows, which was not a common practice. We used phrases from Song of Songs in Hebrew and Spanish. It was a small wedding for Mexico—only 250 people who, we knew, were happy to be there with us from all over the world.

I had made 1800 white butterflies out of plaster and feathers, hanging from fishing lines over the tables. For our first dance, Ilan and I did the bolero (we had taken a dancing class). It was lame, but we did it! Then the hora went on for about an hour. It's wild, insane. They put you up on chairs, people get hurt—it's crazy! I had to redo my hair and makeup. The dinner, which had to be glatt kosher, began at 10:30 p.m. The band gave out many different prizes to the guests, and there were performers who danced on stilts and mariachis. People drank a lot. We served breakfast at six o'clock in the morning. The celebration ended at eight. We still get comments from people who were there.

MOROCCO

Rachel Jacobson

Moroccan Jewish wedding events might be the most elaborate in the world. As in other countries, some Middle Eastern Jewish wedding traditions are similar to those of the surrounding culture—the henna party, the prewedding trip to the hammam, the multiple charging of caftans during wedding events, the bride's entrance on a kind of throne, and the scrumptious items of cuisine. The blessing of the guests by the bride before the wedding ceremony is a traditional Jewish custom, while the priestly blessing of the guests that Rachel mentions is a less common element. Rachel, who has not forgotten her Moroccan roots, teaches Hebrew and Jewish studies in the Boston area, where she has lived for more than forty years.

My great-nephew Steeve married his wife, Esther, in 2007 in Casablanca. Steeve's grandmother, Marie, is my oldest sister. She is the only one of our twelve brothers and sisters who stayed in Morocco. The whole family left for Israel in 1948, before I was born. Marie was seventeen and already married.

For the most part, the Jews of Morocco are well-off financially and have been protected by several generations of rulers. Like his father and grandfather, the current king, Mohammad VI, has supported the Jewish community and has worked behind the scenes for Arab-Israeli peace. Although there have been isolated instances of violence, antisemitism is not evident. Like my sister Marie's family, everyone in the Jewish community follows the same modern Orthodox practices. They all keep strictly kosher and are *shomer Shabbat* (keepers of the Sabbath). They all send their children to Hebrew day schools, which are known to be the best in the country.

I arrived from my home in the United States a week before the wedding, joining some of my siblings who were able to come from Israel and other parts of the US. I missed the engagement party but went to many other traditional celebrations for Steeve, who was twenty-seven, and his bride Esther, who was twenty-one. (Often in Morocco, the bride is much younger than the groom.)

Esther and Steeve under canopies carried by bearers at the henna party

The mikveh was a low-key affair attended by women only—about fifteen to twenty close family members and friends. After immersing, Esther put on a beautiful, embroidered caftan with bright cheerful colors. There was a lot of singing and the comfort of being together before the elaborate marriage celebrations. Along with many other special pastries, my favorite was served— baby eggplants candied in honey and sugar.

For his part, my great-nephew was the center of a *Shabbat Hatan* (groom's Shabbat), which is held in the synagogue the Shabbat before the wedding, when the groom-to-be is called up the Torah and the family receives congratulations.

I was there for the ketubah signing four days before the wedding, when the groom's family brought him to the bride's home, walking through the streets, accompanied by the loudest drums and horns I ever heard. There was so much noise! At the bride's home, they signed the ketubah, along with the rabbi and two witnesses who traditionally are not family members. Both Esther and Steeve received expensive gifts from their future in-laws.

Next was a huge henna party for five hundred people in Marrakesh, two hours away, sponsored by the groom's family. The women wore gorgeous caftans (I bought one in Morocco) and many of them changed garments four or five times during the course of the event. The bride entered the ballroom on a canopied throne carried on poles on the shoulders of four men. The groom entered the same way, dressed in a white *tarboosh* (tasseled hat) and a white *jalabiya* (long robe). There was a French band and a Moroccan band, and singers who sang in French, Arabic, and Hebrew. As the bride and groom sat under their canopies, they were showered with lavish gifts, which were shown to all the guests. The bride received bracelets, necklaces, and earrings, which she put on until she was covered in gold and diamonds. Then a family member applied henna to the palms of all the guests—women and men—who wanted it. This is a testament that the couple is willing to marry, and, as henna stains the hand for as long as six months, that they will not be forgotten and are blessed. There was nonstop eating and entertainment in every corner until the early hours of the morning.

The day before the wedding, twenty women went to the *hammam*, the steam bath. We went into a huge room filled with steam and laid down on wooden beds. For forty-five minutes, someone used a special brush to peel the dead cells from my skin. It's amazing to see what comes off! Then creams are applied, and you feel that you have baby skin.

On the day of the wedding ceremony, the bride traditionally blesses every person who needs help, laying her hand on the person's head. On that day she is closest to G-d and is pure. There were three hundred people in the Great Synagogue of Casablanca, the women and men sitting separately. Family members and attendants came down the aisle ahead of the bride, who was veiled and wearing a simple white bridal gown without jewelry, which was her choice. Rabbi Lau, the Chief Rabbi of Tel Aviv, officiated, reading the ketubah. Under the chuppah, the bride circled the groom seven times, and members of the family read the sheva brachot. At the end, the bride came close to the ark for the *birkat kohanim*, the priestly blessing. Women cannot look and have to shield their eyes. Then off to a very fancy reception at the Hyatt Hotel for even more guests, where there was music, dancing, kosher Moroccan food, and incredible desserts.

For a week after the wedding, people hosted the family for sheva brachot (seven benedictions, like those recited under the chuppah). Every night we went somewhere else, including the Chabad house. When I finally returned home, I was completely exhausted!

PAKISTAN

Zvia Epstein

It may be surprising that a thriving Jewish community existed in Pakistan, a Muslim country known as one of the most hostile to Israel. Built in 1893, the Magain Shalome Synagogue in Karachi, where Zvia's cousin Dorothy married, was demolished after the emigration of the entire Jewish community year by year following Pakistan's partition from India and the founding of Israel in 1948. Zvia, a retired high school English teacher, has lived in Israel since 1971.

When she was eighteen, my cousin Dorothy came to live with us in Karachi. She came from a little town in southeastern Pakistan called Sukkur, where she lived with her parents and six brothers. Her father was my mother's brother.

She tells me that my mother did everything for her, including finding a special young man for her. At that time, some marriages were love matches, but hers was arranged by the families. The boy's family came to my family's home and formally put in a request for the marriage. Then the young couple met, had a few chaperoned outings, and agreed to marry.

Soon after, the bride-to-be was taken to the home of the bridegroom-to-be, Enoch Eliyahu. There, as tradition required, she was given a full set of clothing. Now she was considered engaged. The couple was free to be seen about town together.

The day before the wedding was a special one. First, the bride was covered from head to toe with a mixture of turmeric, saffron, and milk. Then came a bath, giving the skin a special glow. Dorothy's friends came to our house to prepare food for the party to follow, including ghari, a kind of fried doughnut made with yeast and rice flour.

That evening was the *mehndi*, a women's henna party, which proceeded according to tradition. Amid the happy friends and family of the bride, the groom's family entered. They came with a tray of henna paste to decorate the hands and feet of the bride and any of the guests who wanted to be similarly adorned. (The little girls loved it, of course.) In addition to henna and delicious sweets, they brought jewelry and two outfits for the bride. Among the gifts was a *sera*, a jeweled veil that a bride ties to her forehead to cover her face at the wedding ceremony. (My own family has one generations old, made of solid silver.) With merriment and laughter, the bride was then taken to the mikveh, where more sweets were distributed. Meanwhile, the groom, who had not seen the bride for a week, was having his own party at his house, equivalent to today's stag party, I suppose.

The next day, her wedding day, Dorothy and her husband-to-be fasted as required. The wedding was held on a Sunday in 1953 in the synagogue in Karachi, complete with bridesmaids and flower girls. The ceremony was a traditional Jewish one, including the reading of the ketubah with everyone holding their breath to see how much money the groom would be required to pay in case of divorce, a time-honored component.

The wedding feast was held in the hall of the Jewish Sports Club. The couple then went back to the bride's house where she was given her dowry—kitchenware, cutlery, and crockery. After changing into one of the outfits given to her by the bridegroom's family, my cousin left her father's house for the last time.

All that was long ago when I was a youngster. Dorothy and her late husband had six children who now live in Israel along with many grandchildren. My thanks to her for recalling and telling me about these rituals that I did not experience myself.

UZBEKISTAN

Alanna E. Cooper

Alanna, an anthropologist and chair of Jewish studies at Case Western Reserve University, had the opportunity to witness a little-known bridal custom usually reserved for close family and friends. The Bukharan qosh chinon is reminiscent of the thorough cleaning of the hair and body (chafifah) required prior to immersion in the mikveh. But while self-cleansing before the mikveh ritual is common to traditional Jewish brides throughout the world, removal of hair on the face is an unusual requirement. Alanna's own painful prewedding eyebrow tweezing was (almost) entirely voluntary.

A friend suggested it. My mother suggested it. It seemed like something a bride should do. So a few days before my wedding, I went ahead and did it. I drove myself to a beauty salon to have my unruly eyebrows tamed.

I had never had my facial hair plucked or waxed, and I was surprised by how much it hurt. I held the chair tight and winced. The cosmetician went about her business, oblivious. How had I gotten myself into this situation, where I was paying a stranger to pinch and pull my lovely delicate hairs?

When her work on the first eyebrow was complete, I considered leaving. But I was too embarrassed to walk out of the salon with one side manicured into a shapely arc while the other was still its same old bushy self. So, I stayed in the chair, stinging and unhappy. The process certainly would have been easier if I had brought my friends and family with me and made a party out of it.

That's how a Jewish bride would have done it in Uzbekistan. She would not have had her facial hair manicured alone in some impersonal salon. She would have had it done at home, surrounded by the women of her family and neighborhood. I learned that while conducting research among Central Asia's Bukharan Jews.

There, having one's eyebrows tamed prior to getting married is more than a suggested beauty treatment. It's considered obligatory. As long as a girl is single, she is forbidden from having her facial hair manicured. Then, just prior to her wedding, she undergoes the ceremonial removal of the brow—*qosh chinon*—and emerges as a bride. (Those who flaunt social convention and do it before the proper time are stigmatized as a girl who loses her virginity before marriage.)

The first *qosh chinon* I attended was during a hot, dry summer I spent doing research in Uzbekistan. It was 1994, the Soviet Union had recently dissolved, and the region's Jews were leaving en masse for Israel and the United States. I had come to document the final chapter of the community's millennium-long history in the region.

I was a stranger in the Jewish quarter of Samarkand but had quickly befriended a few locals who helped me with my research, including Sasha. He owned a video camera and was often hired to film family events. When he heard that a *qosh chinon* party was to be held in the neighborhood, he arranged for me to attend.

The bride did not seem happy—I wrote in my notes—her hands were shaking, and she looked nervous. But unlike me during my eyebrow-plucking experience, this bride was surrounded by women relatives and friends, who would help her through the ordeal. Her mother and mother-in-law-to-be, her aunts and cousins and sisters escorted her with song to a chair in the center of the family courtyard. There, the cosmetician wrapped a colorful scarf around her forehead, bedecking her in a crown.

The cosmetician then wound a thread around her own fingers and got to work. She moved rhythmically, leaning in toward the bride and then away, catching each hair individually in her grip, pulling and releasing, and pulling again, carefully shaping the brow, concentrating on each detail despite the throng surrounding her. The women guests jostled with each other for a turn to come close, to hold the bride's head steady, and utter a blessing ("may you and your husband have a long, happy life together"), a piece of advice ("be aware that marriage is not always easy"), or a word of wisdom ("do not forget that your husband's family will now become your own").

After each guest came forward to offer her words, she placed a bill in the bride's silken crown. When the cosmetician was done, she would take these bills as payment for her services—a personal and tender financial transaction. But first, before the scarf was removed, the bride was handed a large mirror to hold. A soft, shiny piece of material was tossed over her so that it draped across her head and the mirror. In the privacy of the cloth's folds, she spent a few moments gazing at the image of her new self.

Today, these customs are no longer practiced. With the dissolution of the Soviet Union, Central Asia's Bukharan Jews emigrated en masse and resettled in the United States and Israel, where young women no longer wait until marriage to have their facial hairs ceremoniously cleaned. As for me, when the cosmetician finished my eyebrows, I handed over my plastic credit card, signed the receipt, then got into my car alone. I drove back to my parents' home, where I was staying in the days leading up to my wedding. My eyebrows were shapely and tamed, but the skin above them was smarting. I felt exposed and was embarrassed for people to see my red swelling. I went downstairs to my childhood room and closed the door. Alone, I looked at myself in the mirror. How surprising a change in eyebrows can make. I appeared more sophisticated and mature, even glamorous. The woman staring back at me was a bride. She was also a bit of a stranger.

More than twenty years later, my wedding dress is packed away somewhere in a box, my daughters' brushes and curling irons are scattered around the house, and my eyebrows are again untamed and a bit bushy. I like them like that. I think my husband does too.

YEMEN

Tzipi Avizemer and Dafna Avizemer Rabbo

In 1949 "Operation Magic Carpet" brought fifty thousand Yemenite Jews to Israel, fleeing a perilous situation in their homeland. The elaborate costume of Yemenite brides, especially the towering headdress adorned with flowers, has often served as an iconic representation of Yemen's ancient Jewish culture. For centuries, Jews were consigned to work exclusively in certain trades, including silver smithing, weaving, and tailoring. Perhaps this expertise contributed to the origin of the gorgeous silver-threaded bridal attire that Tzipi, a first-generation Israeli, and her daughter, Daphna, wore for the henna ceremonies they describe. The modern white dress that Daphna wore at her wedding is bland in comparison.

Tzipi

The henna ceremony before the wedding is for women only, a ceremony that signifies a kind of separation from the family—and also a bachelorette party. In 1980, it was important for me to have this ceremony in order to preserve the Yemenite tradition of my parents' home. There were dozens of women around me, led by a woman who dressed me in a special costume, and a singer. I smeared henna on the palms of the women as a sign of good luck. Then I joined the singer in traditional songs about love, along with my mother, my aunts, and my grandmother. The other guests danced as we sang.

I loved all the attention, but my feelings were a mixture of happiness and sadness—sadness because of the imminent separation from my family and happiness because I was going to build a new family with my beloved husband. So the words of the songs amused me, yet also brought tears to my eyes. I told my mother that I wasn't abandoning her and would come to visit and help her.

Meanwhile, my husband-to-be had his own ceremony in his parents' home. There was no singing, but he also wore a special costume. The leader of the community, the *mori*, put henna on each of his hands. My husband covered his hands and protected the henna all night. The next day, the mori came back to remove the henna from his hands.

My close male relatives joined the festivities later. My sisters and brothers each gave me a blessing and smeared henna on my palm. This ceremony was more important to me than the wedding. It was authentic, special, and very emotional.

Dafna

The henna ceremony was an especially stirring experience for me. In my home, I had been exposed to Yemenite songs, food, and traditions. The connection between the henna ceremony and those traditions was very strong. For a few hours on the evening of the henna ceremony in 2013, I felt I had stepped into my grandmother's shoes in the time of her youth in Yemen. Suddenly, my grandmother's remembrances of dances around the well in her childhood home became a reality for me. I am very happy to have gone through this experience and thank my parents who helped to bring it to fruition.

SEVEN

—⟋⟍—

THE WEDDING VENUE

IN TRADITIONAL JUDAISM, it was preferable for a wedding ceremony to be performed outdoors under the stars. This symbolized the hope that the couple would produce a large family according to God's promise to Abraham to "multiply your children as the stars in heaven." Many German synagogues were built with a *treustein*, a stone in the corner of the building facing a courtyard where weddings took place. The stone was incised with initials of a biblical passage from Jeremiah: "the sound of the bridegroom and the bride . . . in the courtyards of Jerusalem." At the end of the ceremony, the groom would throw a goblet against the stone.[1]

Times change, and in her well-known wedding guide, Anita Diamant tells us that "there are almost no rules about where you can or can't raise a huppah."[2] This openness to indoor or outdoor spaces of nearly every sort enables the couple to make choices that are meaningful to them. Oftentimes, the choice is a synagogue to which the bride and her family have a long attachment, such as the Patronato in Havana, founded by the father of the author from Cuba, and Bet El Synagogue in Buenos Aires, where the bride from Argentina married amid the violence of a military junta. (The hall in Argentina where the reception took place was lovingly decorated by the bride's friends, a reminder of the interest of the entire community in helping Jewish couples meet and marry.) Occasionally, the groom's synagogue has special significance and that determines the choice, as for the husband of Anaëlle from France.

Other venues are chosen for a variety of reasons, some financial and political. During the great economic depression of the 1930s in the United States, author Marian's mother married her father in a secret ceremony in a rabbi's study, for they had no money for a celebration. The hush-hush home wedding of Larisa, the bride from Ukraine, was necessary at a time when such Jewish practices were forbidden. The wedding venue in Austria was particularly meaningful to Regina, whose parents had married in the same synagogue seventy-six years before. Like brides who had babies immediately after the Holocaust, a revenge against Nazism, this bride was demonstrating that Jewish life was continuing in the very country that had decimated the Jewish people. Katalin's Hungarian wedding at the synagogue of the only rabbinical seminary in the Soviet bloc was particularly significant when the majority of Jews had left the country or had opted to hide their Jewish origins.

Destination weddings have gained in popularity in the last few decades, as illustrated by Rabbi Abramowitz who writes entertainingly of his experiences conducting outdoor weddings in Bermuda. The sand-covered floor, as well as beautiful original woodwork and chandeliers, attract wedding couples to the historic synagogue of St. Thomas in the US Virgin Islands, whose rabbi also contributed to this chapter. Not surprisingly, a common element in these stories is the difficulty caused by weather events of wind and water.

Wedding venues in this volume include local beaches, hotels, gardens, family homes, and backyards—anywhere a chuppah can be raised. Some of these places involved investigation with particular features in mind—space for the number of guests, cost, beauty, accessibility, intimacy—as described by author Andrea in this chapter, who finally found the perfect venue for her daughter north of London. For other brides, the choice of where to hold the ceremony was not in question, as it was based on family history, connection to Jewish institutions, or local natural surroundings.

ARGENTINA

Irene Münster

Between 1976 and 1983, when Argentina was under the rule of a military junta, Jews were among the prime targets for kidnapping and torture. Irene's story illustrates the temporary refuge that weddings represent—a reprieve from the daily stress of the political situation that Irene's family and guests must have felt. Since her wedding, Argentina's Jews, the seventh-largest Jewish population in the world, have had their ups and downs. Following the bombing of the Israeli embassy and the Jewish community headquarters in the 1990s, thousands of Jews left Argentina, as they did after economic turndowns in 2001 and today. Nevertheless, the capital, Buenos Aires, has a multitude of Jewish institutions and synagogues. Bet El, where Irene married, is the country's first Conservative synagogue and one of the largest. Irene, a university library director, is researching the impact of Jewish immigration in Latin America.

I got married in 1978, two years into the most murderous dictatorship Argentina ever had—the year the world soccer championship was played in Argentina, my home country. People were enjoying the games and were delighted when Argentina got to the finals and won. In reality, this was a way to avoid looking inward and acknowledging what was occurring in the country: People were disappearing; people were tortured and murdered. How could we celebrate under such conditions? I admire my parents and those surrounding them, including the rabbi who married us, for taking a step forward amid the fear and for not giving up on our future.

My parents were founders of the Tarbut School in Buenos Aires, a high school based on Jewish humanitarian principles. They wanted our wedding party to be in the same school dining room where years before we had celebrated after my bat mitzvah. To be honest, I wasn't thrilled with the idea, but we weren't in a position to rent a ballroom in a hotel, and the political situation wasn't conducive to it either. Now, looking back, I am so happy we had the party there. Many friends came that Friday evening to decorate the hall and have it ready for the occasion. With warmth and attention to detail, they turned a high school dining room into a charming and beautiful wedding space.

On the evening of the wedding, I got dressed and had my hair and makeup done. When I looked in the mirror, I didn't recognize myself! Disconcerting everyone, I went into the bathroom, washed off what they had put on my face and hair, and announced that I was ready to go to the synagogue. Water was pouring out of my hair, we were late, but I was ready to walk to the bimah as myself. Meanwhile, my dearest husband, Ricky, waiting for me at the synagogue, was informed that I hadn't arrived. The *gabbai* (sexton) started to tease him that maybe I had second thoughts and decided not to come.

We got married at Bet El synagogue on a rainy evening in August. We were the third in a row of weddings for that night. The ceremony began with my soon-to-be husband and his mother walking toward the bimah, followed by my mother and father-in-law. My father escorted me to the chuppah, as always my guide and protector. Another treasured person was invited to join us under the chuppah—my husband's beloved grandmother. The rabbi escorted her to the bimah, and to this day we remember her happy, smiling face. Our charismatic rabbi sang the sheva brachot and explained the rituals to those present—Jews and non-Jews—making it a unique experience for many.

Once the ceremony was over, we stayed for greetings and congratulations and then left for some photos. We arrived at the party almost at midnight, very excited. Everyone cheered for us, and my husband and I danced our first waltz. Then we danced for hours to Israeli folk and Argentinean music, our parents and friends gave speeches, and the food was superb! A unique part of the menu was the chocolate table. My uncle, who owned a chocolate factory, prepared chocolate animals that represented my mother's zoo. Since my parents owned a house with a big garden, my mother saved and raised abandoned animals. One of these was a monkey that escaped on one of our early dates, giving Ricky an opportunity to recognize the crazy family he was joining.

One of my father-in-law's dearest wishes was to bring fresh strawberries from one of the northern provinces to serve as dessert. So a few days before our wedding, we drove a long way to the airport to pick up boxes of fresh, very tasty strawberries. But by the time the dessert was served, I was so exhausted that I pleaded with my new husband to go home with me before we headed out for our honeymoon. To this day, my husband won't let me forget that he never got the chance to taste the delicious strawberries that he had gone to so much trouble to get.

As the years have passed, we are still exploring and enjoying life together. Our family has grown, Judaism remains strong in our daily lives, and we celebrate the successes of each member of our family.

AUSTRIA

Regina Espenshade

Regina's poignant story encapsulates the recent history of Austria's Jews, a population who prospered in the hundred years before the Holocaust, playing central roles in the cultural and political life of the country. Regina's parents were among the fortunate ones who were able to flee just before the Nazi takeover in 1938, when the annihilation of sixty-five thousand Jews began. Her ecumenical wedding in the former synagogue of the town where her parents married so many years before, and where she began her studies as an international peacekeeper, brings that tragic history full circle. Her story is ultimately one of forgiveness and exchange of pain for optimism and hope for the future. What could be better accompaniments to a wedding?

Our 2013 wedding was not a traditional Jewish wedding. The decision to marry in Austria stemmed from events that began on April 11, 1937. That is the

Regina and Gene at their wedding banquet in the castle

date of the marriage of my parents, Eduard Lowy and Gizella Braun. They were the last Jewish couple to be wed in the synagogue of Stadtschlaining, a village in the province of Burgenland in eastern Austria. Until it was destroyed by the Nazis, a substantial and integrated Jewish community had thrived there, dating back to the sixteenth century. Jews constituted 40 percent of the population.

Forced to flee, my parents and my older sister, Hedy, found refuge in the United States, arriving in December 1939. I was born in 1943. I remember that my father had dreams, never fulfilled, of returning to Austria, although his mother, sister, and other relatives had perished in the Holocaust. My childhood memories are filled with stories of my family's life in Stadtschlaining.

These memories led me to take my mother back to Austria in 1972. As we walked through the main square of Stadtschlaining, a woman passed us and stopped in her tracks. "Gisi?" she asked in amazement. This was Josefin, a childhood friend who recognized my mother's distinctive deep voice. To Josefin, it was as if her old friend had returned from the grave. Josefin had married a Nazi and turned on my mother, her lifelong Jewish friend. At once, she begged my mother's forgiveness. "I forgive you" were my mother's first words to her friend of many years. In the hours after this chance meeting, Josefin showed us traces of the Jewish past that had been virtually destroyed. The synagogue had chickens running around in the courtyard. The gravestones in the cemetery were broken and scattered.

Fast forward to 1999, eight years after my mother's death. My sister Hedy had also dreamed of returning to the place she was born. So Hedy, her daughter, Lisa, and I traveled to Austria together. As we drove up to the village, the principal landmark of Stadtschlaining caught our attention—the fifteenth-century castle next to my mother's former home. From the dusty, derelict relic I saw in 1972, it had been transformed! A sign at the entrance announced that it was now the European University Center for Peace Studies. We learned that it was a destination for students from all over the world to study peace and conflict management.

And the castle was not the only restoration in town. The formerly desecrated synagogue was now the Peace Library, a graceful structure that remarkably retained elements of its former Jewish identity, including the women's gallery above the main sanctuary and brilliant blue and white stenciling on the walls and interior dome. A beautiful granite gate with a Hebrew inscription now marked the entrance to the Jewish cemetery. I had an overwhelming sense of relief.

That trip was an epiphany for me. The very next year, I decided to return to study peacekeeping at the center, an unparalleled opportunity to pursue my passions for peace in the Middle East and for racial and gender equality in the United States. My studies led to assignments as an international peacekeeper, work that became an intellectual and emotional touchstone of my career.

In 2001, using genealogical data, the village invited the descendants of former Jewish residents to return for a weeklong reunion. Village officials and I planned a meeting that would focus on forgiveness and reconciliation, as exemplified by my mother and her friend Josefin years before. People came from around the world, including some villagers who had attended my parent's wedding. The local schoolchildren presented a project recalling in song and pictures the customs of the former Jewish community. In the final convocation, the Bishop of Burgenland formally requested our pardon for the sins of the past committed against the Jews. The reunion transformed the lives of those who attended.

In the years since, people from the village have come to visit newfound friends in the United States, Scotland, and Israel. As an alternative to military service, young Austrian men serve at Holocaust memorials in twenty-three countries. Young men who have served at the Holocaust Museum in Washington, DC, have become our surrogate Austrian family members.

So when my husband asked in 2013, "Where do you want to get married?" there was only one response—in Stadtschlaining. On my seventieth birthday, attended by friends and family from the United States, Austria, Israel, Peru, and Japan, Gene and I were married. Conducted in English and German, our ecumenical wedding took place in the synagogue where my parents had married seventy-six years before. The wedding banquet, including joyous music and dancing, took place in the same castle where I had experienced another major turning point in my life.

BERMUDA

Rabbi A. Nathan Abramowitz

A subtropical British Overseas Territory six hundred miles off the coast of North Carolina, Bermuda has a share in the burgeoning warm-weather "destination wedding" market, as Rabbi Abramowitz's entertaining stories confirm. When the average wedding in the United States costs upward of $28,000 according to a 2021 survey by The Knot (a popular online wedding site), little wonder that some couples opt for a wedding on a beach with few in attendance. But beware of rainy weather and a chuppah too close to the water!

Rabbi Abramowitz signs a ketubah

I have been going to Bermuda from Washington, DC for many years, conducting High Holiday services and special life cycle events, including weddings. Some have been marriages of local residents, and others have been "destination" events. A few weddings stand out in my memory.

I remember the wedding of a banker and teacher, residents of the community, at one of the exclusive golf and beach clubs that dot the island. The beautiful chuppah was made of native wood and greenery. One hundred chairs covered in white fabric were arranged on a lush green lawn. We hoped for good weather. But just as we were about to begin the ceremony, a storm suddenly developed. As wind and rain swept in from the ocean in an enormous surge, everything that had been set up so carefully was completely destroyed—including the chuppah. What to do? There was no room in the clubhouse for a similar arrangement. Finally, everyone crowded into the one small room that was available. The guests stood packed together as I officiated under a chuppah made from a tablecloth and four broomsticks.

I remember another wedding that took place at a small crescent beach below a condo perched on a cliff where the bride and groom lived. As the ceremony began, the groom, followed by the bride in a long flowing dress, carefully walked down a rustic stairway that led from the cliff to the beach. So far so good. I had my back to the water, while the bride and groom and their guests faced the ocean, which was particularly rough that day. I had to shout to make myself heard above the waves crashing onto the rocks that ringed the beach. Nevertheless, the ceremony proceeded well until the groom broke the traditional glass. Just as he finished, a look of horror came over the faces of the newlyweds. I was not able to see the giant wave as it approached and broke over the beach, soaking me, the bride and groom, and the guests up to their ankles.

When a mature bride and groom entering their second marriage called me from Massachusetts, they asked if I could come to Bermuda to perform a ceremony on a beautiful beach without any guests in attendance. I agreed, bringing with me a portable chuppah composed of a velvet canopy that hung on four telescoping brass poles. When transported, the poles could be shortened, and when in use they could be lengthened, held by people in each corner. (The poles were not long enough or strong enough to be placed on the ground.) Finding the essential four chuppah-holders, Jews or non-Jews, had never presented a problem. But this time it was different. For some reason, the golf club where the beach was located was almost completely deserted. There was no one to ask to hold a chuppah. Down on the beach, the few people I asked made excuses not to participate. I went from one cove to another with a rising feeling of desperation. Finally, as I was about to give up, in a distant cove I saw two men accompanied by two bikini-clad women. As I trudged through the sand to confront them, I knew this was my last chance. My heart sank as the men began the familiar response of a previous commitment. They were interrupted by the young women—they would love to do it! All four covered up and trekked up the beach. The ceremony took place under the velvet and brass chuppah held by four accommodating sun-bronzed strangers.

When another couple called and asked me to perform a ceremony outdoors on the beach at one of the older hotels on the island, I warned them that it was a rainy time of year and that they should have a fallback location inside, as my past experience dictated. As is often the case with a rabbi's advice, they did not take heed. It rained for two days and nights before the wedding without letting up. And it was still pouring on the day of the wedding. It seemed that this would be another rain-soaked event. But, as luck would have it, a few minutes before the start of the ceremony, the sun came out from behind the clouds. It was a beautiful day for a wedding.

Before I was asked to come to Bermuda as the island's only rabbi, I had been there only once before. Now, after so many years, my wife and I have dear friends there who have visited us in the United States. The island is a lovely place with many dedicated people among the 150 Jews who live there. We have seen significant changes, as the community acquired a lease on a former church that now houses a sanctuary for services and a kosher kitchen, as well as a Hebrew school. During each of my trips there, I always enjoyed speaking with the children—and, when called upon, performing weddings.

CUBA

Dalia Kaufman Katz

Dalia's story shows how lives are changed, sometimes suddenly and dramatically, by historical events. After Fidel Castro gained power in 1959, the exile of 94 percent of the Jewish population began. Most settled in the United States, especially in Florida. Currently, about fifteen hundred Jews remain, most residing in Havana where there are three synagogues. The Patronato, where Dalia was married, is the largest and remains a hub of Jewish life, housing a community pharmacy where hard-to-obtain medicines donated by visitors are collected and distributed. The future of the Jewish community of Cuba is uncertain today, as immigration to Israel has increased and religious intermarriage is endemic.

I was born in 1935 in Cienfuegos, a small city on the southern coast of Cuba. There were few Jews there; the Torah was kept in my parents' living room. Both my parents came to Cuba from Poland. They met when my father, who operated a dry goods store in a small town where his brother set him up in business upon arriving from Poland, bumped into my mother's sister and her husband in Havana. They had come to meet my mother's ship when she arrived for a visit from Poland. My father accompanied them to the pier, my parents met, and my mother never went back to Poland.

I was raised in Havana, where my parents moved when I was a young child. I attended Instituto Edison, named after the inventor who had recently died, one of the best secular schools in the country. I graduated from high school in 1952. By that time most of the Jews, including my family, had moved from Old Havana to the suburbs. The Ashkenazi community had built a new synagogue, the Patronato, a few years before. (My father, who became a manufacturer of buttons for the clothing industry in Cuba, was one of the founders.) The Patronato was near our house and had a large social hall where the big event of the year was the Purim Ball. That is where my husband, Beni, and I met when I was nineteen.

Beni was dating a friend of my friend. It seemed that everyone knew him, but I didn't, so we were introduced. Summer came and one warm day I went to the beach club where all the Jews belonged. Sure enough, there was Beni, who came to sit next to me. I felt uncomfortable, and my friend called me soon after, bad-mouthing Beni and telling me not to be surprised if he called me. He did. We started to date, going to movies, dinner, dancing, and to shul. I was at the university studying commercial sciences, and Beni, six years older than me, was finishing medical school. He told me that years before, when his father went into my father's store, he would play with me when I was a baby.

We married at the Patronato a year after we met. As the Patronato had no rabbi at that time, a friend of my father's, the rabbi at the Reform synagogue, agreed to conduct an Orthodox ceremony. As attendants, I chose a girl cousin close to my age who had been rescued from an orphanage in Belgium after the Holocaust and a young flower girl and ring bearer from my mother's family. I wore a white satin dress designed with fabric that my mom and I chose; you did not buy dresses at shops. The bridesmaid and flower girl were in pink. After the ceremony, we had a lunch for 150 people. Then we changed clothes and went to the ship that took us to Miami. From there, we took a train to New York City, where we saw snow for the first time. We flew back home after a visit to Beni's cousins in Minnesota.

I continued my studies at the university, and Beni was on the team of a famous surgeon, Antonio Rodriguez-Diaz, who performed the first open heart surgery in Cuba. In 1959 I remember going to the balcony of my husband's office along with my dad as Castro made his way down the boulevard to the army barracks with his tanks and trucks. "There's something I don't like," my father said. "We have to be vigilant; we have to prepare." At first, we pooh-poohed it, but it didn't take long to prove he was right.

Castro voided the degree I had earned at a private university and called us traitors. I had to go back when he reopened the university. It was scary with so many soldiers around with guns. When my husband came back from a medical meeting in Santiago de Cuba, I saw him standing in the doorway. His first words were, "We're leaving." The Communists had taken over the medical society. Everyone had to go to the countryside to treat the peasants. We wrote to the cousins in Minnesota who sent an affidavit as our sponsors. Beni took an exam in Cuba and obtained a surgical internship at the University of Minnesota. We told everyone we were going to the Mayo Clinic for some training. Only our parents knew that we weren't coming back; you never knew who was a government stooge. We arrived in 1960 with $300. Except for three years in Detroit, where my husband trained in obstetrics, I have lived in Minnesota ever since.

My parents followed us here soon after we arrived, but they found the weather too tough and moved to a condo in Miami. With the exception of the years when my children were young, I always worked in accounting—in a hospital, businesses, and finally as manager of my husband's clinic until he retired. Beni passed away in 2012 at age eighty-one. I remained active and involved, including as treasurer of my synagogue's gift shop. I have three daughters and seven grandchildren. Life has been good.

ENGLAND

Andrea Masters

A simple exchange of vows and rings in a rabbi's office represents one end of the spectrum of Jewish weddings. Andrea's daughter Natalie's wedding represents the other—the intricately planned affair of many young women's dreams. In days past, it was considered preferable to hold the ceremony outside in commemoration of God's blessing to Abraham that his descendants would be "as stars of the heavens." Today, while some Jewish weddings are held outdoors, others are held in a familiar synagogue or the home of a family member or friend. And some like Natalie search for a special space in a hotel, a restaurant, a museum, or a wedding hall. All are acceptable sites. Natalie was lucky to have the assistance of two wedding planners— one particularly close and emotionally involved!

After graduating from medical school in Wales, where she grew up, my daughter Natalie moved to London for further training. It was there, while visiting a friend, that she was introduced to Ian. Romance blossomed and my husband and I were delighted when Ian proposed. They decided to have the wedding in London, as there were more family and friends there than in Cardiff, where we live.

Natalie and Ian wanted to get married in an intimate setting, not some large and impersonal hotel. They looked at a couple of places before visiting one I had found by chance on the internet. It was in Essex, a county immediately northeast of London, a stylish wedding venue on the grounds of a historic country estate. It had an orangery at one end of a large Victorian walled garden, suitable for a chuppa, as well as an impressive old brick-and-beam barn with oak floors for the dinner and dancing. There was also a small cottage on the grounds, an ideal place to hold the *bedeken* (the veiling ceremony) and for the bride and groom to spend their wedding night. As soon as Natalie and Ian were shown around, they knew that this was the perfect place to have their wedding. They

Natalie and Ian under the chuppah Andrea made

were especially pleased about the orangery—like getting married outside but without the cold in November.

So the wedding plans began. But first things first. The most important was Natalie finding the wedding dress of her dreams. So one weekend, my husband and I drove to London to take her shopping. I came armed with a long list of shops, and we started with one not far away. Natalie chose two dresses that she liked. Then a dress on a half-hidden mannequin caught her eye. When she looked closer, she decided that it wouldn't suit her. But with a nudge from me and the shop assistant, she reluctantly agreed to try it on. And yes, that wedding dress turned out to be the one.

I then spent time on the internet looking at different chuppas to rent. The problem was that it had to fit between two wooden beams in the orangery. The answer came to me shortly afterward at another Jewish wedding: Why not make it myself from scratch? After all, it surely couldn't be that difficult, having just four posts and a canopy on top. I managed to find an expandable frame online that would fit snugly between the beams. Next, I sewed forty meters of fabric. Weeks later, I had made a unique and special gift for Natalie and Ian, in memory of my father who was in the *schmutter* (cloth) business. On the day of the wedding, it would be finished off with garlands of flowers.

Then several weeks before the wedding, something unprecedented happened. My daughter received an email from a bridal magazine informing her that she had won the services of a wedding planner! This was an unexpected and invaluable help to me, for it meant that on the wedding day, I wouldn't have to go through a checklist to make sure that the contractors were there on time and the multitude of other details. I could concentrate on my daughter, the bride.

Finally, in November 2012, the big day arrived. And, oh, what a day! There was blue sky and sunshine, a bit on the cold side, but the day before it had rained all day (and in fact there were torrential downpours the day after the wedding). We were truly lucky.

In the cottage behind the barn, I helped Natalie get into her dress. How beautiful she looked! Downstairs, ready for the bedeken, waited her matron of honor, three rabbis, a cantor, and my husband. Ian's face was a picture as he entered the cottage and saw his bride for the first time. As the bedeken ceremony concluded, the ketubah was signed and witnessed, and Ian lowered the veil over his bride's face. He and I then made our way to the orangery where the guests were waiting, and we took our place under the chuppa with the rabbi. As the song *Dodi Li* started to play, the guests turned to the window to see my husband slowly walk our daughter down the long garden path. When they reached the chuppa, Natalie walked around Ian three times before taking her place along-side him. I had to pinch myself to stop the tears that were welling up when I looked at my daughter and son-in-law standing there together. After the glass had been broken and the civil register signed, the wedding service came to an end and the reception began.

While the bride and groom left to have photographs taken outside before it got dark, the guests tucked into crudités and drinks, with entertainment by a magician who kept them all mesmerized. An hour later, the toastmaster asked everyone to move into the barn for dinner and dancing. The flower arrange-ments on the tables and the flowers that wound around the wooden beams were perfect for the setting. As an extra touch, the barn doors had green lights projected from floor to ceiling, in line with the green color scheme we had cho-sen. In keeping with the theme, each table had been named a different shade of green—emerald green, forest green, bottle green, and so on. Fittingly, we had placed the rabbis and cantor at the "sage" table.

When the guests were seated, the bride and groom entered the barn, with everyone singing and clapping to *Siman Tov u'Mazel Tov* (Good Signs and Good Luck). Natalie and Ian had decided to keep speeches to a minimum, without the traditional toasts to the Queen and Israel. So the bride's father, the best man, and, of course, the groom made the expected toasts. But I couldn't let the occasion go without making a short toast of my own. Fifteen years be-fore, I had made a speech in rhyme at Natalie's bat mitzvah. Now I surprised everyone with another one in rhyme—this one following on from where the last one had finished!

Toasts out of the way, a delicious three-course meal was served, followed by benching (blessings after the meal). Here, my daughter and new son-in-law had a surprise for me: They had had the benchers (booklets with the blessings) printed in America, decorated on the front and throughout the pages with photos of them as children and of memorable times throughout their courtship. Their dog even had his own page!

When benching had finished and tables cleared, it was time for the bride and groom to take to the floor for the first dance, *The Way You Look Tonight*, Ian's choice. The band then played one song after another until, before we knew it, it was 11:30 p.m. and time for the party to end. Eight hours had flown by, and we wanted to do it all again. The bride and groom said their goodbyes before retreating to the cottage to spend their first night together.

A year later, on our thirty-fifth wedding anniversary, Natalie and Ian gave my husband and me a most precious gift—our first grandchild. And so life goes on.

FRANCE

Anaëlle Ebrard

Anaëlle's warm description of her wedding in Belfort, her husband's historic home-town, is captivating to those of us who love the French language, landscape, food, and the arts. However, violent attacks against Jews in recent years, including the Charlie Hebdo and kosher supermarket murders in 2015, have tarnished France's aura in the minds of many Jews around the world. The immigration of thousands of Jews to Israel in the last decade has been attributed widely to a sense of vulnerability among the Jewish population. Meanwhile, the majority of French Jews like Anaëlle continue to wed and begin their married lives with optimism in the third-largest Jewish community in the world.

We were married on May 7, 2015, in Belfort, a charming city of fifty thousand in the northeast Franche Comté region on the border of Alsace. My husband, David, grew up there; I am from Paris. Traditionally, Jewish weddings take place in the bride's home area—big cities like Paris, Marseille, Lyon, and Stras-bourg, where most French Jews live—or, gaining in popularity, Israel or idyllic

David lowers Anaëlle's veil

destinations such as the Côte d'Azur, Rome, or Ibiza. So this was a bit unusual. Our invited guests were quite surprised.

We made the decision to marry in Belfort rather than in Paris for many reasons: My husband's family has lived in Belfort for several generations and has always been active in the Jewish community. David grew up in the beautiful synagogue there; his presence was essential for the *minyan* (ten people required for public wortship) every Shabbat. If we had married in Paris, it would have been in a large synagogue without the same personal significance. The Jewish community in Belfort is very small and struggling to survive, so our wedding was an important symbol of its continuing existence.

On the Shabbat following our wedding, according to Sephardic tradition, we had a *chabbat hattan* (literally, a "groom's Shabbat"). David was called up to the Torah in the main sanctuary of the synagogue, usually open only on holidays. (Ordinarily, Shabbat services are held in a small chapel adjoining the synagogue.) Having our guests there made it very special. In Paris, we could never have had a wedding that lasted three days!

I met David through our mothers who had known each other for a long time. My mother and his aunt met thirty years ago at a *volontariat civile* program (a voluntary civilian alternative to military service). Then my mother became friends with David's mother. Although they lived in different cities (my mother-in-law, Kathy, in Belfort and my mother, Isabelle, in Paris), they kept in touch. One wonderful day in 2009, the Blums, David's family, came to Paris for a cousin's bar mitzvah. This was the first time we met. (I'm not sure that his brother's bar mitzvah—when I was eight—counts! I doubt that we talked to each other.) Our story didn't begin right away, but finally, five years later, there we were—married!

Our wedding ceremony began at three o'clock in the afternoon. Three rabbis officiated—Rabbi Levintof from Belfort, Rabbi Daltrof, our rabbi in Paris who coincidentally used to be the Belfort rabbi, and Rabbi Kaufmann from the synagogue in the Place des Vosges in Paris that my family also attends. Rabbi Kaufmann recalled the events of January that shook the Jewish community (the Charlie Hebdo attack) and the positive impact the Jewish community has had on the nation. He also recalled the challenges faced by David's grandmother, Jeanine Blum, a Holocaust survivor who was deported to Auschwitz. She was present at our wedding, one of the best gifts that we received. Sadly, she died ten days later.

After the ceremony, we had cocktails in the garden of Maison Blum, the residence of David's grandparents on the first floor and his parents on the second floor. The weather was fantastic, and the cocktail party was excellent, if I do say so myself!

At about five o'clock the guests met at the resort where the evening party would take place. (We had a bus for those without cars.) We had reserved rooms where they could rest and get ready for the evening. After a walk through the grounds, the guests gathered in a reception room for a welcome aperitif before entering the ballroom for the party. We had a *mehitsa* (a barrier separating the women and men) two-thirds of the time. Then we danced as couples. Our friends had prepared videos and songs for us. We will always have wonderful memories of that.

HUNGARY

Katalin Guttmann-Olti

We can only imagine the strength and determination of those like Katalin's mother and in-laws, who married and began their lives again after losing their families and everything they held dear. With a history of antisemitism dating from the mid-nineteenth century, Hungary passed many edicts that oppressed Jews even before the brutal Nazi occupation. No wonder most of those who survived left the country when they could or hid their Jewish identity. Katalin's story ends happily with the marriage of her son and his Belgian wife in a festive Hungarian celebration very different from her own during the Communist era.

After the Holocaust, most survivors in Hungary did not discuss their Jewish origin; they either kept quiet about it or denied it outright. They perceived that this was in the best interest of their children. Later, during and after the revolution of 1956, approximately 90 percent of religious families left the country. This left very few who openly accepted their Jewish identity and who were more or less observant. My wedding took place in such an environment.

In contrast to the majority, my family and my husband's family always openly accepted their Judaism. My father and my husband's father served as presidents of their local communities after the war. With the exception of my father, our parents (my mother and my husband's mother and father) were married with children before the Holocaust. Each lost their entire family in Auschwitz. After the Shoah, they remarried and had children at older ages, so, sadly, my father died nine months before my wedding.

According to Hungarian law in the 1970s, a religious wedding could be held only after the secular one. Our civil wedding took place on August 10, 1973. Our Jewish wedding was two days later in the synagogue of the Rabbinical Seminary of Hungary, the only rabbinical seminary in the eastern bloc. The world-famous Jewish scholar Sandor Scheiber officiated and signed our ketubah. (When Barbra Streisand was shooting the movie *Yentl* in Prague, she flew to Budapest to meet with this eminent scholar.)

Because my family was within the one-year mourning period, we had a quiet wedding. The ceremony followed traditional religious rituals. We did the bedeken, then I was ushered under the chuppah inside the synagogue by the two mothers. My husband was accompanied by his father and one of his few relatives. I circled the groom seven times, the seven blessings were said, and my new husband broke the glass. Young Peter Kelen sang during the ceremony, accompanied by the organ. (He would later become a well-known opera singer.) The wedding was followed by a small reception for about thirty people. We did not have sheva brachot the week following the wedding.

In 2003, my son Zoltan got married in Budapest to a beautiful woman born in Belgium into a Sephardic family. It was a grandiose event, so different from mine. More than 250 guests from around the world witnessed the wedding under a chuppah set up outside the hotel. A Hungarian Ashkenazi rabbi officiated, and an Israeli Sephardic rabbi represented the bride's side of the family. A band played during the five-course meal and the gender-separated portion of the reception, then a DJ took over, letting the younger generation party into the night. We celebrated the marriage of two people of different cultures in a way that would have been unimaginable in Hungary thirty years before.

ST. THOMAS

Rabbi Michael Harvey

Jews have a long history in the Caribbean islands, where they sought refuge from the Inquisition. One of three islands in the US Virgin Islands, St. Thomas granted Jewish settlers freedom of religion as far back as 1685, when under Danish rule. The synagogue, built in 1833 and known for its sand-covered floor, is the oldest in continuous use under the American flag, furnished with its original mahogany ark, benches, and bimah, as well as its original chandeliers. Its small congregation of residents is augmented with tourists from cruise ships that visit the island regularly. Spiritual leader of the congregation from 2015 to 2017, Rabbi Michael recalls memorable destination weddings at which he officiated, including his own father's.

Rabbi Mike officiates at the wedding of his father and stepmother

Coming to The Hebrew Congregation of St. Thomas in 2015, I conducted many destination weddings. These, along with bar and bat mitzvahs, are the bread and butter of the congregation, so to speak. With only about one hundred Jewish families on the island, most lifecycle events come from seventeen hundred off-island members and their recommendations to others.

The first wedding that I conducted after I arrived took place on Richard Branson's private isle, Necker Island. The bride and groom, son of a wealthy real estate mogul, were from New York. They planned two ceremonies—one in New York and a smaller one on the island. I conducted my normal premarital meetings and counseling sessions with them by phone. On the appointed day, I was scheduled to travel from St. Thomas to Necker Island by a private boat owned by the father's company. But a hurricane was fast approaching. Boating became impossible, and the wedding was moved back a day. So the family hired a helicopter to pick me up in St. Thomas. It landed for customs in Virgin Gorda and then flew on to Necker Island. I had never seen such luxury in my entire life! But I was pleased to be a part of connecting two young people in love. As it happened, the hurricane made travel back to St. Thomas impossible. I got as far as Virgin Gorda, where I was marooned in another luxurious location—a five-star hotel arranged by the family—until the hurricane passed.

I conducted a wedding in our historic synagogue for a young couple who had a family history with the synagogue. Several years before, the bride was traveling with her family on a cruise ship and fell ill with appendicitis. She had to be taken from St. Maarten to St. Thomas for emergency surgery. To make matters worse, she was allergic to the anesthesia. It took weeks for her to recover. While she did so, her family connected with members of our synagogue who supported them and prayed for their daughter's health. The synagogue, therefore, had a special place in the bride's heart, and she wished to marry there. It was a small wedding with so much love in evidence that everyone was delighted. The couple wrote their own vows, which were incredibly moving. All of the guests were in tears.

Finally, I had the privilege of officiating at my own father's wedding. My mother passed away when I was fifteen years old. My father had been with his companion for more than twenty years. When he was about to turn seventy-five, they decided that it was time to think about some practical measures that would provide financial protection for my father's long-time girlfriend. As they had already scheduled a trip to St. Thomas, they simply added a wedding to the itinerary. My siblings flew down, and we arranged for a wedding ceremony on one of the local beaches.

My siblings and I put up tiki torches and flowers in the sand for a makeshift chuppah. Our family stood together as I conducted the wedding of my father and his new wife. It was a pleasure and an honor to do so. The beach and the water that day were particularly beautiful.

UKRAINE

Larisa Khayter Katsman

Larisa, her husband, Anatoly, and their two small daughters were in the vanguard of Jews who left Ukraine when the Soviet Union began to allow Jews to emigrate in the 1970s. This was before the fall of Communism, when the floodgates opened and four hundred thousand Ukrainian Jews left for Israel and the United States. Larisa's hometown of Slavuta, a center of Jewish life before World War II, was resettled by Jews like Larisa's family who fortunately were able to flee to Tashkent, Uzbekistan, during the war and were not among the two thousand residents murdered by the

Larisa and Anatoly share a toast at their reception

*Nazis. During the Soviet era, despite its suppression, some Jewish observance re-
mained alive, albeit undercover, as Larisa's Jewish wedding ceremony reminds us.
A retired respiratory therapist, Larisa lives near Boston with her husband, close to
her daughters, four grandchildren, and many relatives who arrived following Larisa
and Anatoly's pioneering relocation.*

In 1969, I met my husband, Anatoly, at my cousin's wedding in Slavuta, a
small city of twenty-four thousand in western Ukraine, where I grew up. Anatoly lived in Kiev but was visiting his brother in Rovno, a large city near Slavuta,
on his vacation. My cousin's family members came to Rovno to buy fish for the
wedding. They needed help bringing it back and, as they were related in some
way, asked if Anatoly could come with them. So he stayed for the wedding.

After we met, I went back to medical school in Odessa, and he went back to
Kiev. We started to call and write, and less than a year later, we decided to get
married. My grandfather and his father were religious men who wanted us to
have a chuppah, a religious ceremony. This was unusual in those days. We had
a shul in Slavuta, but it was only for old people. My parents never went. Sometimes around Jewish holidays, kids would sneak in. If they were caught, they
could be expelled from school for a while as punishment.

But, as I always tried to please my grandfather, I agreed to a religious ceremony in my parents' house in August 1970. It was not legal. We waited until
dark. We pulled the window shades down and also covered them with towels
to block any light. People came at different times so they wouldn't attract attention. Only close relatives were there—my parents, Anatoly's parents, my
grandparents, and my two uncles. My aunt, a member of the Communist party,
was afraid to come.

The rabbi brought a chuppah that we set up. I had on a nice dress, and they
put a white scarf over my head. I don't remember the ceremony very well. We
repeated the Hebrew words the rabbi said. Anatoly broke a glass, and everyone
said mazel tov. Afterward, we sat in the kitchen and had wine that my grandmother made, vodka, and sponge cake. When everyone started to sing Jewish
songs, my mother became upset and said not to sing so loud—someone walking by might hear and report us. I remember how hot it was with the windows
closed in August.

Three days later, we had the civil wedding. It was a rainy day. We went to the
dvorets brakosochetaniy (wedding palace), a building where we signed papers
and a justice of the peace presided over a little ceremony of ten or fifteen minutes. About twenty-five relatives and friends were there. I wore a short white
wedding dress, and Anatoly wore a suit and tie. Then we went to a restaurant

where 150 people were waiting for us. We had a meal and Russian dancing and music—no horas. We didn't go on a honeymoon trip, as Anatoly was in college and had many government documents to submit for his transfer from Kiev to Odessa, where I was living. A year later we took a trip to Moscow. We came to the United States in 1978 with our daughters, then four and a year old. Our daughters have had Jewish weddings so different from ours!

UNITED STATES

Marian Leah Knapp

Marian's story illustrates the influence of the economy on individual lives, including the Great Depression of the 1930s that required her parents to hide their marriage and the advent of World War II that signaled economic recovery for the nation and for her family. Marian is justifiably proud of her blind great-grandmother who nurtured her mother when her mother was young and in need. Perhaps that is one of the reasons she is a champion of elders as former chair of her city's Council on Aging executive committee and author of several books on issues of aging, including her latest Prohibition Wine: A True Story of One Woman's Daring in 20th Century America *(Shewrites Press, 2021).*

My mother, Anne Goldberg, married my father, Louis Noah Gilbert, in a rabbi's study in Boston on December 26, 1931. I have no pictures of their wedding because none were taken. I don't know what they wore or if my mom had flowers. I imagine my father had on a yarmulke. They managed to borrow a room for a one-day honeymoon in a building on Commonwealth Avenue. It was all simple and secret, not because Anne and Lou wanted to be defiant. Rather, they wanted to avoid any expense. Only their friends Lillian and Max, who were witnesses, knew of the marriage and where they spent the night after the brief ceremony.

It was two years into the Great Depression and Lou, who was twenty-seven, was having trouble finding a job and had no money to contribute to even a modest event. Anne was lucky to be working as a secretary, but she lived at home with her mentally ill and widowed mother, and her paycheck bought only household essentials such as coal.

Earlier that year, Anne's grandparents, Leah and Abraham Anapolsky, had celebrated their seventy-fifth wedding anniversary at the Hebrew Home for the Aged in Dorchester. He was ninety-five, and she was ninety-three. My mother was particularly close to her grandparents. Unfortunately, Anne's mother had lost the ability to care for her children adequately. Every Friday afternoon, my mother and her sister took the ferry from East Boston to the West End to their grandmother's house. There, Leah bathed them with warm water in a tub in the kitchen, washed their hair, fed them a hot meal, and baked cookies. She did this even though she was blind.

My mother's grandparents kept her childhood manageable and sane. They represented love and constancy in contrast to her unsettled home situation. So it was extremely difficult for my mother when her friend Lillian, who had witnessed the ceremony and knew where she was, called the morning after the wedding. She called to tell her that her grandfather, Abraham, had died. No one had been able to contact her.

Even with grandfather Abraham's death, the marriage remained a secret. The bride and groom went back to their mothers' homes. Six months later, their marriage came to light after a relative happened on the certificate at city hall. After that, my dad bought my mother a simple white gold wedding band from a wholesale jeweler. The couple lived in other people's houses and run-down rooms and apartments in the Boston area before moving to Providence. It wasn't until 1943, the beginning of World War II, that life began to look up financially. My dad was able to buy a diamond engagement ring and wedding band after more than twenty years of marriage.

I doubt that my parents ever regretted not having a wedding with lots of people, elegant clothing, expansive food, and formal photographs. They were determined to be together and to make things work. My father was a bit of a romantic, in contrast to my mom who was realistic and practical, perhaps as a result of surviving childhood with an unstable mother. The wedding story passed down to me was about the determination it took to carry out the simple act of marriage. Years later, after my dad died, my mom sold the diamond ring and divided the money among her five grandchildren. She had the original, unpretentious white gold ring on her finger when she died.

EIGHT

—ꟷ—

THE KETUBAH

THE KETUBAH, USUALLY TRANSLATED as "marriage contract," dates back to the first century CE, when it was first written in Aramaic. Anita Diamant explains that traditionally the ketubah was not a contract between the couple but a document signed by two nonfamily male witnesses who testified "that the groom 'acquired' the bride in the prescribed manner and that he agreed to support her. [It] set out terms for divorce, and [stated] that she entered into the marriage of her own free will and as a virgin."[1] It was given to the bride as a guarantee of her rights. One of the stories in this chapter hearkens back to 1841 in New Zealand, where the ketubah of the first Jewish wedding in the country—performed without a rabbi or synagogue—survives, illustrating the significance of the document for a Jewish marriage.

In Orthodox circles, the ketubah is often still written in Aramaic with few changes from the original text. But even among the most traditional, the ketubah has undergone changes in the last decades, with additions pertaining to mutual devotion and commitment of the couple to their union. In liberal branches, the language of the text is Hebrew as well as the language of the brides' and grooms' home countries. The story from American Geri Garfinkle describes her negotiation between the traditional mandates of the ketubah, written in Hebrew, and her liberal ideals of marriage, written in English. Clearly, the ketubah has become more than a document testifying to the groom's fulfillment of his responsibilities. Couples can choose to modify the text in many ways appropriate to their unions, whether heterosexual, same-sex, or interfaith. Anita Diamant offers many examples of ketubah texts, including a "mystical ketubah" and one authorized by the Conservative movement that adds at the end a so-called Leiberman clause that requires both a civil and religious divorce (*get*) if the marriage should end.[2]

Around the world, the ketubah is commonly signed by the rabbi or other officiant as well as the bride and groom and other honored witnesses. Usually, it is signed before the wedding ceremony, but in some communities, the signing takes place during the ceremony before the ring-giving. And in keeping with tradition in some places, it is read aloud to the guests during the ceremony. Geri, the bride mentioned above, solved a problem by having two Jewish men sign the Hebrew portion of the ketubah as well as two nontraditional signers for the English portion—a woman friend and a non-Jewish friend of her husband-to-be.

An integral part and proof of Jewish marriage everywhere, the ketubah in the United States and elsewhere was mainly a nondescript boilerplate document until about forty years ago. (This was not the case in Sephardic communities, where decorated ketubot have always been the rule.) Now, the ketubah is regularly viewed as a work of art, providing opportunities for a large number of artists to design original ketubot in a variety of styles. In the story from Poland, an artist friend of the bride decorated the ketubah in an imaginative and meaningful way. It was signed by the rabbi and four witnesses. In the past, the bride might tuck her ketubah into a drawer or perhaps keep it on the wall to remind her husband of his obligations. Nowadays, it hangs on the wall as a beautiful piece of art.

NEW ZEALAND

Patricia Philo Kopstein

Perhaps no other Jewish community is as well acquainted with its first wedding as New Zealand's: The wedding of Rosetta and David has not been forgotten in almost two hundred years. Its date is the earliest in this volume. From pioneers like the couple featured in Patricia's story, the small Jewish community has become a vital presence in New Zealand, producing leaders in trade and government, including an early premier and a recent one. A world traveler, psychologist, and rabbi, Patricia has served congregations in California, Australia, and Hong Kong, as well as in Auckland.

The first Jewish wedding in New Zealand is commonly talked about with a chuckle. The wedding between Rosetta Aarons and David Nathan took place in Kororareka, the first permanent European settlement and port (now known as Russell), on October 31, 1841. That year Rosetta arrived in New Zealand from London with no relatives or friends ashore. David, who owned businesses in Auckland, happened to be visiting his shop in Kororareka and heard of Rosetta. They met and married in the same month. With few Jews in New Zealand, most Jewish men married overseas or married local Maori or Christian women—frowned upon by the small community who made their homes there. So David must have seen his opportunity and seized it quickly.

As luck would have it, Rosetta had her ketubah with her from her earlier marriage to Captain Michael Aarons, who had died at sea. At the time, though religiously observant and able to recite prayers, not many people read and understood Hebrew. With no rabbi and no synagogue to rely on, they faithfully copied Rosetta's ketubah written in Hebrew, changing only the name of the groom, the date, the marriage celebrant, Israel Joseph, and the witness, George Russell, for whom the town is now named. There was only one problem: the original ketubah stated that Rosetta was a virgin (*betulah*). It remained unchanged. So the first New Zealand ketubah was written for a groom and his widow-virgin bride. The ketubah is preserved in Grey's Avenue Orthodox Synagogue in Auckland.

Today, the New Zealand Jewish community remains small in number—about seventy-five hundred—but mighty in spirit and literate in Hebrew! The country is home to seven congregations, both Orthodox and Progressive. My husband, Rabbi David Kopstein, and I very happily served Progressive Congregation Beth Shalom in Auckland from 1998 to 2001. In general, many wedding ceremonies in New Zealand take place in a shul or social hall, but often they happen on a beach or somewhere outdoors in beautiful, pure New Zealand air. They tend to be informal but always include a ketubah and recitation of the sheva brachot under the chuppah. Men and women are usually seated together for the ceremony, with kosher or vegetarian food, and dancing afterward. The country is more observant and stricter than one might guess—very liberal socially, but not very flexible in regard to traditional rituals.

Like Rosetta Aarons, some brides are recent arrivals from elsewhere. But unlike Rosetta and the early pioneering women of New Zealand, these traveling brides do not come to stay. They are the headliners in destination weddings, tourists who will soon leave with memories of vibrant cities and still unspoiled landscapes.

POLAND

Lena Rubenfeld Koralewska

In the last few decades, thousands of young Poles have discovered their Jewish roots, hidden by previous generations out of fear and necessity. They are the descendants of the 10 percent of Polish Jews who survived the Holocaust, the decimation of one of the largest Jewish communities in the world. Often recipients of deathbed confessions by family members, some of these young people have reconnected with Judaism and formally converted. Among the converts are a minority like Lena who do not have Jewish forbears, but have connected to Judaism culturally, spiritually, and politically. Krakow, where Lena and her Canadian husband, Michael, married, was a center of Jewish life starting in the fourteenth century. Now, in Krakow and elsewhere, efforts like Lena's are underway to redress the tremendous losses the community sustained.

I met my Canadian husband, Michael, at a Limmud program in Montreal in 2009. As a graphic designer and cofounder of Beit Krakow, one of the first Progressive Jewish communities in Poland, I had been invited to speak about the Jewish revival in Poland and its connection to the arts. Michael, an actor, playwright, and producer, was presenting a session on a new play about his family's roots in Poland that he was creating with his own mother. We had an immediate affinity; we were fascinated with each other and with each other's projects. When I returned to Poland and he went back to Toronto, we continued to speak and our relationship deepened. A bond formed between us that revolved around a shared interest in Jewish Poland: my desire to encourage a more nuanced understanding of my country, and Michael's desire to find new connections to his own Jewish identity.

In 2006, I converted to Judaism. Growing up in Poland, I was educated in Communist half-truths about its untainted "noble" history that I found hard to accept. I always had Jewish friends, and as I discovered more about Jewish culture and learned Yiddish at university, I found that for me, Judaism was an essential way to express my values and connect to my Polishness. I wanted to be part of a community that encouraged and debated contradictory opinions. When I was twenty-four, I went to Los Angeles to finalize my conversion, as there were no Reform rabbis in Poland at that time.

A month after Michael and I met, I flew to Canada to meet Michael's family. Soon after, Michael came to Poland with his mother. When he saw my environment and met my family, he realized that Polish culture was a much larger

Lena and Michael's first dance

part of his identity than he thought. His family used Polish words, ate Polish foods, and through conversations with his grandmother, Ewa, I learned that, despite living through the tragedy of the Holocaust, her life in Poland before the war was something she cherished. Michael's family's residual trauma from the Holocaust, however, was something he started to work through in order to unravel internalized stereotypes about Polish-Jewish relations. This journey eventually led him to start identifying more and more as a Polish Jew.

After two and half years of going back and forth between Toronto and Krakow, we decided to get married. We had a picnic on Toronto Island and Michael proposed. Our next step was to think about the wedding, and where we should have the ceremony. After exploring several options, including Las Vegas, we decided on Poland. It was the country that connected us, and we felt it would be most meaningful to be married there. Michael began to think seriously about living there.

Our wedding was on April 1, 2014, in the oldest synagogue in Krakow, aptly named the Old Synagogue. We wrote our own vows in Polish, English, and Hebrew. A friend, a Jewish artist, created our ketubah featuring griffins, the symbol of Galicia, and a lion and an eagle symbolizing our two worlds enhancing each other. We signed it before the ceremony along with four witnesses and the rabbi. The synagogue was open to everyone, so there were more than one hundred people who witnessed the ceremony conducted by Rabbi Tanya Segal, the first woman rabbi in Poland after the war. Ours was the first Progressive wedding in Krakow after World War II. We did the traditional parts of the ceremony: circling my soon-to-be husband seven times, drinking the wine, receiving the ring, the seven blessings, and breaking the glass.

After our *yichud* (seclusion) moment, we paraded down Szeroka Street, the former center of Krakow's Jewish district of Kazimierz. We were accompanied by our families, friends, and all who witnessed our union to a nearby reception at a local Israeli restaurant. As we celebrated through the streets, accompanied by a klezmer band, it felt like a scene out of prewar Poland. At the reception with our family and friends, we ate, drank, shared blessings, and danced until six o'clock in the morning. It was legendary.

Michael made the decision to move to Poland, and we live together in a flat in the former Jewish district of Kazimierz. Together, we made the decision to start a Jewish arts and activist organization called FestivALT. We develop and program artistic and activist programs in Krakow as a way to contribute to the growth of Jewish culture and understanding between Jews and non-Jews in Poland and around the world. We are raising our son, Lev, as part of the next generation of Jews in Poland.

UNITED STATES

Geri Garfinkel

Marriage events everywhere place the bonds among women front and center, from henna parties, to gatherings of women at the mikveh, to showers for the bride. Geri describes a particularly lovely tradition prior to the wedding ceremony, the kabbalat panim ("greeting of the faces" in Hebrew) in which the bride is honored by her "sisters" as she sits on a throne-like chair. In Geri's case, this involved gifts, songs, and anointing her feet. Some of the other wedding rituals she describes, like the egalitarian bedeken, liberal ketubah, and exchange of flowers in place of rings, are personalized variations that she and her husband, Sam, created by choice or necessity.

I proposed to Sam on the nude beach at Gay Head in Martha's Vineyard, Massachusetts. The year was 1992, and we had been officially dating for seventeen days. (We had had a long string of nondates, what Sam-the-mathematician called "Epsilon dates" for about six months or so, but those didn't count.) Really, the truth is that even on that first official date, sitting in the park on top of Summit Avenue in Brookline, Massachusetts, overlooking the whole city of Boston, we had been discussing marriage. I just made it official that day on the beach.

But, with Sam in graduate school, and other complexities, we would not be able to marry until the following May. Which gave us time to plan. Maybe too much time to plan. We became disciples of author Anita Diamant, studying *The New Jewish Wedding* to discover meaningful rituals and symbols to remake them in our own image.

So many questions. Where would the wedding be held? In Florida, so my grandparents could attend. Who would officiate at the wedding? We chose a Conservative rabbinical student. Oy! She was neither clergy nor Justice of the Peace. So while she would serve just fine from a Judaic standpoint, she could not make our wedding legally binding. That meant that we would have to be married by a judge or someone, either in Florida before the wedding or in our home state of Massachusetts.

Well, which state had more liberal marriage laws? We broke out the legal texts and discovered that, not surprisingly, the Massachusetts laws were more to our liking. So we found a Justice of the Peace whose office was not far from our apartment. We made an appointment for March 14, 1993.

Mother nature has a funny way of complicating things. On March 13, a huge storm hit the East Coast from Georgia to Maine. I got busy cooking baked ziti,

Geri and Sam gaze at each other during the crowning ceremony

so we wouldn't go hungry if the power went out. The next morning, we woke to sixteen inches of snow at our front door! So we went out the back. The car took hours to dig out with only an ice scraper. But we were motivated. It was our wedding day.

After freeing the car of snow and ice, and digging out the back wheels for good measure, we donned our wedding attire. I wore a handmade lace skirt with a raw silk top and an amazing cummerbund to pull it all together. Sam wore an Indian kurta, a white two-piece outfit. The bottoms were loose and held up with a drawstring waist. The top was a long tunic embellished with embroidery and rhinestone studs serving as fasteners. After adding our L.L. Bean boots, we were ready to go.

But not really. We didn't have our rings yet. So what would we exchange during the ceremony? We drove up and down the area, looking for businesses that were open, but finding mostly dirty snow plowed into eight-foot drifts. But such luck! We found a florist shop open and bought four large bunches of tulips to exchange with our vows. To this day I still give Sam tulips to recognize our March anniversary.

The Justice of the Peace married us in his office, which was decorated with medieval weapons. Sam insisted that we read the Preamble to the Constitution since it was a civil wedding. We exchanged tulips, vows, kisses. And boom! We were married. We and our two witnesses returned to our apartment for baked ziti and dancing in the living room.

But it didn't end there. The United States might have seen us as married, but I didn't really, so we continued planning our Jewish wedding, to be held in May of '93. Round and round we went with the rabbi and my closest friend who was creating our ketubah. Who would witness our Jewish wedding and sign the ketubah? I wanted Cheryl, a Jewish woman, to sign as my witness. Sam wanted David, his best friend, to sign. But this friend wasn't Jewish. Not a problem for us, but what if we had kids? What if our kids wanted to make aliyah to Israel? What if they had to prove their Jewish heritage? Oy!

After much negotiation, we decided all together. The ketubah would have a liberal text in English, which would be witnessed by Cheryl and David. I love our text, which included the line, "We promise to provide for one another equally, and as we are able." These words have shaped our marriage for many years. On the same page, above the English text would be a slightly more traditional text in Hebrew. And this was witnessed by two Jewish men. So that problem was solved.

We gathered in Florida at the end of May. A day or so before the wedding, I dunked in a traditional mikveh without much fuss or celebration. But the morning of our big day, David took Sam to the Atlantic Ocean, where, as dawn was breaking, Sam broke with his single life and prepared ritually to become a married man. Upon his return, he met with all the married men to gather up what wisdom they had to offer. To this day, Sam recalls what my father told him, "Remember, it's all your fault." He meant that anything that ever goes wrong would be Sam's fault—that by making this big commitment, he was also committing himself to take whatever blame was necessary, whenever necessary!

At the same time, I met with the married women in a ceremony called *kabbalat panim*, or the greeting of the faces. The women surrounded me with beauty, made a throne for me to sit on, and anointed my feet with fragrant oil. They gave me gifts symbolizing friendship, and gifts of value as well. It was overwhelming! I was deeply honored and went to my wedding canopy surrounded by the song of these wonderful women.

Finally, it was time. With our beautiful ketubah, our rabbinical student who was officiating at her first wedding ever, and our friends and loved ones, we gathered to sign the ketubah and observe a modern version of the bedeken. Generally, the bedeken is used as a veiling ceremony when a groom ascertains that he is marrying the right woman. For us, it was matching *kippot* (head coverings). He crowned me and I crowned him. We sat, just a few feet from each other, watching as our facial expressions changed. I'm not sure if we saw seventy-two faces (like the seventy-two faces of God), but we truly *saw* each other. We recognized each other in a way we had never before and probably have not since.

From there we proceeded to the actual wedding ceremony. Fifty-five guests stood around the chuppah to bear witness to our rituals. Under the chuppah, we circled around each other, symbolizing that we would serve each other in our married life. We prayed together and sang blessings to each other. We exchanged rings, and were finally married according to the traditions of our people.

After the ceremony, and a few minutes of seclusion in a yichud room, we danced, ate, and celebrated with our loved ones. It had been an exhausting few months, but it didn't stifle the jokes that we should get married again—a third way!

NINE

—⚭—

THE WEDDING CEREMONY

THE WEDDING CEREMONY is typically the culmination of a bride's dreams, plans, and preparations. It is the centerpiece of an emotional journey that begins with first setting eyes on her future husband and represents the bridge to her life as a partner in marriage. According to tradition, Jewish weddings include a set of ritual elements. These include a chuppah (wedding canopy), a ketubah (marriage contract), the recital of blessings, the drinking of wine, the placing of a ring on the bride's finger, and breaking a glass at the end. Traditionally, these elements were included in a two-part arrangement of marriage—the kiddushin, also called *erusin* (betrothal, broken only with a divorce) phase, and the *nisuin* (marriage) phase, which could be a year apart. Nowadays, they are combined in a single ceremony. But, as the stories in this chapter show, ceremonies are not all the same, differing even in regard to those traditional elements and in their order, and often reflecting traditions introduced from the surrounding cultures.

A full range of practices have been defined for the period immediately before the wedding. Orthodox brides and grooms traditionally do not see each other for the seven days prior to the wedding. Couples also refrain from eating on the day of the wedding until after the ceremony. Both of these customs are designed to heighten the positive tension and anticipation of becoming wife and husband. The story from Switzerland, as do others in this collection, describes the bedeken (veiling) of the bride by her groom before she meets him under the chuppah. This ritual usually takes place in a space separate from the wedding ceremony and for religious couples may be the first time they have seen each other in a number of days. The bedeken may recall the biblical story of Jacob, who thought he was marrying Rachel but was tricked into marrying her sister, Leah. Rather than making sure of the identity of the bride, today's ritual is more likely to represent the groom's joyous first look at his beautiful bride, who is then escorted to the chuppah.

Most Jewish weddings worldwide take place under a chuppah, a canopy with a "roof," often a keepsake tallit, supported by four poles, sometimes held by honored family and friends. The chuppah is often a work of art adorned with flowers and other beautiful elements. A blog by Rabbi Barbara Aiello, who wrote the story from Italy in this chapter, notes the origins of the chuppah in the Bible (Joel, chapter 2 and in Psalm 19).[1] The chuppah symbolizes the home that the bride and groom will create together, and the open sides remind us of Abraham's welcoming tent. Rabbi Barbara's story describes a lovely chuppah tradition among families in the Italian "boot," many of them *anousim* whose ancestors were forced to live secret Jewish lives. As in Italy, almost all of the Jewish weddings documented in this book take place under a chuppah—with one notable exception. Elizabeth Joshua's story reveals an unusual marriage tradition of Kerala in India, where brides usually do not marry under a chuppah.

The stories in this chapter and elsewhere reveal the great variety of the brides' attendants in processions to the chuppah, as there are few guidelines. An online photo exhibit shows wedding pictures of ultra-Orthodox brides with opaque veils concealing their faces, requiring mothers and other female relatives to guide them to the chuppah.[2] Nan Weiner's second-marriage story from Canada lovingly details a full complement of family members who preceded her down the aisle, as does the story from Peru. In some stories in this volume, those in the procession hold candles. In others, people play musical instruments or sing.

The ketubah, another important element in Jewish weddings as noted above, was read in the past (and still is in some communities) during the wedding ceremony and sometimes signed then, as in the stories from Spain and India. But, as the previous chapter illustrates, the ketubah is most often signed before the wedding ceremony and oftentimes not read aloud. It is, however, an indispensable component of Jewish marriage.

Traditionally, when she reaches the chuppah, the Ashkenazic bride circles her groom seven times. Some say it signifies a wall of love around the couple or the building of a new home, with seven being the kabbalistic number for completion. Other brides circle three times, symbolizing righteousness, justice, and loving kindness from the Bible.[3] Many brides today choose to forgo this custom or reform it, with the bride and groom circling each other. The television miniseries *Unorthodox* has popularized a traditional wedding song, "Mi Bon Siach," sung as the bride enters the chuppah.

The bridal couple traditionally shares two cups of wine. The first is after a double blessing by the officiating rabbi—the usual blessing over wine as well as a special blessing over the union. In Judaism, wine is associated with joy and sanctification, both at a wedding and on Shabbat, which is often likened to a bride.[4] The story from southern India reveals a little-known custom, perhaps unique to that community, regarding the wine goblet and the ring.

The giving of a ring to the bride is central to the ancient erusin phase of marriage. Jewish law originally required a bride price, which could be something of little value. Since the Middle Ages, a ring has represented the fulfillment of that requirement. The ring should be a plain band, usually gold or silver without ornamentation, placed on the right index finger of the bride as the groom says in Hebrew, "Behold, you are consecrated to me with this ring according to the law of Moses and Israel." Liberal branches of Judaism allow brides to give rings to grooms, as the women make the same pronouncement or another of their choosing. The story from the Czech Republic regarding a special ring is another example of a wedding ritual particular to a certain community.

Weddings everywhere typically blend old traditions with contemporary concerns. A good example can be found in the Canadian story, with the bride "reworking" the traditional sheva brachot (seven wedding blessings) to reflect contemporary language and values, a not uncommon practice. These blessings, spoken or sung over the second glass of wine by the rabbi or shared among honored guests under the chuppah, are at the heart of the traditional nisuin part of the wedding ceremony. They are an ancient set of Jewish principles concerning God and marriage, sourced from the Bible with unknown origins. The bride and groom may be wrapped in a tallit as they listen and take a sip of the wine, signifying their unity as husband and wife.

Perhaps the most well known of the customs surrounding Jewish weddings is the breaking of a glass by the groom at the end of the ceremony. Anita Diamant cites a paragraph from the Talmud about a father breaking an expensive goblet at his son's wedding to make the rabbis, who were apparently having too much fun, "sober" (Berakhot 5:2). The broken glass may also be viewed as a reference to the destruction of the Temple in Jerusalem or the frailty of marital relationships, as well as a sexual connotation regarding a "breaking" on the wedding night.[5] Contemporary egalitarian couples, like Nan and Issie from Canada, may break the glass together. An unusual customary extension of the ceremony kept the bride from Ethiopia and her new husband under the chuppah after he broke the glass.

Throughout Europe, Latin America, the former Soviet Union, and else-where, governments require a civil ceremony as proof of marriage. As numerous stories in this volume demonstrate, these are usually brief ceremonies conducted by a clerk in a government office. Sometimes they are attended by close family members and other guests, but mostly they are pro forma procedures that take place prior to or occasionally after—as in the story from the Czech Republic—the Jewish weddings that are generally more significant to the participants. The story from Ecuador documents an exception, when an official from the marriage registry came to the home of the bride's family and the ceremony was conducted there without a chuppah. Following tradition everywhere, however, guests then enjoyed a repast of special foods.

CANADA

Nan Weiner

Jewish weddings are not one-size-fits-all. They vary according to the needs and desires of the bride and groom, their families, and the person conducting the ceremony, even within the same branch of Judaism. The sheva brachot (seven blessings) are sung or recited during a traditional Jewish wedding. Nan and her husband, Issie, chose to update them for their ceremony to better conform to their own principles. Judaism encourages remarriage after the loss of a spouse.

Second marriages are different. One is older and maybe wiser. This means that second wedding ceremonies may also differ. I had been divorced for thirty-three years, and my husband had been widowed for three. Our ceremony took place in August 2014 in an outdoor courtyard at the University of Toronto. When Issie and I were planning our wedding at ages fifty-seven and fifty-eight, I knew what I wanted: family! Not just family in attendance, but family members fully involved in the ceremony.

Friends who are like family were involved too. My friend Myra was a witness, a function she took seriously, having practiced writing her Hebrew name carefully for the ketubah. Max, my friend since we were ten, was our behind-the-scenes coordinator, getting everyone in the wedding procession in the correct order.

It started with my nephew, who used his trumpet-playing skills to sound the shofar signaling that the ceremony was to begin. The processional began as our mothers were escorted down the aisle by family members. Then came the chuppa holders—all nieces and nephews of mine. Next came four little ring

Nan and Issie under the chuppah

bearers—the youngest grandchild of each of Issie's sisters and my youngest niece, two children entrusted with each ring.

We felt that a group that sings together becomes a community. Led by our future daughter-in-law, one of my nieces, and accompanied by another niece on the flute, everyone sang "Dodi Li" as we came down the aisle, Issie escorted by his two sons.

We had reworked the sheva brachot (part of traditional Jewish weddings), maintaining their meaning but updating their language. As we stood under the chuppa, each of our seven siblings read one of the blessings:

- *Wine.* Blessed is the creation of the fruit of the vine, symbol and aid of our rejoicing.
- *Individual.* Blessed is the creation of one, the individual.
- *Being human.* Blessed is the recognition and appreciation of being human.
- *Men and women.* Blessed is the design of human beings into men and women complementing each other in their differences.

- *Community.* May rejoicing resound throughout the world as the homeless are given homes, persecution and oppression cease, and all people learn to live in peace with each other and in harmony with their environment.
- *Love.* From the Divine, we call forth an abundance of love to envelop this couple. May they be for each other lovers and friends, and may their love partake of the same innocence, purity, and sense of discovery that we imagine the first couple to have experienced
- *Happiness.* We acknowledge the unity of all, and today we highlight joy and gladness, bride and bridegroom, delight and cheer, love and harmony, peace and companionship. May we all witness the day when the dominant sounds throughout the world will be these sounds of happiness, the voices of lovers, the sounds of feasting and singing.

In a feminist twist, Issie and I broke the glass together.

At the brunch that followed, family continued to be involved. Our future *machetuneyste* (mother of our future daughter-in-law) made the challah. Elders of Issie's family—two brothers-in-law he had known much of his life—said the blessing over the bread.

The brunch, speeches, dancing, and chair-raising all went according to plan. But it was the inclusion of family in our religious ceremony that really mattered.

CZECH REPUBLIC

Vida Neuwirthová

Four synagogues, part of the Jewish Museum of Prague, are major tourist attractions for both Jews and non-Jews. Vida mentions one of them, the beautiful Spanish Synagogue, the site for some Jewish weddings. Vida's son and his French wife married there in 2017, the first wedding conducted in the Czech Republic by a woman rabbi, a friend from Paris. Her own Old-New Synagogue (Altneuschul) is located in Jewish Town near the others but is not administered by the museum. Vida, an actress and founder of a Jewish children's theater during the Communist era that continues until today, learned she was Jewish as a teenager and studied secretly with a rabbi in Prague. Decimated by the Holocaust and marginalized during the Communist era, Jews in the Czech Republic, formerly half of Czechoslovakia (the other is Slovakia), now number only about three thousand. They have encountered relatively

little antisemitism in the years since the Velvet Revolution ended Communism in
1999, and the Czech Republic has been a staunch friend to Israel since its founding.

Weddings in Prague are held in one of our three historic synagogues. The
Orthodox Old-New Synagogue, completed in 1290, is the oldest active synagogue in Europe. The Jerusalem Synagogue (also called the Jubilee Synagogue)
is an architectural treasure built in the Moorish style. And the Reform Spanish
Synagogue is considered one of the most beautiful in Europe. I go to services at
the Old-New Synagogue when I can, as I like to be in touch with its history and
I know many others who belong to it. The synagogue has a new wedding chuppa
decorated with 153 Jewish stars representing the number of Jewish communities
in our country before World War II.

It is still the custom for the couple to be separated seven days before the wedding to enjoy their special day even more. In the past, as part of the wedding
ceremony, the groom gave the bride a large silver ring with a compartment on
top in the shape of a house with a peaked roof. Every bride, rich or poor, was
given this ring. When the roof of the house was raised, the real wedding ring
was inside, the one the bride would wear for the rest of her life. Although rare
now, some brides preserve this wedding custom.

Another custom involves the ketubah, the wedding contract. The groom
prepares it and usually reads it during the ceremony. Often the guests receive
copies. Following the wedding ceremony in the synagogue, the couple go to
Prague town hall where they present documents from the Jewish community.
The state now regards the marriage as official.

The wedding feast is the same as other Ashkenazi wedding celebrations in
Europe—speeches, eating, drinking, singing, and smiling.

ECUADOR

Evelyn Zentner de Falck

Like most countries in Latin America, Ecuador requires a nonreligious civil mar-
riage ceremony for validation of the union. Throughout the world, brief ceremonies
are conducted by an official representing the government, such as a judge or clerk,
often in a town hall or other government office. A religious ceremony afterward is
optional. The decision by Evelyn and Miguel, both Jews, to forgo Jewish ritual under
a chuppah in favor of only a civil ceremony was probably unusual. However, thanks
to Evelyn's prenuptial insistence, their sons experienced rituals signifying entrance

into the Jewish community that numbered fewer than four thousand at its peak and now far less.

My parents came to Ecuador from the Czech Republic after the Shoah in 1948. Immigrants were admitted to the country, one of the few to give visas back then, but you had to say you were going to farm. My father was actually a salesman who became a cattle dealer. He never talked about the Holocaust, but we know that he survived Theresienstadt, Auschwitz, and Bergen-Belsen. He passed away when I was in college.

I was born in Ecuador. I went to school there and then to college at a women's two-year school in Boston. My parents knew a girl from Ecuador who went there, and they wanted me to get away from a non-Jewish boyfriend. My husband, Miguel, whose Belgian mother and German father emigrated to Ecuador before the Shoah, also went to college in the United States. After graduate school, he was unable to get papers to stay in the United States, so he went back home to Quito. As it turned out, we both came back in October 1969. Our families knew each other, but Miguel was three years older, so although he lived nearby in the same city, we weren't friends. He remembers that when he was a little boy playing soccer, he accidentally broke a window in my house.

Three months after we returned to Quito, we were invited to the same party. We have been together ever since. Miguel was a mountain climber, so I went hiking with him in the countryside, although I had never done it before. My parents wanted me to find a nice Jewish boy, and I did!

We married in 1971 when I was twenty-one and Miguel was twenty-five. We did not get married in a Jewish ceremony under the chuppah, as Miguel is not at all religious. I consented as long as he agreed that if we had a boy, he would be circumcised and have a bar mitzvah. For our wedding, a delegate from the Registro Civil (the office that registered marriages) came to my mother's house where about forty guests were gathered. In those days, the registry office was shabby and dirty, so middle- and upper-class people did not get married there. The representative of the registrar read the obligations of marriage, and we signed the official documents along with six witnesses—close relatives and friends. One synagogue leader, a good friend of my family, gave a blessing, and we exchanged rings. Then we had lunch prepared by a caterer. It might have been Czech food. Miguel's father was in the hospital, so we went to visit him afterward.

Due to my father-in-law's illness, we canceled the honeymoon we had planned and instead went to the beach in Esmeraldas, a beautiful green province about five hours from Quito. We went in a trailer that Miguel had made from a VW van. He was fond of mechanics. A few months later, when Miguel's father had recovered, we went to Machu Picchu for a month, sleeping in the trailer.

Two and a half years later, our son Arturo was born, followed a year and a half later by his brother, Roberto. As promised, they were brought up as Jewish boys and now live in Massachusetts and New York with their families. I have always been a member of our small Jewish community in Quito. There were more members in my parents' time, as many as five thousand, as some families used Ecuador as a "bridge" country before emigrating to the United States or elsewhere. Now there are about one hundred families. We have a huge community center that is underused. The Conservative synagogue has an Orthodox rabbi from Brazil and of the students at the Jewish day school, only 25 percent are Jewish. There are many mixed marriages. My generation is the most active, and, fortunately, some younger families are getting involved. We come to the United States once a year to see our sons and their families, but Ecuador is our home and we have no intention to leave.

ETHIOPIA

Adena Winer-Avraham and David Winer

This story is based on an interview with Ethiopian-born Adena and American-born David after their move from Israel to Massachusetts. David is a chef, and Adena manages their kosher Israeli restaurant while raising two small daughters and a son. Currently, there are more than 125,000 Jews of Ethiopian descent living in Israel, the first group having arrived in Operation Moses in 1984 after harrowing journeys on foot from Ethiopia to Sudan. Adena remembers her jarring plane ride to Israel as part of Operation Solomon, which brought a second wave of Ethiopian Jews in 1991. Ethiopia's Jews transported with them a rich array of customs, rituals, and traditions.

DAVID: She came into my coffee shop in Tel Aviv one rainy Saturday night in February. I was there to make sure everything was going OK. She was the most beautiful person there. It was love at first sight. I knew her friend, and I ran out to take their order and brought them wine. I just stood there from the kitchen, staring. A few of my workers said to do something. So I wrote my name and number on a piece of paper and said "You are beautiful."

ADENA: My friend's ex-boyfriend was playing music there. It was no place I normally would go. I was saying, "Why am I here?" After he gave me his

David breaks the glass as Adena and her mother look on

number, my friend said he was a good guy. We started to see each other. We didn't really go on "dates." We went to the beach, he cooked for me at his house every Friday. I asked, "Can I bring challah?" We became serious. My family loved David.

DAVID: I met her niece first, then I met her father. He was jailed for a year in Ethiopia for helping Jews to escape to Sudan. He deserves so much respect.

ADENA: I was born in Ethiopia and came to Israel when I was four. I am number nine of ten children. We came with Operation Solomon. We have a video of my brother boarding the plane to Israel that was part of a documentary. It was scary; I remember the seats on the sides of the plane and the shaking. We lived in Acco for a year, then in Bnei Brak (a city of mainly ultra-Orthodox Jews). This was unusual. Most of the Ethiopians lived in Netanya and Ashdod. But my father wanted to mix with everyone and wanted more opportunity. It is still not easy for Ethiopians in Israel. I studied in an Orthodox school and did my National Service working with kids in a kindergarten in Tel Aviv. Then I went to work in the bursa, the Israeli diamond exchange.

My mother was fourteen when she married in Ethiopia. In those days, brides and grooms didn't know each other. The whole village would cook and celebrate together by eating and drinking for a week. Seven days before the wedding, the groom's family would go to the bride's family with gifts, including cows and goats.

My father went to a farm a month before our wedding. According to custom, a rabbi says a blessing over the animals and the people who are there. Then the animals are slaughtered. It is emotional and symbolic. After that, the special work to prepare food begins. Everyone gets together and helps and makes it a party. You get a whole lamb that needs to be cut up. Foods include *injera* (flatbread made from teff flour), *dabo* (a round loaf eaten on special occasions such as a wedding), *shiro* (ground chickpea stew), *misr* (lentil stew), *wat* (a spicy meat or chicken stew made with berbere, a roasted and ground spice mixture), and *tella* (an alcoholic drink made from grain). The food for the celebrations was put into two large refrigerators.

DAVID: My family came from the United States a few days before the wedding in March 2013. The two families met on the Friday night before the ceremony and exchanged gifts. It was very emotional and warm. I was given a watch, and Adena received a pearl necklace.

ADENA: I went to the mikveh the day before the wedding with my close friends and relatives. We walked there and talked on the way. The rabbi's wife checked everything to make sure I was absolutely clean. I dropped into the water seven times. It was very spiritual for me as I asked God for blessings. I dressed in white clothes afterward, and everyone threw the candies that my sister had brought. Then everyone danced. We didn't do a henna party, but some do.

DAVID: The wedding was in Gaash, near Netanya. We had about three hundred people. This is small for Israel, where guests come in sneakers and jeans and everyone you know is invited. It was at a function hall that looks like a castle. The families greeted the guests at the entrance.

ADENA: Once the ketubah was signed and the bedeken was over, we walked outside together toward the chuppah to Amharic music and everyone clapping. Some older women were wearing traditional gold jewelry and dressed in white. Some of the religious men were wearing white also, traditional at a wedding. With our parents at our sides, an Ethiopian Chabad rabbi officiated in English, Hebrew, and Amharic. Men of the families said the sheva brachot, we drank the wine, and David broke the glass. After the ceremony, we stayed under the chuppah and gave each guest a blessing one by one as they came up and embraced us. As we walked out, two men sounded long shofars.

At the party afterward, we danced to Ethiopian music. Certain songs have different dances. One is *eskista*, a special dance for celebrations. As we and our parents danced, guests came up to us, said mazel tov, and put money on our foreheads. Someone in the family collects it. This is an Ethiopian tradition.

In Ethiopia, the whole community comes to the bride's and groom's families for more celebrations after the wedding without the bride and groom. Now, people you don't know still come to celebrate. Our wedding was on a Tuesday, and every night there were more celebrations with eating and drinking, including a Shabbat Chatan (groom's Shabbat) when David was called to the Torah. At each of these celebrations, dabo is cut, which you accept with both hands.

INDIA

Elizabeth Joshua

Thirty years ago, when Elizabeth's family arranged her marriage to Gershon, a Jewish man from Kerala, a state on the south coast of India, it must have been an unusual match. Even then, not many so-called Cochini Jews resided in Kerala. Today, as emigration to Israel has taken its toll, only about fifty Jews remain in the area, leading some to believe that the community in situ is almost extinct after two thousand years. We are fortunate to have Elizabeth's firsthand account of her remarkable wedding with its unique traditions—including the unusual lack of a chuppah—in a world-renowned synagogue.

Our wedding in 1987 was far from an intimate affair. We were joined by friends and family—as well as members of the press. It was the first wedding conducted at the famous Paradesi Synagogue in Cochin, a city in the state of Kerala, in thirty years. So it was a rare sight. Built in 1568, on land given by the Maharaja of Cochin when Portuguese persecution forced the Jews to leave their ancestral home in Cranganore in the north, the synagogue is said to be the most beautiful in India and the entire Commonwealth.

My husband, Gershon, was born in Kerala. After completing his education, Gershon and his father established a business in Chennai, a day's travel from Cochin, where they came to celebrate Jewish festivals and High Holy Days. I am a Bene Israel Jew, born and raised in Bombay, where I was educated. Before we met, both Gershon and I had visited Israel and attended an ulpan when we finished our schooling.

As there were no eligible Jewish women to court in Cochin, Gershon came to Bombay to look for a bride. Marrying within Judaism was so important to most of the Indian Jewish population that matchmaking was very widespread. Through common relatives and friends, we met and became a couple in what we call an "arranged marriage." I was twenty-nine and Gershon was thirty-one. We had no religious differences. Language and food preferences were challenges, however. Until today, I cannot speak Malayalam, the language of Kerala, and Gershon cannot speak Marathi, the language we spoke in Bombay. Our common language is English.

The Jews of Kerala have not adopted many traditional customs from the larger Indian culture. If the wedding had taken place in Bombay, I would have been the focus of a pre-wedding *mehendi* ceremony in which henna is applied in intricate designs to the bride's hands and feet. In another celebration, both the bride and groom have yellow *haldi* (a paste made from turmeric) applied to their bodies. In Kerala, we celebrated two traditional Shabbats. The one before the wedding is the Shabbat Kallah, honoring the bride. The one after is the Shabbat Chatan, when the groom reads from the Torah. Both are festive occasions, with joyous prayers, singing, dancing, and lots of food and wine.

The marriage was conducted by Mr. Samuel Hallegua, a learned and respected member of the Paradesi congregation. It was not conducted under a chuppah, which Indian Jews believe is essential only outside under an open sky. Gershon and I had flower garlands around our necks, a core Indian custom. I was seated on the "bridal chair," my head and face hidden under a circular, thick, tent-like veil, one I couldn't see through. The tradition of this kind of veil is unique to the Kerala Jewish congregation. (Bombay Jews have weddings similar to modern Western ceremonies in which the bride can view all the proceedings through a thin veil or none at all.)

The ring was placed in a golden, two-hundred-year-old goblet filled with wine. The groom sips from it and offers it to the bride. The ketubah, handwritten in Hebrew, was read out in its entirety and signed by us. Mr. Hallegua lifted the veil so that I could drink the wine and sign the ketubah. The prayers were those prescribed by Jewish law, similar to other ceremonies across the globe. Only after Gershon broke the glass did I come out from behind the veil. Then we exchanged rings and Gershon covered me with his tallit, signifying our union.

I had been thrilled with the preparations leading up to the wedding, but also nervous about the large number of people I had not met before. When the day arrived, everyone was busy getting ready for the much anticipated ceremony. I remember feeling overwhelmed, surrounded by so many helpers, each with ideas on what needed to happen next. When I finally arrived at the synagogue and could take a breath, I felt a rush of adrenaline and exhilaration about what was to come. I could not see much of what was happening through the veil, but I could feel the power of the prayers as our bond as husband and wife was formed.

Once the glass was broken, it was time to be merry, celebrate, greet hundreds of guests—and smile for the press! There was a grand dinner with drinks, good food, and singing of Hebrew songs, along with table thumping and laughter.

Indian Jewish history is unique; we have never faced any kind of discrimination. Although we live among a vast medley of cultures and traditions, we have proudly kept our identity alive through the years.

ITALY

Rabbi Barbara Aiello

The first and only woman rabbi in Italy, Rabbi Barbara serves congregation Ner Tamid del Sud, The Eternal Light of the South, the first active synagogue in Calabria in five hundred years. In 2017 the synagogue was recognized as a member of the Reconstructionist Jewish movement. Rabbi Barbara welcomes people of all backgrounds, including anousim (from the Hebrew for "coerced," as their ancestors were forced to give up Judaism) who are discovering and embracing their Jewish roots. Some of the wedding traditions she and her Italian informants describe are modifications of Jewish ones that have been passed down through generations unaware of their origin. Rabbi Barbara is a board member of Kulanu, an organization that supports communities of anousim who are returning to Judaism, many in Latin America who fled the Iberian Inquisition, and others in Africa who claim ancestry from ancient Israel.

Rabbi Barbara recites the family blessing for the newlyweds and their mothers

Gianna F. is older now. Her steps are less firm and her eyesight is not what it used to be. But when she speaks about Italian Jewish wedding traditions, her bright smile fills the room. Gianna's family is *bnei anousim*, which means that five hundred years ago, during Inquisition times, Gianna's ancestors were forced to accept Christian conversion. Families like Gianna's became Christian in name only, pretending to practice a new religion, while observing their Jewish traditions in secret. As Gianna says, "Our Jewish traditions never died."

Gianna recalls,

> I remember we had a tradition to make a blessing *sotto la coperta* (under the cloth). You see, one of the women, like my great-grandmother, would spend nearly a year crocheting a beautiful bedspread, big enough for the bride and groom's double bed. But the first time anyone saw it was on the wedding day. Four men of the family would each take a corner and hold the *coperta* over the heads of the wedding couple. The two fathers would make a blessing in a secret language. Later on I learned that the blessing was in Hebrew, the language of the Jews.

Today, Jewish families, particularly those in the "toe" of the Italian "boot," continue the ancient chuppah tradition. Beautifully hand-crocheted canopies are often passed from generation to generation as family heirlooms.

The basic structure of the chuppah, a canopy supported by four poles, can be as decorative or as simple as suits the taste of bride and groom. However, for Italian Jews, tradition dictates that vines, olive branches, and ivy, rather than flowers, decorate the chuppah canopy and poles. In addition, brides and grooms often tie a small sack of earth to each of the front poles of the chuppah. The earth comes from their respective family homes, or from the villages where they or their ancestors were born. This anousim tradition celebrates the earth, which nurtures their Jewish roots that, regardless of difficulty, never die.

Many Jewish wedding traditions include the family tallit, but in the Italian tradition the *tallet* holds a position of honor. "The tallet is from my grandfather," says bride Valentina who carefully unfolds her Jewish family heirloom. Valentina looked forward to that moment in the ceremony when she and her groom, Ferdi, would be wrapped shoulder to shoulder in "Nonno's tallet" as they exchanged their wedding vows.

Following the promises and ring exchange, a beautiful southern Italian tradition takes place: I invite both mothers to join their children under the chuppah for the Family Unity Blessing. The tradition features a braided gold cord which both mothers use to bind the hands of their children. As the mothers place their hands over the bound hands of their children, I make a special Italian blessing that unites both families in love and support of the new family created this day by their children.

"It was a magical moment," says bride Rosemary who stood with her groom, Lorenzo de' Medici, descendant of the famous Renaissance family, under the chuppah erected on the beach at Nocera. "When my Korean mother and Lorenzo's Italian mother wrapped our hands together, we understood that nothing in this world is stronger than love."

PERU

Molly Neufeld

Molly's lovingly detailed description of her wedding ceremony and celebration at age nineteen provides a shock at the end. Twice divorced and a mother and grandmother, she told us that she had not lost hope of finding her bashert (partner who is meant to be). If she does, this upbeat optimist "might consider the possibility of a fourth wedding." She did not disclose whether she is one of millions of divorced and widowed women who have tried online dating websites, including many created especially for seniors. Although the Jewish population of Peru has been dwindling since the 1970s when Molly left for Canada, three thousand remain.

I met Robby in 1970 after breaking up a long-distance relationship with my first boyfriend. Robby had just returned from New York where he had attended Yeshiva University. I was on the rebound and initially used him to prevent myself from going back to my unfaithful boyfriend. I was eighteen, and Robby was twenty—a good guy and very naive. I was the first girl he ever kissed.

Robby was born in Hungary and came to Peru with his mother, father, and an older sister following the revolution in 1956. His parents were Orthodox, but Robby was not religious. We dated for almost two years when we decided to become engaged. Our families had a *tenaim* (literally "conditions") ceremony. Traditionally, a prewedding contract is read aloud and signed. I only remember my mother and his mother breaking a plate on the corner of a table, a symbol that the engagement was official.

After that, I started saving money for my wedding dress, for linens, and other stuff for my future home. (In retrospect, how tiresome was that? My daughters are in their thirties, still single, and have traveled extensively, while at nineteen I was saving to buy linens!) My mother-in-law, a very organized, efficient, and graceful hostess and cook, took charge of the wedding arrangements. My mother, a working widow, did not have the means to pay for the whole wedding as was customary. My in-laws agreed to pay for half, and my mother and two uncles contributed the other half. I remember that the wedding cost about four thousand US dollars—a lot of money, probably more than I made in a year. We invited two hundred people, a relatively small wedding at the time! I thought it was perfect.

I had three wedding showers. The first was given by the "girls" from my office—lots of fun. My aunts gave a tea in the Hotel Crillon, a fancy downtown hotel, attended by older women. The third was organized for both men and women by our best friends and cousins. As the oldest cousin in the family, most of my friends and relatives were still single.

It was customary for people to send a boxed gift to the bride's home before the wedding or to give a cash gift by going to a place (usually a store) that collected the money and kept a list of contributors, a *colectivo*. Nobody arrived at a wedding carrying a gift or a check inside an envelope.

A week before the religious wedding, we had a civil wedding ceremony at the city hall. Only close family and witnesses were invited. We probably went for lunch somewhere afterward, but I can't remember where.

My mother's family is Sephardic, and Rabbi Benhamu, the Chief Rabbi of Peru, would not have married me unless I went to the mikveh. This was the one and only time I did. Two days before the wedding, I became sick and couldn't stop coughing. The doctor put me on strong medicines that suppressed the cough but kept me in bed, sleeping for two whole days. I missed my wedding rehearsal, but on the day of the wedding, I was feeling fine. (But I was not allowed to drink liquor that night or on my one-week honeymoon to Cuzco and Machu Picchu.)

The morning of the wedding, I had my hair done and I went to a makeup artist who made me look gorgeous! My wedding dress had long sleeves, not only because it was winter in Peru in August but also because strapless dresses were a no-no. My mother-in-law had bought the material for my dress in the United States, and the dress was made by a seamstress. Everybody had clothes made by *costureras* (seamstresses). We didn't go to stores to buy ready-made dresses.

The ceremony and the reception took place in Sharon Synagogue on August 26, 1973. The synagogue was close to Robby's parents' home, so we had pictures taken at his house before the wedding. The custom in Lima was that weddings began at least one hour after the time on the invitation. In my case, the wait was a bit longer because the rabbi was late. His excuse was that he ran out of gas, but he lived very close to the Sharon, so this was probably just an excuse.

The procession began with Robby and his mother, then Robby's father with his sister, my mother with my brother, and my uncle Leon and his wife, Esther. Then came the children—my cousin Evelyn as the ring bearer and my cousin Augusto with my cousin Zina. As my father was not alive, I decided to walk in alone. The ceremony was traditional, but there was no circling of the groom seven times by the bride. I never saw that done in Peru.

After the ceremony, we went to a room where we exchanged rings while the guests went into the ballroom. There was a long head table that included our parents, siblings, the rabbi and his wife. On one side of the table was a most beautiful wedding cake and on the other side was a fruit arrangement. A huge dance floor stood between the head table and a stage where the band was playing. Music and dancing are important parts of weddings in Peru, and all weddings had live bands. People spent a lot of money hiring good bands and even live entertainers.

People didn't stand in line to greet the newlyweds. I remember that we went from table to table kissing the guests and thanking them. The sit-down dinner was probably more modest than dinners in the United States. Each table had a bottle of whiskey and kosher wine. There was only one caterer who could prepare a kosher meal supervised by the rabbi. Even though most Peruvian Jews were not kosher, Rabbi Benhamu wouldn't stay for the reception unless the dinner was kosher. (His blackmail worked really well most of the time.) We danced horas first, and later Latin music until very late. We didn't do the raising of the chairs, but I believe the custom of doing this came from Israel not too long after our wedding. I know it's being done now at every wedding.

There is a cute tradition centered on the wedding cake. All around the cake are white ribbons glued on with sugar icing. Single girls stand around the cake and pull on the ribbons. One of the ribbons is tied to a ring, and the girl who pulls the ring not only keeps it but also is the first one to get married. We also toss the bouquet to the single girls.

Robby and I moved to Canada, arriving in Toronto in April 1976. Six months later Robby died at the age of twenty-six. I was twenty-four and a widow living in a new country. I married twice again in Toronto, but throughout my life, I have always cherished the memories of my first wedding. There is something about leaving your parents' home where you lived as a daughter, acquiring the title of wife, and being the queen of your own castle that makes the first marriage very special.

SPAIN

Esther Muhlfelder

Melilla, where Esther was born and spent her teenage years, is an isolated Spanish enclave surrounded by the area of northern Morocco that was a Spanish protectorate until the mid-twentieth century. Now a troubled flashpoint for African immigrants trying to reach asylum in Spain over border fences, Melilla has been a haven for Jews since the 1500s. Families like Esther's have left for bigger cities like Barcelona and wider horizons, but approximately five hundred Jews remain, some descendants of refugees fleeing the Inquisition, others seeking asylum from Moroccan antisemitism in the late 1800s and later from Nazi persecution. The wedding rituals in Barcelona that Esther describes—notably, the berberiska evening—indicate clearly that her family has not forgotten their Moroccan roots.

I was born in Melilla, a Spanish city of about eighty thousand on a peninsula that juts into the sea from the coast of Morocco. At one time, there was a large Jewish population. My mother's family had lived there for generations since the Inquisition. My father's family came from Sicily in the early 1800s. When I was eighteen, my family moved to Barcelona, where I went to university.

I met my husband, Lewis, from Albany, New York, at an *ulpan* (study center for newcomers) in Israel. He was working at an architectural firm for a year, and I had been there for six months, following one of my four sisters to Israel. We were married in Barcelona a year later in 1981.

Our wedding customs most closely followed those of the Jews of Morocco, although, as I was marrying an American, we didn't observe all of them. The day before the wedding, I went to the mikveh with my mother, my aunt, and one of my sisters. After I came out of the water, they pelted me with *peladillas* (sugar coated almonds), and I ate a little container of honey.

That night was the *Noche de Berberiska*, a traditional Moroccan ceremony. It was held at my parents' home, and there were about seventy guests. The bride makes an appearance after the guests are gathered. Traditionally, she wears a gorgeous velvet costume and headdress sewn with jewels and gold thread. It can cost up to $50,000. Sometimes it is a family heirloom that is passed down as a mitzvah. I was modern and didn't want to wear the traditional costume (although my niece, who married recently, did).

I entered as everyone, both men and women, sang Hebrew and Ladino songs they learned from childhood. My mother put a veil over my head. The women

Esther places the ring on Lewis's little finger held by her mother

had henna applied to the center of their palms for good luck. Then trays were brought out to me with all kinds of gifts—gold necklaces, diamond earrings, chocolates, perfumes, petit fours. The veil was lifted, and I opened the jewelry boxes and thanked everyone.

The rabbi was there and conducted a ritual that signified the first step of our marriage contract. We each held a corner of a white handkerchief—my soon-to-be husband, my father, the rabbi, and myself—as the rabbi and my father, who was a *Cohen*, said a blessing. This was followed by a lot of food, more than you ever see here in the United States—ten kinds of fish, ten kinds of meat, gorgeous platters of petit fours, baskets of *fishuelas*, a traditional sweet, and *puritos almendras*, a cigar-shaped treat made with thin dough, ground almonds, and honey.

The next day was the wedding in the Sephardic synagogue in Barcelona. My husband didn't see me until the ceremony at 6:30 that evening. I wore a typical white wedding dress, made by my uncle in his factory in Barcelona. As customary, the bimah was in the center of the sanctuary. Men and women sat together. As a sign of modesty, my head was down and my veil was down as I entered, and I did not look around. Parts of the ceremony included the Cohen benediction, the sheva brachot, and the reading of the ketubah, which we then signed under the chuppah along with two of my uncles. (Parents cannot do it.) In the Sephardic tradition, the bride puts a gold ring on the little finger of the groom. We used my father's ring. The bride does not receive a ring as part of the ceremony—although I got a white gold ring later.

After the ceremony, we had a beautiful party on the terrace of a hotel for one hundred people. We stayed at the hotel that night and then traveled around Spain with my parents and my husband's parents from the United States. Seven months later, we went alone to Bermuda.

I raised my family in the US. But my son married a woman from Germany whose parents had come there from Ukraine. They had a destination wedding in Marbella in southern Spain.

SWITZERLAND

Ariella Tishler

Ariella's story connects past generations with her own. The seven-week period between Passover and the festival of Shavuot is an introspective and rather mournful period and one during which Jewish weddings are not held. The festival of Lag B'Omer, on the thirty-third day of this period, is an exception to the wedding prohibition, decreed coincidently by her father's ancestor, an illustrious sage of the past. This day and this ruling carry deep personal significance for Ariella. Her maternal grandparents' wedding in the local Hungarian orphanage—held on the same day as her own decades earlier, on Lag B'Omer—is one of the most remarkable wedding venues described in this collection. Like Ariella's family, a number of Geneva's six thousand Jews are Orthodox.

Carl lowers Ariella's veil at the bedeken ceremony

When you stand under the chuppah, you find yourself at the most fascinating of intersections. You've been to the mikveh, been reborn in a sense, and now the next phase of your life is about to begin. But there you are, just for a few minutes, with a foot in each camp. You stand there as the sum total of your upbringing, backstory, and DNA—the people and experiences that made you. On the other hand, you are there by the most important choice you have made in your life so far. I imagine that this is the case for everyone, but I can only speak for myself. The date and location of my wedding—part of that backstory—were especially meaningful. Carl and I were married in Geneva, Switzerland, on the fourteenth of May 1998.

I grew up in Geneva. My mother's family first arrived there from Budapest, miraculously escaping the horrors of war and the Bergen-Belsen concentration camp on the Kastner train, named after Rudolph Kastner, a Hungarian Jewish lawyer and journalist who negotiated with Adolf Eichmann to allow sixteen hundred Jews to escape to Switzerland in exchange for cash, gold, diamonds, and trucks. The train brought them to this beautiful country. With unfathomable resilience and courage, my grandparents started a new life in Switzerland. They were grateful to the country which took them in, to the community they helped build, and to family and friends who stood united and unbowed.

My father had grown up in England, where his family had immigrated from Poland a generation before, also escaping the war. While traveling through Switzerland as a student, he met my mother, fell in love, and has been in Switzerland since they married.

So those are the two sides of my family—one from Switzerland via Hungary and the other from England via Poland. My husband is from Boston, where his father's family has lived for generations. His mother's family came from Washington, DC. Interestingly, for both sides of my family, as well as for my husband and me, our wedding date had particular significance.

Under the chuppah, the past, present, and future swirl together; they certainly did that day in May. According to our *luach* (Hebrew calendar), it was the eighteenth day of the month of Iyar, the holiday of Lag B'Omer. On each of the forty-nine days between Passover and Shavuot, we count the *omer*, a practice dating back to the Temple period, when an omer (a measure of grain) was brought as an offering. In subsequent years, this period became marked by sorrow. The Talmud tells us that all of Rabbi Akiva's students died during the first part of this period, often attributed to their lack of respect and consideration for each other. Traditionally, therefore, Jews do not hold weddings during the counting of the omer, nor listen to live music, nor do other things that we associate with joy.

But for Ashkenazi Jews like us, Lag B'Omer is an exception. The students stopped dying on the thirty-third day. (The Hebrew letters for thirty-three are *lamed* and *gimmel*, which together spell out *Lag*.) On this day, you can be married; on this day, you create joy, you commemorate understanding between people, you look to unite and to celebrate together. This is a particularly special day for my family because my father's ancestor, Rabbi Moshe Isserles (known as the "Rema"), declared in the sixteenth century that Ashkenazi Jews could, in fact, be married on Lag B'Omer. And on my mother's side, my grandparents were married on Lag B'Omer in Budapest in 1937. Sixty-one years earlier, my grandmother, sitting close to me, was married on this very day.

Both my husband's family and mine are communally active and inclusive. A beautiful Chassidic custom is to invite everyone—the whole community—to a wedding, and this is what we tried to do. Making our wedding a communal celebration, especially on Lag B'Omer, was very important to us. People used to take two hours for lunch in Geneva, so families like ours could eat lunch together at home most days. Having the wedding at that time of day allowed the maximum number of people to attend. Everyone was invited to the ceremony and reception. Then there was a long break before a small dinner in the evening.

Sixty-one years earlier and one thousand miles away in Budapest, my maternal grandparents had a similar idea. They were grateful for being able to invite the community, but they wanted to go a step further. Specifically, they wanted the orphans of the community to share in the *simcha* (celebration). So they arranged to have the wedding celebration in the orphanage! I have always thought that was an incredible example of generosity and goodwill.

Ours was a traditional Orthodox Ashkenazi wedding. My husband wanted a *tisch*, a traditional gathering of the groom and his well-wishers, prior to the bedeken (veiling) ceremony. Perhaps forty or fifty men attended, a diverse group. The tisch is like that—you have a group of people who may not know each other but are united in their common joy. That, together with whiskey and some food for everyone (except the groom), goes a long way, as does the singing and dancing. After the tisch came the bedeken, when the groom enters the room where the bride has been waiting, checks that she is the right person, and lowers the veil over the bride's face. This part was very emotional for me. From there, we were separately escorted to the chuppah by our respective parents who were holding candles.

While much of the religious ceremony would have been similar, if not identical, to those conducted elsewhere throughout the world, there is a further secular aspect to marriage in Switzerland. Here, you must have a civil ceremony in addition to a religious one. Ten days earlier, we had a civil wedding ceremony in Geneva's former town hall, a beautiful building close to where I grew up. There, under the auspices of the Ville de Genève, we were officially married. The civil ceremony was also special. My grandmother and local family members attended, as well as good friends of my husband, who were themselves on their honeymoon in Switzerland. One of them acted as a witness. My aunt was the other one.

The two ceremonies—civil and religious—formed a composite experience that was local as well as transcendent, rooting us in a time and place while at the same time connecting us to generations past and emerging. Gratitude is the great enabler of joy.

TEN

—ᴍ—

AFTER THE CEREMONY
AND BEYOND

THIS CHAPTER OFFERS a varied group of exceptional bridal stories that span the time from immediately after the ceremony—*yichud* and the celebratory festivities—to the years after marriage.

An interesting postwedding custom is called *yichud* (seclusion), which in Jewish law restricts the private meeting of a woman with one or more men under any circumstance. An Orthodox man who finds himself alone in a room with a woman (other than his wife, mother or sister) opens the door to transform the space from yichud to public. In the context of this book, however, yichud refers to the brief—approximately ten minutes or longer—period that the bride and groom spend alone together in a separate room immediately after the ceremony. If they have fasted during the day, as is customary among some groups of Jews, the couple typically have something to eat. They emerge from yichud whenever they are ready and join their guests.

In ancient times, marriages were consummated immediately after the wedding ceremony. When that practice ended, yichud became a symbolic substitute. A Chabad website offers the idea of yichud as a brief time to process the momentous event that has occurred and a message about the importance of private time in a marriage amid the hustle and bustle of daily life.[1] However, many people are curious as to what happens during a particular couple's yichud. If the private time together is drawn out, guests may begin to giggle and gossip about what might be going on. Even the rabbi might participate in joking about yichud, as we can see in the story of the bride from Nova Scotia, Canada.

Throughout the world, celebrations after the wedding ceremony typically include eating, drinking, music, and dancing. In traditional circles, guests may entertain the couple with songs and antics. At Orthodox parties, male and female guests celebrate and dance separately. Nowadays, lifting the bride and groom (and sometimes their parents) on chairs has become a popular center-piece of the merriment, although the origin of this ritual is hazy. Surprisingly few stories in this collection mention such joyous elevations, so perhaps the custom has gained in popularity comparatively recently.

Many postwedding parties incorporate elements of the surrounding culture. The Talmudic concept of *dina d'malkhuta dina* ("the law of the land is the law") implies that Jews should be open to the ways of others, that there is no hostil-ity to the customs of the countries in which Jews live so long as those customs do not compel Jews to violate their own laws. Thus, the wedding celebration in Venezuela that the bride's mother describes in detail featured local good-ies, Latin music and dances, and like all Latin American good times, ended at daybreak. Likewise, the wedding party in Beijing included an array of Chinese customs and ceremonies, a blending of Jewish and Chinese traditions that ex-pressed the cultures of the couple and their unusual and dearly loved adopted environment. The Afghani-Ashkenazi couple's story reminds us that the inte-gration of customs from various traditions is selective. After an Ashkenazic ceremony, the couple came home to find traditional Afghan decorations. This story, along with others in this volume, notes the sheva brachot, customary fes-tive meals hosted by family members and friends in the week after the wedding, where the blessings recited or sung during the wedding ceremony are repeated.

Several stories in this chapter document the years following the wedding ceremony. We appreciate the candid reflections of the author from Brazil who has chosen a rewarding childless lifestyle and those of the plucky author who married in Iran and divorced in the United States. Another spirited woman began life in Russia and ended up as a plantation manager in Jamaica. As told by her grandson, this is an extreme example of the changes that accompany the transition from bride to wife. The Serbian story is one of the saddest in our col-lection. Good relations between Jews and non-Jews, who attended each other's weddings before the Holocaust, did not result in the survival of the majority of the Jewish community.

AFGHANISTAN

Daphna Shemesh

When immigration became possible in 1951, most of Afghanistan's four thousand Jews left for Israel. The rest followed in 1979 after the Soviet invasion. Daphna mar-ried in an Ashkenazic ceremony in Israel, but her story highlights several unusual

betrothal and wedding traditions of her husband's family, some still observed by
people far from their ancestral home—a cake crowning the bride's head, a dance
with beribboned sticks, an embroidered sheet as a dowry gift, and sugar cones as
wedding decorations. The henna party she describes is common throughout com-
munities from former Arab lands, although specific details differ, such as how and
where the henna is applied and who is invited.

I met my husband, Mottie, at a dance club frequented by students at Hebrew
University in Jerusalem. I was a student after finishing my military service in
the intelligence corps. My father is Israeli, and my mother is from Philadelphia.
After several moves with my family, I lived in Israel from age eleven. Mottie's
father was born in Afghanistan and came to Israel in 1950. His mother, whose
family came from Afghanistan, was born in Israel, where Mottie and his five
siblings were also born.

The day before our wedding in 1993, I went to the mikveh with my girlfriends
and then headed home. This was different from the mikveh celebration for Mottie's niece. At that party, the women relatives brought cakes and sweets that
they had made. After our niece got dressed following immersion in the mikveh,
there was dancing and singing and at one point a round cake was put on her
head like a crown. Then we went back to her parents' home for the traditional
henna party with men and women guests. One of her sisters-in-law prepared
henna and applied it to everyone's palms, which were then tied with a cloth.
We had cakes and sweets baked by her future in-laws, as well as dried fruits,
nuts, and chocolates. There was more happy singing and dancing. Another
cousin's henna party included a dance with sticks decorated with ribbons that
were clicked together. At both of these celebrations, some of the men played
traditional frame drums, *tof miriam*, that belong to the family.

Our wedding took place at the Larom Hotel in Jerusalem. It was a typical
Ashkenazi ceremony with 450 guests—everyone we knew, including the guy
from the convenience store down the street. My mother-in-law told me that in
Afghanistan, the bride and groom would walk through the streets as a procession beat drums and danced. The bride would be wearing a shiny, elaborately
embroidered galabeya, a long gown with wide sleeves. As a dowry, she would
be given a white sheet embroidered with messages of love, as well as clothing
that the family had sewn. We did not observe those rituals, but when we got
back to our apartment, we were surprised by another Afghan custom. Our
apartment had been beautifully decorated, filled all around with sugar cones
hung with candy on silver and gold threads and placed on silver and gold trays.
We ate the candy.

For the next seven nights, my husband's family hosted us, taking turns reading the sheva brachot (seven traditional wedding blessings) at their homes. There were forty or fifty people every night until late. We ate rice with carrots and chicken or meat, and gondi, meatballs made with ground meat or chicken, onions, and cardamom. We were exhausted by the time we went to Turkey for our honeymoon.

BRAZIL

Mônica Guttmann

Jews have made their homes in Brazil since fleeing the Portuguese Inquisition in the fifteenth century. Now numbering about 160,000, the Jewish population—the second largest in Latin America after Argentina—came in successive waves from Europe and the Middle East, escaping war and expulsion. They enjoy a comfortable standard of living despite a recent economic downturn and have experienced little antisemitism. As Jewish women in the Americas and Europe have pursued higher education and entered the workforce, a greater number, like Mônica, have remained childless. Her story highlights the positive aspects of nurturing entire communities of children in a loving partnership.

Judaism is strong in my family. My father grew up in Hungary and my mother in Brazil, the daughter of Hungarian Jews who had emigrated to Brazil. The women on my mother's side worked to earn money and have success in their careers. My maternal grandmother became a well-known fashion designer. The women on my father's side were housewives who dedicated themselves to caring for the family. But both of my grandmothers were observant Jews whose husbands were cantors during Shabbat and High Holiday services. Like my mother, I was brought up to marry a Jewish man, become a Jewish mother, and follow Jewish traditions.

I met my husband, Celso, at a rabbinical course at a Conservative synagogue. I wanted to study Judaism at a deeper level, and he wanted to be a rabbi at that time. We got married under a chuppa, sharing our joy with family and friends. We created our own ketubah with an alternative text, and I painted the watercolor image in it.

Although we are not Orthodox, I wanted to walk around my bridegroom seven times. According to the rabbi, the groom had to face the rabbi and not look at his bride entering the hall. I must confess it was the only disappointing moment of the ceremony. As I was walked down the aisle with my mother and brother (my dad had passed away), I was unable to see my future husband's face as he waited for me under the chuppa. Nevertheless, as I walked around him seven times, I fully felt my sensuality and my womanly strength as I revolved around my man.

Judaism has remained a part of our lives, although we have not created a traditional Jewish family. We are a Jewish couple without children. We did not create space for children in our lives, focusing parental energy on children and young people in our community—my husband as a healthcare professional and dental professor, and myself as a therapist, writer, and educator.

Although a childless marriage is not highly valued in Judaism, our marriage is a loving partnership wherein each of us works separately, knowing that we have common values and interests that must be respected and cultivated. We must nourish these values with particular care and attention, not losing sight of the other or being distracted by the demands of the outside world.

As a Jewish wife, I feel connected to the strong legacy I received, even if daily demands often divert me from it. When entering the Sabbath, I feel that my soul knows it, my body recognizes it, and my heart welcomes it, even if my ego is distracted by routine. We should not forget Shabbat, the Great Bride, as an element in a loving marriage.

CANADA

Lina Zatzman

Like many Jews who grew up in Canada's small maritime province of Nova Scotia, Lina left Nova Scotia and now lives near Toronto. Halifax, the capital of Nova Scotia, once called "Canada's Ellis Island," still has approximately fifteen hundred Jews. The clothing shop in Yarmouth, whose owner provided Lina's wedding dress, still exists, now run by a son of the founder, but few Jewish families remain in that small town, which no longer has a synagogue. Lina mentions yichud, seclusion of the bride and groom immediately after the ceremony. Observed most often in Orthodox circles, traditionally it is a time for the couple to relax together before the wedding festivities and to share a light meal, the first as husband and wife, after fasting on the wedding day.

In December 1949, when I was four years old, my parents, Sol and Hilda Gilis, and my infant sister, Ruth, left Glasgow, Scotland, for Southampton, England. There, we boarded the SS *Aquitania* for its last sailing to Nova Scotia. My parents had decided to start a new life in Yarmouth, Nova Scotia, where my father had obtained government grants to start a knitting factory. My mother's childhood friend, Rose, had married Hermie Shapiro, a Canadian soldier from Yarmouth, who opened a dress shop there when he returned from the war. So although they left family and friends behind, they had a connection in Nova Scotia.

At that time, Yarmouth had a synagogue, a rabbi, and between sixty and seventy Jewish families. Ruth and I attended Hebrew school and Young Judea, and my mother became active in Sisterhood and Hadassah. We were the only Jewish family on our street, and I was one of two Jewish children in my elementary school. Antisemetic comments and bullying were not uncommon occurrences. There were only three Jewish boys in my high school, and my parents never made a fuss if I went out with a non-Jewish boy. In spite of, or perhaps because of this, I developed a strong sense of Jewish identity.

In 1960, at the age of sixteen, I left high school to attend Dalhousie University in Halifax. On the first day, groups of first-year students were shown around campus by upperclassmen. I noticed a cute young man (CYM) leading another group. Later that week there was a movie and dance for freshmen in the auditorium. Lo and behold, there was CYM, standing in the aisle beside me as we freshmen were being informed of the rest of the week's activities. In a voice loud enough for CYM to hear, I announced to my seatmate that I would not be attending one of the activities. "Why not?" gruffly inquired CYM, who had overheard, as he was meant to. "Because," I replied, "it is Jewish New Year, and I will be going to synagogue." "Oh," he said, "I'll see you there." And that is how my romance with David Zatzman began.

We had an up-and-down courtship with many breakups and reconciliations until 1965, when we decided we really were meant to be together. Studying at different graduate schools, we saw each other whenever we could. We set our wedding date for June 11, 1967, in Yarmouth.

I picked out a wedding dress in Toronto, sent Uncle Hermie the information, and yes, he got it for me wholesale! In the days of large skirts and lace, I chose a simple gown with a medieval feel to it. My mother hid the dress in her closet, as her friends knew it would be "different," and they were curious to see what I chose. My sister was my maid of honor, and my teenage future sister-in-law Julie and my friend Ellen were my bridesmaids. David's friend Frank traveled from Toronto as his best man, and friends Brian and Ernie served as groomsmen. Yarmouth no longer had a resident rabbi, so Reverend Greenspan drove from Halifax with Ernie to perform the ceremony. (He might have been an ordained rabbi, but we always called him "Reverend.") He arrived late, as he had performed a bris that morning, so we hurriedly signed the ketubah at the kitchen table before leaving for the synagogue.

Our synagogue held only a hundred people, so the children of the community (who could not be invited) gathered outside to watch me go in. Inside were aunts, uncles, and oldest cousins of David's large family, residents of Halifax and St. John, New Brunswick. My aunts, uncles, and cousins lived in Scotland and Israel and so could not attend.

I walked down the aisle to the chuppah on my own, joining David, my parents, his mother, grandmother, and Uncle Charlie who stood in for David's father who had died two weeks before. David and I sipped from the same cup of wine, held first by my mother and then by David's mother. I remember that Reverend Greenspan explained the symbolism of the chuppah to the guests, many of whom were not Jewish. He said that our parents had welcoming homes and that he was certain we would have the same. After breaking the glass and signing the civil marriage register, we went to a small room in the back, as tradition dictated, and had a few minutes on our own to catch our breaths. When David asked what we should do there, Reverend Greenspan laughed and replied, "If you don't know, you shouldn't be getting married."

We then drove a few miles out of town to Braemar Lodge, one of the grand old rustic retreats famous in Nova Scotia, for the reception. My mother's friends had arrived earlier that day, set up name cards, and brought homemade baked goods for the sweet table. Because of the death of David's father, my mother had canceled the music, much to the disappointment of the band that had spent many hours learning to play "Hava Nagila."

What I remember most is the feeling of real community. Though none of my extended family were there, the bride's side was filled with people I had known all my life—members of the Jewish community, neighbors, friends, and people who worked for years in my father's factory. It was a truly *heimische* (warm and friendly) occasion, a fitting start to our life together. David died in 2021, just before his eightieth birthday.

CHINA

Nancy A.

A small Jewish community, founded by traders from India or Persia, established itself a thousand years ago in Kaifeng, a city on the banks of the Yellow River. But acceptance and consequent assimilation took its toll, and by the time the synagogue was destroyed in a flood in 1840, hardly anyone cared. In the 1990s, a few hundred people, descendants of six original families, began to reclaim their heritage. But except for several hundred Jews like Nancy's son, Alex, and daughter-in-law, Shira, who participate in an expat Jewish community, Jewish life and customs are not on

display. Nancy, who wants us to use only her first name, describes in detail an un-
usual wedding and attendant festivities that merged Chinese rituals with traditional
Jewish ones. Since we interviewed Nancy, Shira and Alex have moved to Canada
where they are raising their family.

My American son, Alex, and his Canadian wife, Shira, met in Beijing, where
they were both working. Alex had been in China for four years, and I was not
expecting him to marry a Jewish girl. They met through Kehillat Beijing, a
Jewish community of mainly young expats who meet for Friday night services,
holidays, and other gatherings at the Capital Club, the first private business
club in China. The couple became engaged while on vacation in the Caribbean
with Shira's family. Alex wrote in the sand, in Mandarin "Will you marry me?"
They decided to have the wedding five months later on May 31, 2015, in Beijing.

Several of us from Alex's and Shira's families arrived from the United States
and Canada a few days early to recover from jet lag and help with last-minute
details. Surprisingly little remained to be done, however, as Alex and Shira,
with assistance from a Chinese wedding planner, had organized every last element. It was quite a feat!

The first event began with a Friday night service at the Capital Club, led
by a visiting rabbi from New Mexico whom the couple knew from his previous engagements with Kehillat Beijing. Shira's father delivered a lovely d'var
Torah. The service was followed by dinner and dancing to music played by a
klezmer band comprised of talented Kehillat members. The next day, after a
trip to the Great Wall, the families and close friends returned to Beijing for
a rehearsal dinner at a favorite Chinese restaurant. By then, the families had
gotten to know each other better and enjoyed each other's company as well as
the excellent food.

The wedding ceremony took place at a beautiful classical Chinese-style hotel in the center of the city. In the library of the hotel before the ceremony, the
bridal couple, two witnesses, and the rabbi signed the ketubah, a gorgeous
document in Hebrew, English, and Mandarin, created with Chinese paper
cuts. During the brief bedeken, the rabbi recited a blessing while Alex lowered his bride's veil. Then the traditional Jewish wedding ceremony began. As
the K.B. musicians played, Alex's father and I escorted Alex down the aisle to
the waiting bridesmaids, dressed in black with red Chinese scarves, and the
groomsmen. Shira followed in a perfect long white gown, accompanied by
her parents, toward the chuppah, a combination of Jewish and Chinese elements: traditional embroidered Chinese banners in red and gold and a canopy

of Shira's bat mitzvah tallit. With guests wearing gold, red, and blue yarmulkes, the room was a sea of brilliant color.

Under the chuppah, each holding an end of a red scarf, Shira and Alex circled each other seven times, symbolic of Joshua breaking down the walls of Jericho and the couple breaking down any walls between them. One of the loveliest moments occurred when Shira's mother and I wrapped the couple in her father's tallit. As the ceremony progressed, Alex and Shira drank wine from a kiddush cup that Alex received on his bar mitzvah, they exchanged rings, and their siblings and cousins recited the sheva brachot. The ceremony ended as Alex broke the glass, then everyone shouted mazel tov and the band struck up "Siman Tov."

The one hundred guests then trooped outside to the expansive lawn of the hotel for hors d'oeuvres, not knowing the surprises that awaited them. As we milled about conversing, we heard drum beats from the far corner of the property. As the sound increased, we watched in amazement as a procession came closer. It was led by two huge red Chinese "lions," followed by musicians in traditional colorful garb thumping drums, crashing cymbals, and playing horns and instruments that resembled bagpipes. In the middle was a red and gold closed sedan chair on poles, perched on the shoulders of four strong men. As the procession approached, Alex went out to meet it, calling "Shira, come out," according to custom. After the traditional refusal and repeated requests, Shira emerged. Then the lions, actually two men in each huge costume, began an astounding acrobatic dance, doing flips and somersaults and shaking their bright red fur in time to the music. Alex thanked the lions by "feeding" them traditional lucky red envelopes of money.

As the Chinese wedding ceremonies continued, Alex was presented with a bow and arrows and instructed to shoot one arrow at the sky and another at the ground, signifying that he will always protect Shira. In another ceremony, Alex and Shira stepped over an apple and a saddle, apparently a play on the Chinese word for "safety." More confusing still to Westerners, the emcee handed Shira a date, a prune, and finally a peanut—foods having something to do with fertility. Hmm . . .

Finally, it was time for the tea ceremony. As I sat with Alex's father at one end of a red-clothed table and Shira's parents sat at the other end, our children gave each other's parents cups of sweet tea, which we accepted with both hands. The best part of the ceremony, at least from the perspective of an American parent, is that the bride and groom each thanked their respective parents for raising them—a very nice, and very Eastern, touch. Next came another bit of Jewish tradition. As the klezmer band played, the newlyweds and both sets of parents were raised on high as the guests danced around them.

Then it was back into the hotel for dinner. There were many toasts to the bride and groom, which they translated from Mandarin to English and English to Mandarin. Shira's father made a particularly memorable toast featuring a video Shira had made two years earlier, before her departure for China. She was playing the violin and singing Hodel's song from *Fiddler on the Roof*, "Far from the Home I Love." There wasn't a dry eye in the room.

A fan-shaped menu at each place setting listed fourteen different items in Mandarin and in English. We feasted on braised cuttlefish with nuts, roast lamb with vanilla, beef with black pepper sauce, crispy sesame chicken, and so many other delectable dishes. But that wasn't the end of the festivities. For the finale, the newlyweds changed into tee shirts sporting their special logo: a traditional Chinese wedding "chop" or seal with Mandarin characters signifying double happiness, to which they'd added a double Jewish star. They ushered their guests outside again and, in true Western style—or maybe it's One World style—a DJ had everyone dancing in crazy hats until two in the morning. It was a truly memorable and marvelous wedding.

IRAN

Shanaz

We are grateful to Shanaz, who wants to use a nom de plume, for the description of her Jewish divorce, a personal subject addressed only in this one contribution to our collection of stories. Although divorced in the civil legal system, a Jewish couple remains married religiously until the husband gives her a get. Until then, the wife is unable to remarry according to the Orthodox and Conservative branches of Judaism. For many years, the get has been the focus of discussions related to the problem of the agunah—the "chained" wife whose husband refuses to give her the get. Prenuptial agreements have been forwarded as a solution. Shanaz's receipt of their ripped ketubah (marriage contract) from her now-former husband may be a dramatic local ritual.

In 1950 and 1951, when I was a small child, my family was forced out of Iraq along with the entire Jewish community. Some families went to Israel, England, or the United States, but my family went to Iran where my father had business contacts. We lived in a neighborhood in Teheran where almost all the families were originally from Iraq. Most of them rented their homes in the hope that one day they could return.

Shanaz (right) with her future daughter-in-law and son at
their henna party

I went to college and graduate school in the United States, where I met the
man I married. My parents' decision to allow me to study in the US was unusual, but they wanted me to have an excellent education. Typically, marriages
in our community were arranged by the family. They did not accept my desire
to marry an American at first, and it took me a year to convince them. Finally,
they gave in and sent platters of sweets to family and friends, the traditional
way to announce an upcoming marriage.

In our community, there was only one flavor of Judaism—Orthodox. The
engagement is actually part of the wedding. It is a big deal legally: if the couple
does not go through with the marriage from that point, then a Jewish divorce
is necessary. At a gathering of relatives and friends, the ketubah was signed by
ten men, mainly close friends, and the rabbi. We said vows in Hebrew and my
husband-to-be broke a glass, like at the end of a wedding ceremony. I wore a
beautiful long dress. Then there was a festive dinner in my parents' house with
kebabs and tebeet, a long-simmered chicken and rice dish with spices.

A party when henna is applied to the fingers is traditional right before the
wedding, but I did not have one. When my son and daughter-in-law got married a few years ago, however, I organized the celebration I did not have. There
were elaborate costumes for the bride and groom, a procession led by family
members, belly dancers and singers, traditional foods, and, of course, henna.

My wedding in Teheran was on a Tuesday, an auspicious day. I wore a
Western-style white dress and veil, made by my sister-in-law, an accomplished

seamstress. I went to the hotel where the wedding took place, riding in a car decorated with flowers. There, three hundred people were waiting, men and women seated together. Following a procession led by men with torches, I came down the aisle accompanied by my father. My bridesmaids carried my long veil up to the chuppah composed of a large tallit held by the groomsmen. After the reading of the ketubah in Aramaic, the exchange of rings, the sheva brachot, and another breaking of the glass, we celebrated at a reception at the hotel. My parents went all out, with delicious kosher food, Iranian and Western music, dancing, and merrymaking. That night we stayed in the bridal suite of the hotel before going back to our studies in the United States.

My husband is a good person, and we had some wonderful years, but after more than thirty years of marriage, we divorced amicably. The husband has to give permission for the *get* (Jewish divorce). After speaking beforehand with the sympathetic head of the Boston bet din (rabbinic court), I invited my cantor and brother to accompany me. During the procedure, the three rabbis on the court asked why we wanted to divorce and made sure our names on the documents were precisely correct. I then held out my cupped hands, and my husband transferred our ripped-up ketubah to me. My witnesses were shaken, but I was not. My ex-husband and I have remained good friends.

JAMAICA

Ainsley Henriques

Marriage is always life-changing, but some marriages result in more significant transitions than others. Only a resilient bride like Ainsley's grandmother, Pearl, born in a Russian village, could have successfully adapted to life on a distant sugar plantation with no running water and a house full of her new husband's relatives. Little did she know that generations later, her grandson (recipient of her husband's name and her own vigor) would be the guardian of a rich Jewish heritage that began in the seventeenth century with escapees from the Inquisition. Ainsley has been a leader of the Jamaican Jewish community and its institutions—a sand-floor synagogue, a school, a museum—for sixty years, persevering even as the resident Jewish population has shriveled due to emigration and assimilation.

My little grandmother, Pearl, all of four feet eleven inches tall, was a wonderful lady with a twinkle in her eye. As children, my brother and I took her stories for granted, assuming they were like those of anyone else's grandmother. In reality, this was not the case.

My grandmother was born in Shepotovka, a Russian village near Kiev in present-day Ukraine. At twelve, fleeing Cossack raids, hiding in hay carts as her family crossed borders, and finally voyaging in steerage, she arrived in Philadelphia, joining her father, a coal seller, who had immigrated earlier. In Philadelphia, she lived near the docks in a modest house with her parents and four younger siblings.

Pearl's next-door neighbor and best friend had married a Jewish man with Jamaican roots. When this man's friend came to Philadelphia from Jamaica for a visit, she was invited to dinner. My grandmother was the blind date. The story goes that Ainsley, my future grandfather, was immediately struck by her looks and personality. Escorting her home, he told her that he was going to marry her. She laughed at his impetuousness and thought that that was the end of him. It was not to be. He pursued her through visits and letters.

Well, Jamaica was a distant country in those days and, worse, my grandfather lived on a sugar plantation, Serge Island Estate in eastern Jamaica, purchased by his father in 1897. There was no gas light, only oil lamps, no tram cars, only horses and buggies, and no running water. Forbidding! But eventually, she fell for his importuning. In 1916, after a small family wedding in Philadelphia, she and her new husband were off to Jamaica and the plantation household, comprised her husband's parents, a spinster aunt, a dominant grandmother, and her husband's sister, Ivy. Although she had grown up in an Orthodox family, it was not possible to be so observant in those days in Jamaica. So she adapted, learned to play bridge, and lived a life of relative ease.

In 1918, Pearl's husband returned to Philadelphia, hoping that he would find employment there and an opportunity to take his wife and young child (my mother) back to America, away from the isolation of rural plantation life. Tragically, he succumbed to the Spanish flu that was ravaging Philadelphia.

So a few years later, after the deaths of her husband and her husband's parents, Pearl, along with her sister-in-law Ivy, took over the management of the plantation. Having no one to assist them, they ran the plantation as a remarkable sister-in-law partnership. Together they raised my mother, and later, after my mother's brief marriage ended, the three of them raised my younger brother, Richard, and myself.

My grandmother, Pearl, died in 1978. She was about ninety-two years old—a thoughtful, caring, and resilient woman with a homespun philosophy. I still miss her. Indeed, I still miss both her and my great-aunt Ivy, an inseparable pair for over half a century.

SERBIA

Ana Lebl

What terrible irony that Ana's grandmother, recipient of Serbia's highest medal for her work building a church, was murdered in the capital of her country by that government. An article in The Times of Israel *(March 30, 2016), which reported that "Serbia returns property taken in Holocaust to tiny Jewish community," adds a striking addendum to Ana's story about the wedding of her grandmother, Ana, and her grandfather, Leon. The article is headed by a photograph of a dignified gentleman—Aleksandar Lebl, son of Ana and Leon, born in 1922, and father of Ana, the author of this story. The article describes how Aleksandar was among the tiny minority of Serbians who escaped the country, joined the Yugoslav partisans fighting the Nazis, and came back to reclaim his home in Belgrade in 1945. The article reports that few survivors remain to take advantage of a recent Serbian law to restore property to Jewish owners.*

Only 15 percent of the Jews of the former Yugoslavia survived World War II. My story is one of vanished traditions. The former Yugoslavia had a large Jewish population, both Sephardic and Ashkenazi. Even before World War II, there were some mixed marriages between Jews and non-Jews and a range of religiosity. Jews in Serbia lived and worked together with non-Jews, so it was not so unusual that my grandfather had a non-Jewish girlfriend (my father told me that she was the daughter of a Serbian Orthodox priest!) before finding his Jewish bride. His job involved a lot of traveling and living in towns where there were no Jews. Likewise, my grandmother's family, living and working in a local sugar factory in Belgrade, shared their lives with non-Jews and attended each other's celebrations.

My grandmother, Ana Robicek, married my grandfather, Leon Lebl, in 1921. The Ashkenazi chief rabbi of Yugoslavia, Dr. Ignaz Schlang, originally from Poland, performed the wedding. It took place in the Ashkenazi synagogue in Belgrade on a very hot July day. Most of the guests went from the synagogue by horse-drawn carriages to the wedding party at the sugar factory. Many were non-Jewish friends and colleagues. The bride's father, Aleksa Robicek, was a vice director of the factory and that is where the family lived. My father, Aleksandar, was born there in 1922.

Leon was a mining engineer who worked for various mines, so the young couple and their baby son moved many times from one Serbian town to another. At some point, they settled in Aleksinac, a small town where their daughter,

Jennie, was born in 1927. As they were the only Jewish family in town, my grandmother became friendly with her Serbian Orthodox neighbors and became actively involved in the social and cultural life of Aleksinac.

Tirelessly working as secretary of the local Serbian (non-Jewish) women's society *Gospodje Knjeginje Ljubice* (Ladies of Princess Ljubica), this Jewish bride and her little daughter Jennie raised funds for building a local memorial church. A plaque inscribed with Ana Lebl's name remains at the entrance to the church as the only Jewish donor. For her work, she received the state medal of St. Sava, the highest in the country.

The family moved back to Belgrade in 1933 where Ana again became involved in charitable, educational, and cultural volunteer work, this time with the Ashkenazi women's society *Dobrotvor* (Benefactor). One of its first presidents was a relative, along with two others on the board of directors. All were killed in the Holocaust, as was my grandmother who had been honored by her country and had given so much to both the Jewish and non-Jewish communities where she lived.

VENEZUELA

Judith Goldstein

Wedding celebrations that begin late and end in the early morning, hundreds of guests beautifully coifed and dressed in the latest fashion, lavish meals and entertainment, rousing dances: These are the hallmarks of Latin American weddings like the one that Judith meticulously planned for her daughter Michele in the "good ole times" before Venezuela's economic plunge at the end of the 1990s. Amid rising violence, antisemitism, and exorbitant food prices on the black market, the majority of Jews have left the country for the United States and Panama, while Israel is making efforts to help an increasing number of the nine thousand remaining Jews to make aliyah. Judith, who lives in Florida among a large community from Venezuela, reports that Venezuelans have brought their predilection for elaborate weddings with them.

I grew up in the United States and lived in Caracas for thirty-four years. Caracas is a cosmopolitan city with Jews from different backgrounds, both Sephardic and Ashkenazi. The Sephardic community is composed mainly of Jews originally from Morocco. Before the late 1960s, it was considered a *shanda* (shame) if a couple from the two different cultures wanted to marry. It was an intermarriage! Nowadays it is common for Sephardim and Ashkenazim to

Michele

marry, bringing a rich mix of customs related to the ceremony and events before and after. I have attended many elaborate *beberiska* celebrations for brides-to-be dressed in gorgeous golden gowns, with henna, traditional prayers and chants, and wonderful Moroccan food—like a wedding itself. But we are Ashkenazim with roots in Eastern Europe, and my daughter and son-in-law's wedding was in our own tradition.

My daughter Michele met her husband on a visit to her brother, Danny, at Brandeis University. Danny's friend Joey, an American whose family lived in Miami, liked Michele, but at the time she had a boyfriend in Caracas, where we lived. Months later, when Danny learned that Michele was boyfriend-free and available, he invited his friend Joey to come with him to Caracas during vacation time. That was when Michele and Joey's romance began.

Michele married Joey in February 1993, still the "good ole times" in Venezuela. Wedding events took place over four days. Many friends and relatives of Joey's family and my own came from the United States. Who wouldn't want to travel to Venezuela in February? When out-of-town guests arrived at the

Hotel Tamanaco on a hill overlooking the city, they were greeted with little bags of local goodies including Toronto chocolate balls with a hazelnut inside and Susy wafers with chocolate. These came with an itinerary of events for the weekend. On Thursday evening we had a small dinner at home, and on Friday we arranged bus tours of the city for those who wanted to do more than lounge around the pool. That evening, the groom's family hosted a beautiful Shabbat dinner at a club we frequented. And the next day, guests could lounge in the sun, enjoy another bus tour, or show up at the hair salon (an important appointment for many), which we had arranged.

The wedding was held at La Quinta Esmeralda, a beautiful venue in Caracas known for its fabulous décor and food. By Caracas standards, the wedding was small—450 guests. In contrast to the US where guests are strictly counted, in Venezuela it is considered a mitzvah for invited guests to bring their friends if they are visiting. If the groom's family had been local, the number of guests would have been double or triple. The women in the family were all decked out in dresses created by a designer who now has an exclusive shop on Madison Avenue in New York. The economic situation has changed in Venezuela, and it probably wouldn't be possible to do that now.

A traditional Ashkenazi wedding ceremony was held outside in the garden. As usual, it didn't begin until ten o'clock in the evening. (Everything in Latin America begins later than in the US.) The parents of the bride and the groom stood under the flower-decorated chuppah as Michele circled Joey seven times. I recall that the rabbi recited the sheva brachot.

At the party that followed inside, there was no assigned seating other than a table for the bridal party and family. As customary, guests mingled and sat wherever they liked. Food stations and buffets were set up around the elaborately decorated room, along with tables of magnificent sweets, most prepared by friends of the family. It is traditional for women in Venezuela to gather in groups to bake homemade desserts—petit fours and other small marzipan pastries—along with a lot of gossip and camaraderie.

The party began with a hora and continued with Jewish music and dancing. At one point, the bride and groom were tossed in the air. This was followed by Latin music—salsa, merengue, congas, and sambas. The party was quite a production, going on until the wee hours when breakfast was served—typical fare of hot chocolate and churros, delicious fried dough sticks covered with sugar, somewhat like a doughnut. Sunday morning, tired and happy, we hosted a brunch for our visitors at the hotel. Hopefully, our guests left with wonderful memories, because we certainly did!

ELEVEN

ARRANGED AND FORCED
MARRIAGES

NOW AND IN THE PAST, the selection of a Jewish woman's marital partner
has been accomplished in three ways: The potential bride can be forced or de-
ceived into marrying a certain person, she can be introduced to a person with
the intention that a marriage will ensue—commonly referred to as an arranged
marriage—or she can set out on her own to find a mate.

Many people are confused about the difference between forced and arranged
marriages. The most important distinction is that the bride, often very young,
has no say in a forced marriage. This type of marriage, without the bride's consent and against her will, has been called a form of enslavement, condemned by
the United Nations as a human rights abuse, and by governments worldwide.[1]
In contrast, both partners in an arranged marriage have accepted the assistance
of their parents or a matchmaker and have consented to the marriage.

Jews are prohibited from engaging in forced marriages. For this prohibition,
we can thank the family of the biblical Rebecca. The Torah describes her marriage (Genesis, 24) in the following dramatic way: Abraham's servant Eliezer
meets Rebecca and proposes to take her back to Canaan to marry Isaac. In
response, Rebecca's family says, "Let us ask the maiden." This interaction is the
basis of the Jewish law that no one may be married against her (or his) will.[2]
According to the most important code of Jewish law, the fifteenth-century
Shulchan Aruch, a marriage that takes place without the bride's consent is not
legal.[3] Furthermore, the Talmud prohibits a father from arranging the marriage of a young daughter to an old man, as it may encourage her "licentious"
behavior with others.[4]

Child marriage is extremely rare among Jews in the modern age. Nevertheless, as a few of the stories in this chapter show, adherence to Jewish law

regarding forced marriage has not been universal, and the line between "forced" and "arranged" may be blurry. In this chapter, Rachel Wahba writes that her mother, a member of the Baghdadi Jewish community of India, "had no choice" but to marry her father's associate, a good man smitten with her, but one she hardly knew. In Iran, Farideh Goldin's mother had been "married off" when she was thirteen, a fate independent Farideh was determined to escape. Gina Waldman's Libyan mother was seventeen, above the age of a classic forced child marriage, when she had to abandon her true love to marry her much older cousin as a cruel act of family obligation. Similarly, in the story from Morocco, the sixteen-year-old potential bride had no say when her family decided that she should break off her engagement to a sweet fiancé and a few years later marry her own uncle. Herb Selesnick labels his grandmother's marriage in Lithuania "arranged," but "forced" might be a better descriptor of a marriage based on a father's promise of his twelve-year-old daughter to a potential business partner.

In Jewish society worldwide, arranged marriages—the meeting of prospective mates facilitated by parents, other family members, or professionals—were the norm until the modern historical period. Indeed, many of the stories in this collection demonstrate that families have not entirely ceded their influence on brides' choices, even in the modern age. Family members may "fix-up" meetings of eligible young people, and approval of the potential mate may be a factor in the bride's decision to marry.

In contrast to the informal strategies of the majority of families today, the Haredi (ultra-Orthodox) segment of Judaism has "institutionalized" finding mates for marriage as part of a widely accepted system of *shidduch*. In Haredi communities, the practice of using a *shadchan*, a professional matchmaker, produces what might be called "assisted marriages." Potential marriage partners are introduced, sometimes in the presence of their parents. They then get to know one another, however briefly.[5] In some strict communities, couples may meet only a few times; in others, meetings may take place over months. But the choice is ultimately that of the couple, who have the right to say yes or no. In some cases, the man and woman tell their parents and not each other that they wish to become engaged. The shadchan then conveys the news.

This chapter features three rather successful arranged marriages. Aimée Aviva Cohen writes about her parents' late marriage in Tunisia, a "marriage of convenience" that improved the lives of an "old maid" and a lonely widower, arranged by an unofficial matchmaker.[6] Yitzhak Bakal's mother had an excellent education, but deferred to her father's discretion following a thorough investigation of her character and background by her future husband's female relatives, as was customary in Iraq. We do not know how she felt initially about the match, but we know that she raised a fine family who honor her memory. Twenty-five years later, Yitzhak's uncle's marital choice, aided by a matchmaker, may illustrate the family's transition from nearly forced to nearly free choice of marital partners. Following the tradition of the culture around them, Indian Jewish brides like Noreen Daniel no doubt expected that their marriages would be arranged by their families. Luckily for Noreen and her husband, Romiel, leaders of the Indian Jewish community in New York, their long union has been "a match made in heaven."

INDIA

Noreen Daniel and Romiel Daniel

Noreen and Romiel come from prominent Bene Israel families, the most numerous group of Indian Jews who, according to tradition, arrived in India more than two thousand years ago. While a large percentage have immigrated to Israel, about five thousand Bene Israel live mainly in Mumbai (formerly Bombay) and surrounding areas. Noreen, a former health counselor, is a translator and consultant on India's Jewish communities and founder of the Indian Jewish Congregation of the USA. Romiel, who trained first as a cantor, is the only ordained Indian rabbi in North America and, judging from his account of his fifty-year marriage to Noreen, a true romantic.

Noreen

Our mothers are first cousins, so my husband and I are second cousins. After my college graduation, my mother and Romiel's mother arranged our marriage. It was three years before we got married. In the meantime, we both earned master's degrees, mine in embryology in Bombay and Romiel's in chemistry in the United States. It wasn't until he returned from the United States and began work as a manager in a textile mill in Gujarat that preparations for the marriage began.

These preparations started with a special ceremony to invoke the blessings of the departed souls of our family. We said the *Hashkaba* and *Kaddish* prayers as we remembered our deceased relatives. As customary, in the room was a tray with puris (pieces of fried unleavened wheat bread), an egg beaten and fried, pan-fried chicken liver, and a small glass of brandy. Bits of aromatic wood called *oud* were added to burning coals in a censer and taken to all the rooms of the house along with a bowl of jaggery (dark brown sugar made from the sap of palm trees) and another of turmeric.

Noreen and Romiel

After this, wedding invitations were sent and shopping began in earnest for sets of jewelry, a sari for the henna ceremony before the wedding (green silk with gold embroidery) and a sari for the wedding itself (white silk with silver brocade).

The henna ceremony was held after sunset on the Saturday before the wedding. For the first part of the ceremony, I wore old clothes, and turmeric paste was applied to my hands, legs, and face by my mother, aunts, and cousins. They had fun—I did not. After about a half hour, I went to the mikveh in my home to wash off with hot and cold water, herbal shampoos, and sandalwood soap. Then I got dressed in the green sari, with green glass and gold bangles on both arms, earrings, and a necklace. My long hair was styled in a bun on which garlands of jasmine flowers were arranged.

When I came into the living room, it was full of guests. There were two chairs, one behind the other facing west to Israel. I sat in the front chair, with my younger brother in the chair behind. Then followed a custom of invoking the blessings of Elijah the Prophet. This is a common practice in the Bene Israel community, asking for his protection and a blessing for a special occasion. On a center table was a platter with seven fruits and fragrant flowers surrounding a *malida*, a dish prepared with parched puffed rice, freshly grated coconut, sugar, and sliced dry fruits. Everyone present recited prayers. These included the blessings given by patriarch Jacob to his sons, chanted three times, and ending with Psalm 121. This was followed by the distribution of the flowers. The guests inhaled their fragrance after reciting a blessing. The fruits were also distributed along with the malida. A few fruits and malida were given to the bride in a handkerchief with a blessing that she be fruitful. A simple dinner followed.

As the henna ceremony began, five young women carried in a tray with a mound of henna surrounded by flowers. On the tray were a cup of rice and pieces of jaggery. The flowers were tied to my forehead. My aunt applied henna to the index finger of my left hand. Then she fed small pieces of jaggery to my brother and me. She took a few grains of rice in both hands and threw them over my shoulders and head, as an appeal for plenty of food in my future home. Next, she took some money in her right hand, waved it over my head three times, and put it on the tray. Other women did the same thing. I was told that this was to ward off evil spirits. (The money was later given to charity.) Everyone expressed wishes that my brother would be the next groom.

It was late at night when Romiel's family came to our house. They brought a silk sari for me to wear when I went to their house after the wedding. They also brought jewelry with pearls and rubies for the wedding day. We served colorful sweets and drinks to them. Romiel's niece slipped a letter into my hand announcing, "Uncle Romiel asked me to give this to you." I felt embarrassed in front of all the guests. After they left, some members of our family visited the groom's house with gifts and sweets. By the time they returned, it was quite late and most of us had gone to bed.

Romiel

May 23, 1965, was a day full of expectation. It was the joining of two souls brought about by two strong mothers who had decided that this was a match made in heaven. And you know what? They were right! Our more than fifty-year continuing journey was predetermined by G-d and our mothers.

We had a time-honored Bene Israel wedding in the Magen David Synagogue in Bombay, a grand celebration. As the bride approached the chuppah, I sang a beautiful, traditional wedding song, the "Yona Thi Ziv," composed by Israel Ben Moses Nahara in the sixteenth century. Under the chuppah in the synagogue, we exchanged our marriage vows. My uncle, Captain Joseph Samson, recited the seven blessings, the mainstay of marriage if adhered to. Aunts, uncles, brothers, cousins, friends, and the community were the witnesses. Most of them are not here anymore, but I am sure they are looking down from their heavenly abode and saying that they blessed this wedding.

During our marriage, we have lived in different countries from India to Mauritius, Madagascar, and the United States, where we live now. As we journeyed, we knew we were not alone. Our togetherness helped us overcome obstacles and hardships. I am sure the Almighty knew that when He brought us together.

INDIA

Rachel Wahba

Compared to the other major divisions of Indian Jews (Bene Israel and Cochini), Baghdadi Jews are relative newcomers to India, first arriving as traders in the eighteenth century from Iraq (hence the name) and other Arab countries. A writer and psychotherapist, Rachel has provided an intimate glimpse into the origin of her parents' union (we could swear she was there!), when marriages were arranged by families and Baghdadis were expected to marry only within their own group of businessmen and merchants. Not surprisingly, her parents' wedding was a Western-style affair, as Baghdadi Jews did not adopt the traditions of their Bene Israel neighbors nor those of the Arab lands they left behind. Assimilation and immigration to the West have reduced the Baghdadi population in Bombay and Calcutta to a few hundred.

Katie Sharbani cried for days when she realized she had no choice. Her cousins Molly, Yolly, and Helen comforted her when she cried in a panic, "But I don't even know him, how am I supposed to marry him?"

Maurice (Moussa) Wahba, on the other hand, was madly in love with her. He felt he "saw" her long before meeting her, in a dream, when he was five years old. He claimed to have recognized her face when he first saw her at her father's house at Shabbat dinner. Years later she told me, "Your father is a romantic! I wasn't even born when he was five years old!" They balanced each other out from the start.

Efraim Sharbani, Katie's father, was fond of this young man and appreciated his honesty in business. Nobody noticed Maurice falling deeply in love with Katie over several dinners at the house. Maurice's brother Yacoub approached him one day, saying, "Moussa, you need to go to Egypt and bring back a wife. You are twenty-nine; it's time."

"I already found her," Maurice told his brother.

"Who?"

"Katie, Efraim's daughter."

Maurice was too shy to make the call himself. His brother reached for the phone to set up a formal meeting with Katie's father. Efraim was delighted. He had known Maurice for over a year and approved.

"What?" Katie was shocked; she tried to get out of it. "He is Egyptian. You always said I had to marry an Iraqi!"

"It's lucky you are not marrying an Iraqi," Meeda, her mother, retorted. "Iraqi men are tyrants—much better with an Egyptian!" Her father explained how Maurice was "a very special Egyptian," a very decent man whom he completely approved of despite not being Iraqi.

There was a young British soldier Katie had danced with a few times at the Jewish Club. But an Ashkenazi was not going to be acceptable in this proud Mizrahi/Sephardi family. Although her mother, born and raised in British Singapore, would have been more than fine with a European Jew for her daughter, it was a crush with no future.

Katie cried. Then she bargained for a few "dates" to get to know Maurice. There hadn't been much conversation at the Shabbat dinners at her house. She was busy taking care of her blind grandmother, performing duties expected of her. Maurice was moved by her gentle spirit and her "sweetness and kindness" toward her grandmother.

Katie got her three "alone" dates with Maurice and a chaperone. She liked him, and decided this was someone she "could grow to love, once I got him to get rid of his pastel sharkskin suits and that mustache!" It was hard for her to "have to marry" when she was "not ready." But she had a younger sister eager for her turn, and Katie was already twenty.

The engagement party in 1945 was a huge success, with the Egyptian consulate celebrating with the young couple. The ketubah was signed and the wedding was a Western-style affair as the Jews of Bombay shed their old customs from a past they had fled.

As she hoped, Katie fell in love, sooner than she imagined she would.

IRAN

Farideh Goldin

In 1975, Farideh left the confines of her traditional family in Shiraz to become, as she advises, her "own queen" in the United States, where she is the past director of the Institute for Jewish Studies and Interfaith Understanding at Old Dominion University in Virginia. In Wedding Song: Memoirs of an Iranian Jewish Woman *(Brandeis University Press, 2003), Farideh detailed her mother's life as a child bride who gave birth to her at age fifteen. Her second book,* Leaving Iran: Between Migration and Exile *(AU Press, 2015), is based on a memoir written by her father, the refugee scion of a family of judges and leaders of the Iranian Jewish community, who still number about nine thousand living in Iran today.*

Iranian stories do not start with "Once upon a time." Rather, they start with, "Once there was a person, and then there was no one."

On a dark winter night, when I was about six years old, my grandmother told me the story of Esther, the Jewish Queen of Persia. My grandmother, Tavous, whose name means "peacock," the symbol of the Persian crown, sat cross-legged on a Persian carpet. "*Yeki bood, yeki nabood*," my grandmother started. "There was once a person, and then there was no one. Once there was a beautiful young virgin named Esther, an orphan in care of her uncle. Uncle Mordechai said, 'The king is looking for a new wife. I am taking you to the palace to be viewed. You'll compete with many exotic beauties, but if you win, who knows, maybe you'll be able to help your people in times of trouble.' And when Esther was indeed chosen as the Shah's prize, her uncle told her to stay demure, silent, and to hide her Jewish identity."

"Why did she go?" I asked. "I would not have gone."

"That's impossible," my grandmother said. "When a king decrees, the citizens obey."

"Even now?" I asked her.

Classic image of an Iranian
bride like biblical Esther

"Even now," she answered.

Not a good proposition, I thought. I would not have wanted to be one of
many in a harem, losing my freedom to silk costumes, gold, and precious
stones—what trappings! Queen Esther was afraid of speaking to her own husband. And that husband of hers didn't treat his other wife, Vashti, with love,
respect, or compassion, divorcing her, sending her away after she refused to
dance for her husband's guests, after she refused to be cheapened and humili-
ated. That wasn't a fairytale—not a "Happily Ever After" kind of a story. It was
a frightening tale of helplessness for a young girl. The story remained with me
throughout the twenty-three years I spent in Iran.

This was around the time the Shah of Iran married his beautiful queen,
Farah. We didn't have TV stations in Shiraz to watch it, but the walls of the
city were plastered with their wedding pictures. In the absence of TV, a movie
about their wedding was being shown in the theater closest to the Jewish quarter where we lived. The tickets were expensive; I couldn't see it. But pictures of
the beautiful bride with her white taffeta wedding gown, a diamond tiara, and
a very, very long, silk train, surrounded by numerous flower girls my age, were
plastered everywhere.

The bride, our new queen, had been studying architecture in Paris when
the Shah's son-in-law, who was in charge of students abroad—yes, son-in-law,
because the Shah was that much older—saw the young woman with a bright
future and plucked her for his father-in-law, the king. That was the way it was
done. The Shah had previously given his young daughter to the man who

became his son-law; the son-in-law returned the favor—or at least, that's the way I saw it. Women were commodities.

As the country celebrated their wedding, as young girls were awed by white lace, jewels, and glitter, I shuddered. She should have said no. She should have studied architecture in Paris. Like Queen Esther, Farah's uncle had facilitated her transfer to the Shah's palace by introducing her to the Shah's son-in-law. To be a queen was irresistible, I guess. She couldn't foresee her husband's demise, exile, two children lost to suicide. Maybe her mother, a widow, had persuaded her, the way Mordechai had spoken to the young fatherless Esther: "You must do this. This is for the family, for me, for your people."

When I was twelve years old, I had the chance to make a pilgrimage to Esther's shrine in Hamedan, my mother's birthplace. My uncle, who accompanied us, told me that there was a passage underneath that led to Jerusalem, a passageway to escape just in case of trouble.

I was in trouble. I was approaching puberty. My mother had been married off at age thirteen. I wanted to be in that dark passage underneath the shrine, finding my way out of Iran. I couldn't, of course. Instead, I knelt by the lattice-carved ornamental piece on top of Esther's grave, stared at her resting place, and prayed for Queen Esther's help, prayed that she would help me find a destiny different from hers.

I took Queen Esther's legacy to heart. I left Iran so as not to be subjected to the tyranny of one powerful man after another. What kind of king would be so fickle as to accept the murder of all Jews under his rule? What kind of a king would ask victims to defend themselves without the help of his soldiers? The Shah, the king who married the beautiful Farah, didn't stay in Iran during the 1979 revolution to protect us. He took his money and his jewels and his jumbo jet and let my family and many others fend for themselves.

For all Jewish girls and young women, may you live without the worry of being sold physically and spiritually in order to save yourself and your people. I pray that you will be your own queen and not the helpless princess of a fairytale.

IRAQ

Yitzhak Bakal

Yitzhak's mother and her sisters were lucky to be born to a father who valued education for women, when it must have been far from the norm in 1920s Iraq. As potential brides, however, the sisters had little to say about the marriages that their family arranged for them. Beginning with the Farhud (pogrom) in Baghdad in 1941 to the 1980s, almost the entire Jewish population, a people who had lived in Iraq since biblical times, left the country in response to violence and oppression. Yitzhak, who immigrated first to Israel and then to the United States, is a leader in the field of community-based services for youth and adults, success he attributes in large part to his mother's influence.

My mother and father were married in Baghdad in the early 1920s. My mother's father was a rabbi who saw as his responsibility the marriage of his daughters to men of character, men who were capable of supporting them and their children. My mother was educated in secular and Jewish studies at the Alliance Francaise, the finest and most selective school for Jewish students in the city. There, she must have been exposed to notions of romance and love. Nevertheless, born into a patriarchal culture, she deferred the decision of whom to marry to her parents.

As was customary then, my father was much older than my mother. His father had passed away when he was in his late teens, so he was the breadwinner for his family, running a successful business. He had no experience meeting or socializing with young women; his mother and his older sisters chose a bride for him. Traditionally, it was women's business to investigate and learn about the bride's reputation, her upbringing, and her family background. The bride's character, as well as the groom's, were most important when matches were arranged. Although the use of matchmakers to make a suitable shidduch was prevalent at that time, my mother's and father's families knew each other and dispensed with that service.

In a sense, then, there was no courtship. Before the wedding, my parents did not see each other without a chaperone. And although my mother did not participate in the decision to marry my father, I was told it was a joyous wedding. I do not know much about the wedding ceremony itself. I do know that my mother's parents were struggling financially, so the celebration must have been a modest one. My mother's father, despite his rabbinical background, worked hard as a *sofer*, a scribe of Torah scrolls. With three daughters, his concerns were to provide each with a good education and to save enough money for a dowry (*nedunia*, in Hebrew).

In the late 1940s, when I was a young teenager, I had the opportunity to attend the wedding of my mother's younger brother. Although my uncle grew up in a more egalitarian world than my parents, it was still a time of transition, a time when the new Western culture of romantic love had not taken hold. My uncle met his wife through a matchmaker. My mother and her sisters played an active role in the choice of the bride; again, the focus was on her reputation, her education, and her family's background and history.

The courtship was chaperoned by family members of the groom. The young couple was invited to the homes of many family members who reported their observations to each other. The night before the wedding, there was a henna ceremony when the bride's fingertips were dipped in henna during a celebration. After blessings and prayers by a rabbi, a *chalghi*, a group of musicians who played traditional instruments, serenaded the guests with time-honored Iraqi music. The bride was showered with love and attention by women from both sides of the family. She needed as much support as she could get: The transition from being overprotected by her family of origin to being a wife and future mother must have been hard and scary.

When I think about my family history, I realize that my grandfather's decision to educate his three daughters was courageous and foresighted. Girls were brought up to be homemakers. Yet my mother and my aunts became educated women. Although unable to engage in professions outside the home, they were major forces in directing their children, both girls and boys, toward learning. Thanks to their influence, their children became highly educated and managed to build successful careers in Israel and the United States.

LIBYA

Gina Bublil Waldman

Gina's story is longer than most in this collection, but it combines careful descriptions of many cultural elements with a compellingly frank story of her mother's life and marriage. Although the sad events of her mother's life took place in the twentieth century, they could have happened hundreds of years ago. Gina, recipient of the Martin Luther King, Jr. Humanitarian Award for her human rights activism, is cofounder of JIMENA (Jews Indigenous to the Middle East and North Africa). She and her family fled Libya in 1967.

My mother, Laura, was born in Tripoli in 1929. She was the daughter of Michal and Amos Rabba whose ancestors had been forced to leave Spain during the Inquisition of 1492. My mother's ancestors escaped to North Africa and settled in Libya. Laura looked like a Spaniard. Her long jet-black hair curled behind her ears and was twisted in a coil resting on the crest of her head. Her almond-shaped, chestnut-colored eyes gave away her shyness; she allowed herself only furtive glances when no one was watching.

Laura was the oldest of four children. When she was ten years old, the death of her father abruptly changed her life. On the day of her father's funeral, Laura's mother sat in the center of a room crowded with women relatives whose wails of grief could be heard from afar. Eyes transfixed to the ceiling, Laura's mother, Michal, looked as though she were in a trance. Her swollen eyes looked delirious as she kept repeating to herself, "It's *maktub*!"—the Arabic word for "It's written"—meaning that one's future destiny has already been prescribed by God above. Maktub has to be accepted and cannot be changed by humans, a belief Jews adopted from the Muslim customs of the country where they now made their home. Michal's agony rendered her numb. Rocking herself on the chair, she kept hitting her own face with the palm of her hands. Silence fell in the crowded room except for the occasional, "Maktub—it's your destiny, it's meant to be this way."

Laura felt paralyzed by uncertainty. She was only ten years old, and her world was crumbling. She was overcome by a dreadful loneliness. Her beloved father was dead. It was her maktub. A surge of anger came over her. If God was so compassionate, then why had she been singled out for such devastating maktub? She couldn't understand. Her feelings of betrayal rendered her inconsolable.

Michal, who had no skills and no means of supporting her four small children, was caught in a web of despair. With no other recourse, she sent Laura, her oldest daughter, to live with her sister, Regina. Aunt Regina soon pulled Laura out of school and put her in charge of the household chores. Constantly cleaning for a household of eight, Laura would bend over the wash basin for hours, her small hands turning blue from rubbing clothes against the washboard in cold water. With sadness and despair enveloping her life, Laura nevertheless accepted her fate for fear of adding to her mother's difficulties. But she never forgave her aunt for depriving her of an education.

Every Saturday after Shabbat service at the synagogue, Laura and her teenage girlfriends would walk arm in arm along the Lungomare—a promenade along the seaside. Dido, a handsome young Jewish man, would do the same, and the two occasionally glanced at each other and smiled. In those days, when touching or talking directly with the opposite sex was not accepted, Dido sent secret messages to Laura through his sister.

Occasionally, when Aunt Regina took her afternoon nap, Laura sneaked out to meet Dido in the alleyway near the apartment building in Via Leopardi. In the early afternoon hours, most people took shelter in their homes from the relentless sun. The deserted streets provided a sense of privacy and an opportunity to get to know each other. Dido and Laura fell in love. They wanted to get married and move to Israel. Dido planned to bring Laura to meet his mother, then she could ask Michal to approve a marriage between Laura and Dido, as was customary.

Aunt Regina found out from a gossiping friend and was infuriated. She had other plans for Laura. Using every cunning device she knew, she convinced her sister to have Laura marry her own son, Rahmin. They would continue to live with her. "After all, Laura is like a daughter to me," she said to Michal, with tearful eyes. Michal found herself trapped in the age-old custom of obligation taking precedence over her child's happiness. Ultimately, she should consider herself lucky to give a daughter in marriage without a dowry. In fact, Laura's dowry consisted of a hand-embroidered shirt and Michal's only valuable piece of jewelry—a beautiful gold filigree necklace, given to her as a wedding gift by her mother-in-law.

Laura knew that her cousin, a tall handsome man with green eyes and receding hair that gave him a sophisticated look, was a womanizer with many girlfriends. Why couldn't his mother pick another wife for him? Didn't he have enough girlfriends who could bring him a handsome dowry? Laura would ask herself these questions during her sleepless nights.

So a deal was struck between the two sisters. Laura was never consulted and had no right to challenge her mother's decision. "Your aunt has been supporting you. You should be grateful that she has taken you into her home, like her own daughter," Laura's mother would say. "Besides, it is maktub. Your destiny has already been written and sealed." Laura was seventeen, and her cousin Rahmin was thirty-four, double her age.

Preparations for the wedding followed according to custom. A *zeyana* (a traditional beautician) was hired to remove the bride's pubic and other bodily hair to prepare her for her wedding night. Lemon and sugar were cooked slowly until the honey-colored mixture became like wax. It was then applied to parts of the body to be cleansed of unwanted hair. When it started to dry, it was quickly yanked off, tearing out the hair painfully. "You need to suffer to be beautiful," the zeyana would say.

Next, Laura was taken to the mikveh, the ritual bath where she immersed herself seven times. Leaving the mikveh, Laura felt refreshed. The ritual had revived her soul, even if it was for a short time.

A week before the wedding, a ceremony called henna was scheduled to take place in Laura's mother's house. A ritual carried by Jews from Moorish Spain, only women participate in the henna festivities, the only all-female gathering in Sephardic tradition. The ceremony takes its name from an herb native to the Middle East, which is dried and processed into a fine powder. Coffee grounds, a raw egg, and water are added to the greenish mixture, giving it the consistency of mud. The henna is packed on the hair for several hours and rinsed off. Used for centuries in the Middle East as a dye and a conditioner, it gives the hair a brilliant sheen.

Special desserts and savory pastries filled with almond paste and dunked in honey syrup were proudly displayed on large brass trays in Laura's mother's home. The house, however modest, took on a festive air, with exotic scents of cinnamon, cloves, and orange flower water. Dates filled with roasted almonds, figs, and walnuts were laid out on a silver platter on the small kitchen table. Turkish coffee mixed with cardamom brewed in large pots.

As the hour for the henna ceremony was approaching, Laura's feeling of helplessness moved from anger to despair. Eyes moist, she looked out the window and saw her beloved Dido standing under her balcony calling her name. "Laura, Laura, *Aziza*—my dear." His voice quivered, and his face was ashen. Laura went out into the small balcony, but she was unable to speak. When her gaze met Dido's, she lowered her despairing dark eyes and went back into the house. Resigning herself, she allowed her hopes to evaporate.

It was now time to put on the traditional henna costume. She found herself encircled by a group of giggling female cousins. The traditional robe, the *zdaad*, was made from a five-yard-long, hand-woven burgundy fabric with silver threads. The shimmering burgundy cloth was wrapped and pleated as a skirt on Laura's slender body, leaving about a yard of excess to be draped over her head and shoulders, a necessity in a culture where modesty was a woman's cherished possession. Under the zdaad, Laura wore a white and lavender shirt with wide sleeves, intricately embroidered with symbols such as Fatima's hand, to protect her from the *en*—the evil eye. It was believed—and still is, in most Middle Eastern countries—that the hamsa, the hand showing all five fingers, is the best protection to ward off bad luck, another reflection of how the Jews have woven Arab customs into the fabric of their Sephardic culture.

Laura's mother, Michal, had worn the same costume at her own henna ceremony, and her grandmother, Ruth, had worn it before that. A bright pink scarf interwoven with gold threads was gently wrapped around her head to conceal Laura's beautiful black hair. Moorish-style handmade silver filigree jewelry, handed down from her ancestors, was put around her neck and arms. "*Yella*, stop crying, silly girl," her cousin said, as she attempted to smear kohl, a black powder, around Laura's brown eyes. Rouge brightened her pale cheeks.

Her face covered with a sheer, pink veil, Laura was now ushered into a crowded room. Her mother was spraying orange flower water over the guests. Laura sat at the center of the room crowded with women applauding and ululating, making the high-pitched vibrating *zaghrit* sound that Middle Eastern women make on happy occasions.

Michal, taking turns with her female relatives, applied henna to her daughter's long hair. As a sign of good luck in finding a husband, the bowl of henna was passed around the room for the guests to put on their fingertips. *"Akbal l'ilk*—May you be the next bride," young girls said to each other, as they rubbed the pasty mixture between their fingertips until they turned bright red. Laura's sobs were drowned by the rhythm of the *darbuka*—a Middle Eastern drum.

A week later, Laura was married to her cousin Rahmin. Her beloved Dido immigrated to Israel. "It's maktub, it's maktub," Laura kept telling herself.

A year later, my parents had a happier maktub: I was born.

LITHUANIA

Herb Selesnick

With 30 percent of Jewish marriages ending in divorce today, Herb's story reminds us that in past generations, not all marriages were happy ones, even if couples did not officially divorce. In the nineteenth and twentieth centuries, tens of thousands of Jews like Herb's grandparents left Lithuania for the United States, fleeing pogroms and military conflicts. Almost all of the sizable population of Jews who remained, including those from Vilna (now Vilnius), the "Jerusalem of the North," did not survive the Holocaust. Herb is a management consultant in the Boston area, where many Litvaks (Jews with forbears from Lithuania) make their homes.

My paternal grandmother, Flora, was born around 1880 in Anikst, a small town in eastern Lithuania about sixty miles north of Vilna (now called Vilnius). Flora Weinbren married my grandfather, Harry Selesnick, in 1899, soon after he returned home to Anikst from seven years of service in the Czar's army. Harry was six years older than Flora. It was an arranged marriage.

Flora's father, Jacob, owned a successful hardware business in Anikst. Just before Harry entered the army in 1892, Jacob promised, as a wedding dowry, to take Harry into his business as a full partner. At that time Flora was only twelve or thirteen years of age. Not long after Harry returned home to claim his bride and her dowry, Jacob's hardware store burned to the ground . . . uninsured!

With a newly pregnant wife and no ready means of support, Harry booked passage for South Africa where Flora's two brothers were already well established. They helped their new brother-in-law secure a position designing and supervising the construction of shafts for the diamond mines that still ring

Flora Weinbren Selesnick at age forty, c. 1920

Johannesburg. Harry came from a family of builders and was a self-taught and talented architect. In seven years, he saved enough money to leave Johannesburg, sail for the United States via London, and send for his wife and six-year-old daughter.

Flora's arranged marriage was not a happy one. Settled in the US, she had four more children between 1909 and 1917, including my father, Sydney, her secondborn. She loved baking, gardening, and cats, and had a fine singing voice. She was a sensitive soul who came from a family with musical abilities. (Her brother and a cousin became concert violinists.) Harry had the rough manner that comes from growing up in the building trades, serving a lengthy and arduous military tour as a cavalry officer in the Caucuses, and developing a tough enough persona to deter aggression from the antisemetic Cossacks in his "band of brothers."

Yet, Flora and Harry prospered in America. Throughout the 1910s and 1920s, Harry gained many residential and commercial architectural commissions and invested in real estate. He always credited Flora with sound business instincts and financial management skills, often citing a commercial building she persuaded him to buy while they were prospering. It was the only property that continued to provide them with rental income during the Great Depression.

Unfortunately, in those fateful years following 1929, they lost the rest of their real estate holdings, including their home. And shortly after Harry's sixtieth birthday in 1933, when Flora was fifty-four, they separated and never reunited.

Flora believed to her dying day that Harry still loved her. She repeatedly told her children that he would soon be coming back to her, and even called for him plaintively and hopefully on her deathbed in 1942. Her sons, angry with their father for having left their mother, never summoned him to her bedside.

MOROCCO

Yolande Cohen

A professor of contemporary history at the University of Quebec, Yolande is past president of the Academy of Arts and Humanities of the Royal Society of Canada and recipient of the title of Chevalier of the French Legion of Honor. She generously shared this excerpt from the oral history project she directed about the lives of Moroccan Jews living in Canada. The interview was conducted by Marie Berdugo Cohen in 1987. Rachel E., the subject of the interview, was born in 1926 and emigrated to Canada with her husband and four children in 1967. The story of the marriage of a young woman and her much older uncle, an uncommon union but one not prohibited by Jewish law, is one of the most unusual in this collection. We do not know the outcome of the marriage, which understandably aroused complications in family relationships.

I was born in the city of Fès and lived there until I was nineteen. I was engaged at age sixteen—or should I say that my father betrothed me at sixteen, because it wasn't I who found my fiancé: The father of my fiancé asked my father to give me to his son, the only son of a rich family. My father came to me and said, "Here is a very nice boy, the owner of his own shop, from a good family, very rich" and all that. I had no say in the matter.

So we became engaged. We celebrated the betrothal at my parents' house with a big celebration. The same evening my family went to the home of my husband-to-be, but I had to remain home with our maid and an elderly aunt. I didn't have the right to enter my fiancé's home; it was the custom that engaged young women could not enter the home of their intended husband until the marriage.

As I got to know him, I found that my fiancé was highly educated, very nice, and sweet. He was twenty-two. As he was heir to his family's fortune and his father had died, he had four "tutors" who managed his affairs. He came to see my father and asked him how to deal with these coaches. My father told him, "Listen, I'm going to discuss this with Samuel," who worked in a law office, "and get back to you." When he did, Samuel responded, "How can you give your daughter to that boy? It's not one husband who will marry your daughter, it's four—and with the real husband, it's five! These guardians have to die before your daughter's fiancé comes into his fortune. I do not advise this."

My father, a very intelligent man, succeeded in convincing my fiancé that he could not marry me. It was the end—I have never seen him since that day. It took time to get over this. It was three years before I began to go out with friends. They introduced me to boys, but I did not find what I needed.

Then Samuel, the man who had advised my father not to let me marry, approached me. He was my mother's brother, my uncle. He was thirty-eight, and I was nineteen. It was 1945 and he had just divorced his wife. He wanted to go to Casablanca and asked if I wanted to go with him. I said yes. We went to the home of his parents, who were my grandparents. I remained there for some time.

My father came to Casablanca one day on business. My grandmother left her room to make a request to my father: "Joseph, I am going to ask you something. Do not be upset by my question; whether you say yes or no will not change our relationship. I want you to ask Samuel to marry Rachel. I want you to know that whatever you decide to do, Rachel is my granddaughter and will always be my granddaughter." My father answered, "Yes, I agree."

So we were betrothed that September and married on March 13, 1946. I didn't have a say in anything. It was difficult for me only because my father had accepted for me once again. My mother was a bit more reluctant. We had some of the wedding celebrations in Fès. The whole family was invited, but it was a little complicated. My grandparents wouldn't come because the relatives of my husband's first wife were also members of the family. Everything was a bit on the sly. We had received a lot of insults. You know how it is in families. His first wife was his first cousin, and I was his niece.

We had a big get-together on Saturday with my father's family. We had a party the next afternoon to show the trousseau. Although it was right after the war, my father managed to get table settings and fabric for outfits for me, as well as gowns for the wedding, toiletries—everything. On Monday, I took a bus to Casablanca with my paternal aunts. We found everything ready for the henna party at my grandmother's house. The party had the extraordinary ambiance of an oriental soirée, with an Arab divan, singing, and dancing. My husband's boss, a Muslim, was there too.

But there was one thing that bothered me. It was the fact that I was going to go to bed with my uncle. That was the one thing I couldn't get out of my mind. Of course, I adored my uncle. I loved him, but never thought I'd marry him. I kept asking myself how I was going to go to bed with him, which haunted me throughout the preparations. I became obsessed with the idea. At the same time, I couldn't say anything to my mother.

Wednesday evening the wedding blessings were pronounced in the apartment where we would live, and the wedding ceremony took place at my grandmother's house. We went home in a horse-drawn carriage, as there were no taxis in 1946. I wore a white gown and veil. I didn't remove this veil. I kept it on until we went to bed.

TUNISIA

Aimée Aviva Cohen

Aviva's story is a poignant one. Born when her father was in his sixties and her mother well beyond usual marriage age, Aviva, a psychotherapist living in Paris, has sensitively reconstructed the progression of her parents' lives and late marriage, aided by a small black-and-white wedding photograph and, no doubt, the memories of her widowed mother. Other than the ancient enclave of one thousand Jews on the island of Djerba, most of Tunisia's once vibrant Jewish community of one hundred thousand has left for Israel or France after persecution and terror attacks from the 1940s to the present. Tunisia was the only Arab country to come under direct German occupation in World War II.

Aviva's parents Georgette and Joseph

I am lucky! I was born in Tunisia, far from Europe. I grew up in the second part of the twentieth century; I escaped the Second World War. My father was sixty-three years old when I was born, and my mother was on the verge of her forties. I should have come into the world much earlier, but that was not my fate. I was my parents' first child. It was both tough and joyful for a little girl to live as a survivor, a miracle, as well as an off-time phenomenon.

My parents' story is both tragic and fortunate—a short period, really just a few years, that transformed the lives of two Tunisian Jews from a community of people who had lived in Tunisia for millennia. My father, born in the nineteenth century, had a charmed life as a youth, if I can believe my own idealized version. An intelligent, cultivated, and handsome man, he was observant and politically engaged (his best friend and brother-in-law represented the Tunisian Zionist movement at the Basel Congress of 1924), as well as a successful businessman. He found love with a young woman of "good family," as they said then, a fine match in all respects. It was a good marriage, which, unfortunately, was not blessed with children. And then, wham!—war, failure of my father's business, and sickness and death that took away his beloved wife.

My mother, twenty-five years younger, lost her mother at a young age and her father as an adolescent. Although surrounded by the affection and protection of her extended family, she lacked a permanent home and dragged her suitcases from house to house. Hosted sometimes by her older sisters, who already had families of their own, and sometimes by uncles and cousins, she went from one refuge to another, from under one roof to another. A single woman who was without immediate family, even an attractive and buoyant one (but without a dowry), she found, as the years passed, that she was hopelessly categorized as an "old maid," the name traditional Jewish society called women who were left behind when it came to marriage.

My parents were two wounded souls who were introduced for a late marriage, almost unimaginable to both. Arranged marriages or "marriages of convenience," in contrast to love matches, were common in those years. My mother, though not leading an independent life, which was unthinkable then, still earned a living. She worked in an embroidery workshop, making the trousseaus of young middle-class Jewish girls who anticipated marriage on the arrival of puberty: bridal finery, silk lingerie, sheets of fine linen, lace bedspreads, tablecloths, and napkins finely embroidered with silver or colored thread— magnificent work of which I have a few samples. I have retained a few evocative words pertaining to embroidery: *jours* (preliminary threads in back of a pattern), *plumetis* (a type of embroidery), *festons* (scallops on the edge), *tulle* (a kind of sheer fabric).

It was in this workshop on the rue de la Marne in Tunis (the building is still there!) that my parents' destiny was joined. Madame B, the manager of the workshop, was the sister-in-law of my father, then a lonely widower. Madame B was not a professional matchmaker, but she had a feeling that this older man and this woman who was still young enough to have a child would be good for each other. Their marriage, *inSh'allah*, would avoid a sad future for both of them: the permanent celibacy of one and inconsolable widower status of the other—an unfruitful life and solitary old age for both. And she was right!

I know nothing about my parents' wedding in 1945, just after World War II. It was never a subject of discussion. Were there celebrations, oriental music,

customary merrymaking? Was there a henna party—a good-luck tradition—
the week before the wedding? Was there gluttony on traditional salty, spicy,
honey-dripping delicacies? Did anyone launch into *youyous* (ululations, trilling
of the tongue)? The bride must necessarily have gone to the hammam for the
ritual bath on the eve of her marriage.

Of the religious ceremony, the rabbinic blessing that had to be given in the
synagogue, I have only a little yellowed black-and-white photo with chiseled
edges: There is a very dignified gentleman with gray hair, a thin mustache, and
a dark suit. The bride has brown curly hair. She is wearing a long white gown
with a train and a light veil covering her hair. The mood seems serious; both
look solemn. They stand side by side without looking at each other. Their eyes
are focused on the camera. Are they happy with the turn their lives have taken?
What have they promised? What have they achieved, and what do they dream
of? What hopes do they cherish? It is for each the dawn of a new life.

My mother is finally married! She acquires a certain respectability, a lady
who carries the desirable name of a husband. For her, it represents the attain-
ment of security and stability, perhaps even prosperity, and paradoxically,
freedom: Her wandering life is finally coming to an end. She no longer has
to depend on the hospitality of others. She is going to live in her own home,
under her own roof, even if it is the first wife's house, with her furniture and
her jewelry.

For my father, it is the end of a difficult life alone, and perhaps the reawaken-
ing of hope for a descendant. Isn't the first commandment for a man to have
children, to procreate, to perpetuate his name?

My mother had five pregnancies, of which only two came to term. No doubt
they were waiting for a son, but I was very welcome—expected and desired. My
sister was born five years later. There is no doubt that my parents were courageous and heroic progenitors!

Having a father the age of a grandfather was sometimes painful, especially
leaving school at the end of the day. I was ten years old when he died tragically
on the platform of the Tunis train station on the way to his week of work as a
traveling salesman, work that he had gallantly moved into after his bankruptcy.
My sister was five years old.

My mother's married life was brief, but I like to remember that my parents
got along well, and I hope that they ended up loving each other. Until her last
day in 1997, she remembered her husband with loyalty and pride in the signa-
ture that she adopted after his death: She always preceded her name with the
honorable title, Widow.

TWELVE

INTERMARRIAGE AND INTERETHNIC JEWISH MARRIAGE

IN THE JEWISH WORLD, intermarriage usually refers to the marriage of a Jewish partner to someone of a different religion who has not converted to Judaism. (See chapter 4 in this book for conversion stories.) When Jews think of intermarriage, ideas about it are often inconsistent with ancient Jewish history. In the world of the Torah, ancient Hebrews did marry women from other groups: Abraham married Keturah after Sarah died; Jacob and Leah's son Judah married Shu'a the Canaanite; Joseph married Asenath, daughter of the Egyptian priest Potipherah; Moses married Zipporah, daughter of the Midian priest Jethro. Many of these wives and parents-in-law, such as Jethro, are described with high regard.

Not all intermarriages were looked on favorably, however. (Samson, who married Delilah, the Philistine woman, did not fare so well.) The Bible specifies seven tribes that were off-limits for marriage to Hebrews "for they will turn your sons away from following Me, to serve other gods; so the anger of the Lord will be aroused against you and destroy you suddenly (Deuteronomy 7:4)." This biblical passage is most often cited as the source of the Jewish prohibition of intermarriage.[1]

Approximately twenty-three centuries ago, when the Jews returned to Jerusalem from Babylon, Ezra the Scribe expanded the ban to include all nations and enforced it retroactively, compelling "all Judeans to divorce their foreign wives and excommunicating those who refused to comply."[2] The only marriages to non-Jews that were allowed were to women who converted to Judaism. In the rabbinic period (from the first century to the seventh century CE), the ban on intermarriage evolved into prohibiting intermarriage with *nearly all* and then *all* non-Jews. During the Middle Ages, some European states prohibited marriages between Christians and Jews. Yet, the practice of intermarriage continued.

Fast forward to the nineteenth century, when Napoleon created laws that emancipated the Jews of France and the territories he conquered. Under Napoleon's legal code, Jews could marry anyone they wished to marry. In 1808, Napoleon convened the Grand Sanhedrin (rabbinic council) who ruled that intermarriage was no longer banned. Despite these early signs of Jewish liberality toward intermarriage, these decisions were viewed—and still are viewed—as highly controversial.

Orthodox Judaism has remained adamant that mixed marriages are unlawful. For the most part, the progressive Jewish movements (i.e., Conservative and Reform Judaism) have also kept to Jewish law as codified in the Talmud, encouraging non-Jews interested in marrying its members to undergo Jewish conversion before holding a wedding. That said, many Reform rabbis will marry Jews and non-Jews even without conversion. The trials and tribulations of Jewish intermarriage have made it the butt of entire stand-up routines and books, and have raised policy issues within individual synagogues as well as the organizational heads of the various Jewish branches.[3]

In Israel, the religious ban on intermarriage is enforced by law.[4] Israel's legal code on marriage and divorce is based on the old Ottoman law, which gives Orthodox rabbis a monopoly on marrying Jews. Since there is no legal recourse to civil marriage, Jews who want to marry non-Jews must get around the prohibition by performing their nuptials abroad. When they return, usually from Eastern Europe or Cyprus, proof of their union in hand, the state recognizes their marriage. As we will see in chapter 14 on marriage issues in Israel, Israeli citizens have found ways to get around this law, although the number of intermarriages between Jews and members of other religions remains small.

Although intermarriage disqualifies individuals wishing to become Conservative rabbis, and is still highly unusual within the Orthodox community,[5] intermarriage is a common occurrence among Conservative, Reconstructionist, and Reform Jews throughout the world.[6] A Pew research study of US Jews showed that among non-Orthodox Jews who have married since 2000, 72 percent are intermarried, with slightly more former brides than grooms reporting a non-Jewish spouse.[7]

The stories in this chapter are examples of the enormous diversity of intermarried couples. Of all the bridal stories we have been privileged to learn, perhaps none represents more diversity than Sara and Annie, an "interracial, interfaith, and differently-abled" same-sex couple who shared the writing. The brief story from France by Guershon about his friends' wedding is not about a religious intermarriage, but we thought that the notable interracial wedding of Sarah and Yohanan, a leader of the Federation of Black Jews of France, belonged here. The wedding in Honduras, meticulously organized and described by Rosario, the groom's mother, included all the elements of a Jewish ceremony—with the exceptions of a rabbi and an officially Jewish bride. Ana's story from Croatia, as well as Maxine's from South Africa, suggests one of the findings of the Pew study noted above: the children of intermarried couples are more likely than not to identify as Jews. And according to Tracy's fascinating story, her interfaith and intercultural marriage and residence in Japan have kindled greater appreciation for Judaism and a desire to pass on her heritage to her child.

Although theoretically one cannot label the marriage of a Sephardi and Ashkenazi Jew as an intermarriage, the communities of some interethnic Jewish couples have seen their marriages that way. For this reason, we have included stories from Guatemala, where Deedie's grandparents were initially against her parents' courtship, and from Curaçao, where Josette and her groom had to negotiate differing customs and traditions.

CROATIA

Ana Lebl

A past president of the Jewish community of Split, the second-largest city of Croatia on the Adriatic Sea, Ana dedicates her time to organizing cultural, religious, and educational events that highlight the significant contributions that the Jewish community has made to the prosperity of her city. With the financial help of the World Monuments Fund, she was instrumental in restoring the sixteenth-century synagogue where the wedding she describes took place. Ana's family illustrates the mingling of religions before and after the breakup of the former Yugoslavia, making the terrible hostilities among countries in the Balkan region in the 1990s (at least partly based on religion) difficult to understand. Her story also demonstrates that interfaith marriages—in the US and conceivably in other countries—do not necessarily result in a loss to the Jewish community.

After World War II and the Holocaust, only 15 percent of Jews survived in the former Yugoslavia, of which half moved to Israel between 1948 and 1952. Of the seven thousand who remained, most were not observant Jews. Some had converted to Christianity, and many joined the Communist party. The majority were in mixed marriages of Jews and non-Jews.

Malvina and Omri celebrate their marriage

After the partition of Yugoslavia in 1991, each new country went its own way regarding legislation and the status of religion. In Croatia, religious marriage, including Jewish religious marriage, became fully recognized only in 2008. My parents had a civil secular wedding in 1954, as I did in 1987. There are still very few Jewish weddings, often of foreigners and mainly in the capital city of Zagreb.

When I was young, my plan was to move to Israel to look for a husband. Living in a small Jewish community, the choice of Jewish partners was quite limited. Although there were Jewish summer camps and youth seminars, probably organized to expand opportunities to find Jewish partners, few marriages resulted. In the meantime, I found a wonderful non-Jewish boyfriend and got married. We have two daughters, Sara and Tamara, unmarried students with mixed Christian, Jewish, and Muslim heritage. Although secular, their cultural and traditional identity is Jewish.

My extended family is my Jewish community of Split. When the Germans arrived in 1943, half of the three hundred members of this small community were murdered. After a third of the survivors moved to Israel, we have only one hundred members of our Jewish community left. Before Italian fascists badly damaged it, the last wedding in our old synagogue took place in 1942.

The rate of intermarriage in the post–World War II Jewish community of Split has been almost 100 percent. This does not equal assimilation, however, since many non-Jewish spouses actively participate in our communal life. Many of their children have strong Jewish identities and celebrate Jewish holidays. Some have moved to Israel, and some whose mothers are not Jewish have formally converted.

One of those converts is Malvina Maestro. Born to a Jewish father and a non-Jewish mother, Malvina was raised with a strong connection to the Jewish community. So it was not unexpected when she decided to move to Israel and fulfill the requirements for Orthodox conversion. There, she met her future husband, Omri. When they decided to marry in 2012, they agreed to have the ceremony in Split in our old sixteenth-century synagogue, restored and back in use. The ceremony was conducted by an Israeli rabbi who lives in Zagreb. Guests included Omri's family and many of their Israeli friends, as well as Malvina's non-Jewish family and friends and our Jewish community members. This was the first Jewish wedding in Split in seventy years! For our tiny community and our old synagogue, Malvina and Omri's traditional Jewish wedding was an unmistakable sign of revival and hope.

CURAÇAO

Josette Capriles Goldish

The first Jews, originally from the Iberian Peninsula, arrived in Curaçao in the 1600s from the Netherlands. They established historic Congregation Mikvé Israel-Emanuel, the oldest synagogue in continuous use in the Americas, where Josette and her husband were wed. The sand floor, one of four in the Caribbean, is well known to thousands of tourists who visit the island each year, reminders of the desert wanderings of biblical Jews and homage to Jews of the Inquisition who used sand to muffle the sound of their prayers. If you thought that Jewish grooms, both Ashkenazic and Sephardic, universally step on a glass at the end of the wedding ceremony, think again. Josette's story documents unusual local customs regarding wedding glassbreaking as well as inviting guests.

The strains of "Baruch Ha'ba" float down to the courtyard of the historic Mikvé Israel—Emanuel synagogue where I am waiting with my father to walk into the main sanctuary on the evening of my wedding. These first introductory notes coming from the organ are my cue. Remember to walk slowly, remember to smile, and for heaven's sake, don't trip when you walk in those high, high heels on the sand that covers the floor of the synagogue. Those are my main thoughts as my father pats my hand signaling that it is time to go. "Welcome in the name of G-d," sings the choir, and arm in arm we head inside where hundreds have gathered to watch the ceremony.

But then, as I enter and see all those familiar and beloved faces of family and friends, all the instructions that I have been given are forgotten. I deviate from my route to hug my Aunt Sarah whom we call Chacha, blind since years before I was born. Her husband has found her a spot right near the front at the doorway of the synagogue, and I am so happy to see her there, knowing how difficult big crowds are for her. As I continue and approach the Holy Ark where four young boys are holding up the chuppah, the choir gives way to the soprano soloist, my cousin Ethel, and all of a sudden, the beauty of her voice and the solemnity of the moment hit me.

My husband is standing under the chuppah waiting for me with our parents, two rabbis, and a cantor. He is legally already my husband because before driving to the synagogue, we stopped at the marriage registry in the Pachi de Sola building for our civil ceremony, which is separate from the religious one that is about to commence.

Sheva Brachot ceremony in the Sala Consistorial

Although to the onlookers everything may seem to be as it is always done, he and I know how much it took to agree on all the little things that go into planning a wedding; particularly this wedding between an Orthodox Ashkenazi man and a fairly secular Sephardic woman. Yes—to him walking in the procession with both his parents. No—to me walking with both of mine instead of with only my father. My mother will be escorted by her brother-in-law instead of walking on the arm of my father-in-law as would have been customary here. No—to me walking around the groom seven times. Yes—to a small pre-reception wedding dinner in the Sala Consistorial—the social hall—followed by the sheva brachot (seven blessings) traditionally recited after a meal for the bride and groom. And what do you mean the groom has to pay for polishing the brass chandeliers in the synagogue? Well, that's how it is done here in Curaçao. These chandeliers with their many candles are lit only for *Kol Nidre* and at weddings . . . if the groom has them cleaned. The chandeliers shine, and the candles are ablaze.

Although it all goes smoothly, there is a panicky moment when the rabbi turns to the best man and says, "The ring?" The best man looks around and answers, "Chicu has it." Chicu is my cousin's two-year-old son who, at the beginning of the ceremony, was holding a pillow onto which the wedding ring had been attached by a few loosely sewn stitches. He is nowhere to be found and is finally discovered behind one of the large pillars of the synagogue, playing in the sand and sitting on the pillow with the ring. We can continue!

Following a custom from the nineteenth century, invitations to Curaçao weddings in the Jewish community were never mailed or hand-delivered through the 1960s. As was customary, ours too were printed in the newspapers, and everybody who knew us or our parents showed up for the reception. We have pictures of many of the eight hundred relatives and friends who came to our reception in a private club that could accommodate the large crowd, but none of the procession into the synagogue, none of us under the chuppah, and none of Chicu sitting in the sand with my wedding ring. The photographer, a dear friend of my father's, had a little too much champagne and whiskey at the reception, and ended up losing the rolls of film he took during the religious ceremony.

Maybe we can claim one of the dents in the silver platter as proof that our wedding actually took place in this historic synagogue. My husband thought he was going to be stepping on a wrapped-up glass item to recall the destruction of Jerusalem. Not here! In Curaçao's Sephardic community, the groom throws a fine crystal glass with a strong hand onto the platter, and the people standing in front of the Holy Ark must turn away a bit so that the shattered crystal does not harm them. The congregants accompany this act by shouting *"Besiman tov!"* (may this marriage be under a good sign), and even many of our non-Jewish guests will repeat that saying.

It is only through stories like this that we can confirm that we were married in the synagogue—our *snoa*—where my ancestors worshiped since it was built in 1732. And, of course, we have several marriage certificates: the civil one that confirms that we were legally wed, an Orthodox ketubah brought from Cleveland to make sure that everything was super kosher, and the Mikvé Israel–Emanuel ketubah that confirms that, indeed, we stood there under the chuppah so many years ago.

Much give and take and more than fifty years later, we are getting old together. Occasionally, we like to look at the pictures taken on that day in July when we were married. There are many photographs that were taken at home, at the civil ceremony, and at the reception. But as we have not one picture taken inside the synagogue, we must rely on our memories.

FRANCE

Guershon Nduwa

Guershon, born in the Democratic Republic of Congo, converted to Judaism in 1995 after studying in Israel. An educator for Doctors without Borders, he is president of the 250-family Federation of Black Jews of France, which has led the struggle for recognition of Jews of color. A documentary, spurred by antisemitic polemics of a popular black entertainer, featured Guershon and Jewish leaders discussing the challenges of being Jewish and black in France. Guershon acknowledges Sarah and Yohanan's wedding as one positive sign of progress for the Federation's mission.

A wedding is always an emotional event. This wedding was especially emotional for me because the groom, Yohanan Moche Antchoue is a friend, a brother, a man faithful to his ideals, and vice president of FJN—*Fédération des Juifs Noirs de France* (Federation of Black Jews of France). This was the first time a black Jew had filled the historic Synagogue Nazareth in central Paris, as more than five hundred people witnessed the marriage of Yohanan and his bride Sarah Rose in December 2015. This was a month after a brief civil ceremony required by French law. Sarah is a white Jewish woman born in Paris who runs a family business. Yohanan was born in Gabon, the son of a mother from Ethiopia and a father from Switzerland.

Sarah and Yohanan stood under the wedding canopy and were joined according to Jewish tradition. A ketubah was signed, and they exchanged rings. A joyous reception followed at the synagogue. This kiddushin (sanctification) represented an opportunity to reflect on the meaning of two lives becoming one in happiness and spirituality. In his address, the rabbi of the synagogue, who had met with the couple to prepare and organize the ceremony, alluded to prejudices many still suffer because of their skin color. This wedding allowed us to realize that each of us is essentially divine. As this talented and successful couple wed, it signified a real victory over racism.

GUATEMALA

Deedie Karake

The Guatemalan Jewish population of about nine hundred includes German and Middle Eastern Jews like Deedie's father, who arrived at the beginning of the twentieth century and Ashkenazic Jews like Deedie's mother, who arrived from Eastern

*Europe in the 1920s. The strictures against Ashkenazic and Sephardic relationships,
which Deedie's parents faced, seem strange to us today. Such divisions were not
unusual in the past, however, and some remnants may remain, as families desire
continuity of special Jewish customs and traditions in the families of their married
offspring. Deedie, a business administrator, and her husband, Miguel, are among
the founders of the Gan Hillel preschool in Guatemala City.*

My mother, Rosa Kachler, was born in Guatemala to an Ashkenazic family
originally from Russia and Poland. My grandparents were on their way to the
United States when the ship stopped in Guatemala. They loved the climate and
decided to stay.

My father's family was Sephardic. His mother was born in Palestine, and his
father in Morocco. In contrast to my mother's family, who had been farmwork-
ers before they emigrated, my paternal grandfather was a businessman, and my
grandmother was an educated woman who spoke nine languages.

Both families had stores in Guatemala City, one behind the other. My mother's family sold shoes, and my father's family sold fabrics. Both my mother and
father worked in their families' stores when they were young, so they must have
seen each other from a distance. My father was handsome, and my mother was
beautiful and both had many boyfriends and girlfriends. My father's mother
gave Hebrew lessons at a desk in the back of her store. My mother was one of
her students. She remembered seeing a picture of her teacher's attractive son.

When my mother was fifteen and my father was nineteen, they finally met,
and it was love at first sight. A few years later, they decided to get married. But
both families were against a courtship. This was because Rosa was Ashkenazic
and Eduardo Pérez was Sephardic, from an educated and wealthier family. In
those days, Ashkenazim and Sephardim did not mix—it was like marrying a
non-Jew. They could not be seen together publicly.

But gradually, their families accepted the idea of their marriage. So when
my father's job took him to New York City, my mother joined him. They got
married at Congregation Shearith Israel, also called the Spanish and Portuguese Synagogue, in 1946. My mother was nineteen. Her father came from
Guatemala, but the trip was too expensive for her mother to come too. Both my
paternal grandparents attended. A Rabbi Goldstein officiated. I do not know
if there was a reception after the ceremony. Although it is common now and
completely accepted, this was the first Ashkenazi-Sephardi marriage in the
Jewish community of Guatemala City.

My parents stayed in New York for about a year and then returned to Guatemala. My brother was born there in 1948, and I was born in 1951. As it turns

out, my grandmother gave bar mitzvah lessons to my husband long before I met him, just as she had given lessons to my mother.

HONDURAS

Rosario Losk

Rosario, former honorary consul of Israel and founder of a Spanish language school in Tegucigalpa, the capital of Honduras, expresses unmistakable pride in her family and the part she played in her son and daughter-in-law's marriage, including accompanying her son and a mariachi band to serenade his future wife in the middle of the night. She mentions ritual parts of Cynthia and David's wedding that are widely practiced and others that are less well known. Wrapping a couple in a tallit that signifies their unity is a beautiful practice that is becoming more popular, while the semicircular arrangements of chairs for guests might be a local tradition. Author Anita Diamant (The Jewish Wedding Now, Scribner, 2017, last edition) undoubtedly would be pleased to know of her role in this newsworthy wedding.

The protagonists of this story are my son, David Leonardo Losk, and his wife, Cynthia Maria Haddad. David is a dual citizen of the US and Honduras, as I am originally from Honduras and my husband is from the US; Cynthia is a Honduran citizen. David lived in Tegucigalpa, the capital of Honduras, up to the age of nine, when our family moved to California for my husband's doctoral studies. After graduating from Boston University in 1996, David returned to Tegucigalpa to work for a few years before studying for his master's degree in business.

The night that he returned, he and Cynthia went to a party of friends they had in common. But they did not connect. Although they were sitting at the same table, David was focused on renewing primary school friendships and remeeting old friends. Cynthia thought he was a bit arrogant, so she and her friend moved to another table. A few months later, at another gathering of friends, they met again. This time she did not think he was arrogant. Thus began a lovely friendship, with lots of socializing and mutual support.

The evening before Cynthia's birthday, David decided to hire a Honduran mariachi band to serenade her, a cultural tradition for demonstrating affection. He called a number of friends to accompany him, but they were all busy. As a protective mother, I objected to him going out late and alone with a group of mariachis that he did not know. At that hour, they probably had been drinking. Meanwhile, the mariachis were in front of our house, waiting for David to give them the address and warming up their voices. I insisted that this situation was not safe. David responded, "I'm going to serenade Cynthia! If you want, you can come." That's all I needed to hear. I ran for David's car and, as we lived close to her, very soon I was in front of Cynthia's house enjoying a selection of very romantic songs. I think I am the only future mother-in-law who has accompanied her son on an occasion like that.

Soon Cynthia's parents heard the music and looked out of their window. They saw David and the mariachis and me with them. Surprised, they came out to the street to greet us. It was a nice moment and the beginning of a new friendship. I had done something different, and I think they appreciated and enjoyed the innovation; a mother will do anything to support her children.

Because our son, David, was a young Jewish man and Cynthia was Christian, once they decided to marry we sought solutions for a Jewish wedding that would be meaningful to both. We knew that many rabbis would not agree to officiate at such a ceremony, so we decided to utilize the resources at hand. My husband, David (who has the same first name as our son), had served as *hazan* (cantor) at the B'nai Israel Synagogue in San Jose, Costa Rica, and at the Shevet Achim Synagogue in Tegucigalpa, places where we had lived. He was ready and willing to officiate if David and Cynthia wished.

When she heard the news of their engagement, a dear friend sent me *The New Jewish Wedding*, a book by Anita Diamant. The book's essential message is that each couple can develop their own version of a Jewish wedding, provided that certain essential elements are followed according to our thousand-year-old tradition. That is what we did. The event was so beautiful and unforgettable that at the end of that year, one of the widest circulating newspapers in Honduras included the Losk-Haddad wedding as one of the ten most distinguished of 1999, publishing a number of photos and emphasizing the special aspects of the ritual.

In Tegucigalpa, the Jewish community is small, with limited resources. My husband selected the melodies and music for the ceremony. We then ordered the sheet music from New York and contacted a local string quartet. Its members had never played Jewish music but were willing to learn. They rehearsed with my husband, and the result was incredibly beautiful.

A few hours before the wedding, a friend, the bride's mother, and I were supervising the florist's work. The bride's mother said to me, "Rosario! Something strange is happening. There has been so much work on this wedding and everyone looks so happy. Nobody looks tired." I responded, "That's what it's about. This way everyone helps with the happiness of the bride and groom. Let's continue like this."

To begin the ceremony, a cantor we knew from Costa Rica walked down the staircase of the wedding salon, decorated with flowers and colored leaves of the season, singing "Hinei matov umanayim" in a spectacular baritone voice. It was a lovely way to announce that an exceptional event was about to unfold. An excellent local flutist had also rehearsed with my husband. When the bride entered with her parents, he preceded her, playing lovely melodies and dancing around her. It was a gracious and unexpected detail, ensuring that the bride's entry illuminated the honor that, as queen of the occasion, she deserved.

So that the guests were able to understand and follow the elements of the wedding, we prepared a pamphlet with explanations, placed on all the seats. The chairs for the guests were arranged in a semicircle in fulfillment of the custom that no bad spirits hide in the corners and ruin this special event. When she reached the chuppa, the bride did the traditional walk around the groom seven times, counted one by one.

Prior to the wedding vows, the cantor filled every corner of the salon with the lovely song, "Shalom Rav." The emotion was felt by everyone; there was no room for indifference. The ceremony included all the prayers of a traditional Jewish wedding, including the sheva brachot (seven blessings). In one of the photos, the couple appears at the moment that David's father is bestowing a traditional blessing on them. Both are covered with David's tallit as a symbol of their unity all of their lives. At the end of the ceremony, the groom broke a crystal goblet with his foot, by one interpretation to signify sorrow for the destruction of the temple and by another to signify the delicate nature of the marriage relationship, which should be nurtured and appreciated.

In a Jewish wedding, the officiant does not marry the bride and groom; they marry each other—the commitment comes from the couple. David and Cynthia happily fulfilled every step of their celebration, including the tradition of briefly retiring to their room after the ceremony for a light meal and to catch their breath. They looked happy, lovely, and radiant.

Then the dancing began. We had a live group and a DJ so that the music would be continuous. We wanted to make sure that all of our four hundred guests danced, so we hired an Israeli dance instructor to lead the Jewish dancing during the festivities. Everyone had a great time doing Jewish and Latino dances as well. The bride and groom and their mothers were raised up on chairs as guests danced the hora. "Hava nagila," "Shalom Aleihem," and all the traditional Hebrew songs were heard throughout the night and into the wee hours of the morning. And, of course, we did not forget the boleros, merengues, salsas, and cumbias. It was a beautiful, happy event, a magical evening. All the effort was worthwhile, and the lovely memories are a continuous source of joy.

JAPAN

Tracy Slater

Tracy's story is not about her wedding ceremony (which consisted mainly of signing a series of Japanese documents) but about her unusual marriage across racial, ethnic, cultural, religious, and national lines. While Jewish religious leaders typically fulminate against intermarriage, her story shows that unions of Jews and non-Jews (to say nothing of the additional diversity between Tracy and her Japanese husband) can sometimes enhance Jewish identity and that children of intermarriage can grow up Jewishly. Tracy is author of the award-winning memoir, The Good Shufu: Finding Love, Self and Home on the Far Side of the World *(Putnam's Sons, 2015) and founder of Four Stories, a global literary series in Boston, Osaka, and Tokyo.*

On a typical morning a decade ago, I would wake in my studio apartment in the South End of Boston, with the sun streaming through my large bay windows, and take stock of the life I had planned so carefully over my thirty-six years. Lying content in my soft white sheets, I'd think gratefully of the PhD in English Literature I had earned at twenty-nine, the academic career I had painstakingly built, and the fierce independence I cherished.

On most mornings, I'd linger a while, no complicated marriage or crying child to claim my attention, and luxuriate in the stillness, watching the early light bathe the brownstones of my city. Then I'd climb out of bed, shower, dress, add a swipe of mascara and lipstick, kick on my heels, and dash to my neighborhood café for the chai-soy latte that would fuel my day teaching writing at a Boston-area university.

Before leaving my apartment, I might stop a moment at the bookshelf by my door, run a finger along the spine of my feminist dissertation on gender and sexual violence in early twentieth-century literature, and feel thankful once again that I was a woman in contemporary urban America: safe, independent, and yes, overeducated. On my way out, I'd pass the *mezuzah* my mother had insisted I hang on the doorframe, its tiny Old Testament scroll shrouded in silver, ignored by both me and all my gay neighbors.

But all this changed the day I fell desperately in love with the least likely partner in the world: a traditional Japanese salaryman—who could barely speak English.

My husband and I met when his company sent him to earn an Executive MBA at the university where I taught. Within three days of meeting him, I fell in love, T's calm movements and thoughtful eyes somehow snaring my heart more completely than any man's eloquence ever had. Within three weeks, T said, "Lub you" (which I made him repeat three times before realizing this was "love" with a Japanese accent), and we were contemplating a life together across two hemispheres. Within a year—when the sudden death of his mother sent him home permanently to Osaka—I found myself in an entirely new existence, deeply entwined with T, yet utterly lost in his world.

But through it all, T's calm, quiet love sustained me. "I feel proud you," he'd say, beaming, every time I tried to take a new challenge, or embarrassment, in stride. "I love you first in world and always will," he'd assure me, and somehow that felt more like home than anything ever had. Perhaps more surprisingly, it made me, at age forty-one, optimistic enough to want to start a family with him, even though I had no idea how to manage that in a bi-hemispheric marriage, or how I, once a confirmed critic of modern motherhood's demands on women, could have come to want such a thing—and then undergo four years of rigorous hormone treatments in its pursuit.

Like many Jewish parents today, my mother feared that if I married "outside the faith," I'd lose my only chance at cultivating my ethnic identity. As the BBC put it in a news article, "Intermarriage . . . has been called a threat to the future survival of the Jewish nation."

But I'd like to propose the opposite. Marrying a Japanese man, moving to his country, and having a baby together has given me an appreciation for my Jewish roots—and fueled an insistence on passing them on—in a way few other experiences or places could have.

As someone who has strayed further afield than just across the aisle, I can tell you: Marrying and parenting across ethnic, cultural, or religious lines doesn't mute, muddy, or erase our unique identities, all the different shades of humanity, of life. Instead, if we're lucky, it expands us enough to experience new worlds that only highlight how and why we value where we—and our children—come from too.

Because I gave up my home and lifestyle for my husband's vastly different world, I'm constantly struggling in a very specific way with that fear so many of us share in love and marriage: how to ensure we don't lose ourselves, don't submerge ourselves in the other. For me, one unexpected answer has been to insist that we celebrate the Jewish holidays in on our suburban house outside of Tokyo that our child grows up with Hanukkah dreidels and haroset.

Japan will never be easy, but it proves endlessly fascinating. Perhaps, I come to realize, a life worth living doesn't always have to be easy, comfortable, or a happy reflection of one's intended plan, as long as it's filled with wonder and love.

SOUTH AFRICA

Maxine Hart

Like many South African Jews at the forefront of anti-apartheid activities from the 1960s to the 1990s, Maxine's principles concerning social justice were put to the test when she was imprisoned for them. She showed conviction in a different sphere when she married Jim, a non-Jew, in a ceremony that her Orthodox religious family could not attend. She understood their opposition to her interfaith marriage in a country where 80 percent of the Jewish population of eighty thousand are Orthodox and the intermarriage rate is only 7 percent. Happily, her marriage did not cause the breakup of family relationships: family members came to the brunch after the ceremony, and her mother hosted her son's bris.

My American-born husband, Jim, and I met in South Africa in 1990 while working for the same company, a large manufacturer of chipboard and laminate products used in homes in South Africa and around the world. This was before the end of apartheid. The CEO of the company, a progressive person, believed his company was a microcosm of South Africa, and if we could work together in the company, South Africa could work together as a society in the future. The company consisted of five thousand workers, ranging from heavily unionized ultra-conservatives to liberals, located in urban and rural areas throughout the country. We were hired in a groundbreaking mission to prove that integration could work, even in the presence of so many dynamics of conflict. Jim, a reporter, was hired to work as director of communications and I, a trained social worker and political activist, was hired to build shop floor work teams.

Six years before we met, in September 1984, I was arrested and imprisoned for four and a half months in solitary confinement for my work furthering the aims of the ANC (African National Congress). I was politicized while working as a social worker in the townships outside Johannesburg and seeing at close hand the appalling conditions people were forced to live under. For me, joining the struggle to end apartheid was not a heroic act, it was a matter of doing the right thing. As a prisoner, I was "privileged" as a white person. Despite being interrogated persistently, I was not physically harmed. However, I could only see people from the outside for a total of five hours a week. This was hard for my family and for me mentally. I was finally released and given a three-year sentence suspended for five years. I was arrested again in 1986 under a state of emergency imposed by the government and again held for two weeks in solitary confinement.

Maxine and Jim at their garden wedding

After my release, the national social work organization of South Africa, a very conservative body, wanted to take away or suspend my license to practice as a social worker because of my political activism. This angered social workers around the country who mounted a campaign to prevent this from happening. Social workers organized and started a new opposition group called Concerned Social Workers. The mainstream organization finally dropped the case against me. After earning a master's degree in education in London, I returned to South Africa and got the job with the manufacturing company, where I met my husband.

I never stopped being an activist. In 1994 I was asked by the Independent Electoral Commission to assist in the historic task of organizing the first democratic election. As the deputy director for staffing, I was charged with hiring 226,000 electoral workers. We had four months to organize this first election after apartheid.

Jim and I dated for a year and lived together for four years before our marriage in 1996. Jim is not Jewish, and my family was not in favor of the marriage. My sister is an Orthodox Jew and has eight children.

We had our wedding ceremony in our garden, conducted by a Justice of the Peace. I never wanted a big wedding as I never had a Cinderella fantasy of walking down the aisle in a white dress. My family did not attend the ceremony. I never held this against them, as they did not dislike Jim, and I am sure that my marriage out of the faith was difficult for them, given their beliefs. Each of our twenty-four guests had a part in our modest wedding. One of our friends brought the chuppah, another said a Hebrew prayer. My best friend, a Muslim woman, also said a prayer, and Jim's young son carried the ring. Other friends organized the flowers and the music. I walked around Jim seven times, and he broke the glass. Then we had a catered brunch in the garden that my family attended.

I identify as a Jew. I go to shul services on the High Holidays and have a regular Pesach seder. Our son had a bris in Johannesburg performed by a mohel, and he also had a bar mitzvah. The rabbi who performed the bris had no problem with our interfaith marriage: He said a bris represents a covenant between God and the child. My mother hosted the event.

We came to live in Jim's hometown near Boston in 2002 after having lived five years in Mexico City, where Jim was bureau chief for the *Los Angeles Times*. I am senior vice president of human resources for a community bank.

UNITED STATES

Annie and Sara Goldsand

Annie and Sara's story exalts the advantages of meeting potential partners online. Who can say if Annie and Sara, so different outwardly but lovingly akin emotionally, would ever have met before the internet? According to a large-scale study (Cacioppo, et al., Proceedings of the National Academy of Sciences, 2013), a third of US marriages between 2005 and 2012 began with online dating. The researchers did not report on the religion of respondents, but almost everyone knows of someone who met their spouse through JDate. Sara and Annie are one of more than 125,000 same-sex couples who have been married legally since the historic 2015 Supreme Court decision. While Orthodox rabbis do so rarely, rabbis of progressive branches of Judaism now routinely officiate at same-sex weddings. Annie and Sara are now parents of two daughters.

ANNIE: I was born in Chicago and have lived in Arizona since the first grade. I met Sara in August 2010. Before our initial meeting at Starbucks for a cup of coffee, we chatted online and on the phone. We bonded over our teenage obsession, the boy band *NSYNC, and our deep devotion to our families. I was living with friends at the time and had just received a job offer after finishing school. I was struck by Sara's kindness, beautiful smile, and sense of humor. Sara tells me that she was struck by my character and openness in my online profile, explaining my disability and outlook on life. The two of us dated for a few months before officially becoming a couple.

We spent our first New Year's Eve in Palm Springs, California. Soon after, we moved in with one another. After dating for three and a half years, I proposed to Sara in my parents' backyard. The beautiful part was that everybody helped put together the proposal. Both of our families joined us in celebration of our engagement.

SARA: As untraditional as I boast that we are, Annie does have some traditional ideas that were important for her to act upon. Before our engagement, Annie had conversations with both sets of parents, and even asked my parents for their blessing. She then set out to orchestrate the most amazing evening of our lives (only to be outdone by our beautiful wedding).

Unbeknownst to me, Annie, her sister, her sister's boyfriend, and her parents changed her parents' backyard into a gorgeous romantic landscape. There were candles lining the sidewalk and illuminating the pool; white fairy lights were hanging everywhere, conveying a winter wonderland. After a few white lies, I

Engaged couple Sara and Annie

was coaxed into the backyard. Annie's proposal was meaningful and beautiful. We had dinner, danced, and shared a bottle of wine. Then we were joined by both of our families for dessert and celebration. Our engagement was received with love and was a true family affair.

ANNIE: Over the next two years, we spent time planning our dream wedding with our friends and family. On November 7, 2015, we were married at a hotel in Scottsdale, Arizona. Only a few months prior to our wedding, gay marriage officially became legal in Arizona. We were thrilled to add $76 to our wedding budget for our marriage license!

SARA: Because Annie and I are not a traditional couple in any sense of the term, we found that we had leeway to customize our wedding ceremony. We were married under a chuppah to represent Annie's beliefs and heritage and as a way to symbolize the home we will build. This was important to us, as we intend to raise a Jewish family. During the ceremony, we and others spoke of our past as individuals and as a couple, how our families shaped the women we are today, and the marriage equality laws that had been passed just months before our big day. We wrote our vows to each other, and at the closing of the ceremony, we exchanged rings and I proudly broke the glass. We were thrilled with the way our officiant, Annie's cousin, conducted the ceremony.

Annie was born with spinal muscular atrophy. This has never hindered her or her family from their firm belief that she is as capable as anyone else. My wife is proof that "disability" is really a mindset. I am so proud of the woman she is and grateful that our kids will have such a role model. When we got married, I changed my name to Goldsand. Needless to say, we have had a lot of fun confusing people!

ANNIE: Our wedding day was the happiest day of our lives. We spent it dancing and celebrating our love for one another and everybody we adore. We are an interracial, interfaith, and differently-abled couple. We celebrated our uniqueness, and everyone who joined us on that very special day felt our sense of joy and deep devotion to one another. We honeymooned in the Caribbean.

THIRTEEN

—⚏—

WARTIME AND POSTWAR
WEDDINGS

THE STORIES IN THIS CHAPTER are among the most moving in this collection. They demonstrate the determination and fortitude of women and men to forge loving relationships, support each other, and formally establish their partnerships in Jewish ceremonies under the most challenging circumstances imaginable. These remarkable stories remind us how personal history is inextricably bound by political world history. The Holocaust and World War II are life-altering realities in these wartime stories.

It happens that the majority of narratives in this chapter are from Scandinavia—Norway, Sweden, Denmark, and Finland (which, while not officially a Scandinavian country, is often grouped with them). Many of the brides and grooms found safety in neutral Sweden, where seventy-five hundred Danes, fifty thousand Norwegians, and forty-eight thousand Finnish children, as well as thirty thousand survivors of Nazi concentration camps, found refuge during World War II and after.[1] These dramatic stories show the intersection of personal and political history in this part of the world, a history of World War II and its aftermath that is relatively unknown.

The Holocaust covered a broad swath of time and geography. Hitler published his antisemitic manifesto, *Mein Kampf*, in 1924, and at the height of his power in the late 1930s and early 1940s, he controlled most of Europe and North Africa. The Hitler years of deprivation, austerity, and uncertainty constituted a long period in which it was extremely difficult to marry. And yet, many Jews did marry. They consecrated their relationships with hope for a better world, and they created weddings with ingenuity.

Brides who married during World War II had to be resourceful amid scarcity and insecurity. The Jewish bride in wartime Finland, for example, wore a wedding dress made of parachute fabric. (Soon after the ceremony, her new husband left to fight at the Eastern Front.) Similarly, the bride from England made her own dress and hat for the wedding ceremony before a feast of usually unobtainable goodies. She and her groom were unable to live together for a year after the wedding.

Many of the stories in this chapter describe even more devastating circumstances due to conditions of war, both before and after the nuptials. The story from Norway describes a bride ironing her wedding gown in tears. A refugee in neutral Sweden, she and her sister were lucky to escape their homeland. Hundreds of Norwegian Jews, including the bride's father and more than a dozen other relatives, did not survive in the aftermath of Hitler's invasion. The unusual story from Denmark describes a sumptuous kosher wedding and honeymoon in 1942, largely free from the impact of war. But only a few months later, with "the goose in the oven," the newlyweds had to flee, escaping through a series of harrowing ordeals. Shulamit Reinharz's parents, natives of Germany, spent the war years in hiding in the Netherlands. Unsure they would survive (only a quarter of Dutch Jews did), they married after the war, first in a civil ceremony, then a religious one months later when they could find a rabbi.

The poignant stories by two sisters, natives of Romania who wed in Sweden after the war, show the remarkable resilience, strength, and hope for the future that so many survivors of the Holocaust exhibited despite the horrors they had experienced. The modest weddings of both sisters, filled with both sadness and joy, represented getting on with life. Both sisters, matriarchs of multigenerational families, expressed the same message in their stories: Hitler did not exterminate us!

The story from Israel represents a different wartime experience from others in this chapter. In the shadow of the Holocaust, Jews sometimes used marriage as a way to escape Europe.[2] Some fortunate Jews, those lucky enough to obtain scarce "certificates" that allowed them to immigrate to British Mandate Palestine, obtained false documents for "wives" to accompany them. Some of these fictitious couples did form marital relationships when they came ashore; others, like the "bride" in the emblematic story recounted here by her granddaughter, did not.

DENMARK

Rabbi Bent Lexner

Bent Lexner is former chief rabbi of Denmark. His story presents a personal view of Denmark's remarkable history during World War II. After the Nazis invaded and occupied the country in 1940, they allowed the Danish government and its institutions to function much as before. Thus, Bent's parents' elaborate wedding could take place in 1943 when, as he notes, Jews in the rest of Europe were in the throes of catastrophe. The legend that the Danish king wore a yellow star in defiance of the Nazis describes the spirit of the country but has no basis in fact. (Danish Jews never wore the star.) However, the Danish clergy, government officials, and ordinary citizens did, indeed, conspire to save their Jewish neighbors when word came down to arrest and deport them. We are fortunate to have an account of the Jews' escape by sea to neutral Sweden from one of the participants—Bent's mother, one of seven thousand Danes who evaded the Nazi's "Final Solution."

My parents married in Copenhagen on February 7, 1943. Please notice the year: a Jewish wedding in the middle of the Holocaust. We are sitting on my mother's balcony in the center of Copenhagen as she tells me her story more than seventy years later, and we are astonished that it was possible to hold an elaborate Jewish wedding while Jews in the rest of Europe were victims of the worst catastrophe in two thousand years.

My parents' story begins at the start of 1942. My father's best friend, a non-Jew called Kurt, was getting married. My father, who was born in Copenhagen of Jewish parents who had emigrated from Russia in the early 1900s, was, of course, invited to the wedding. Kurt suggested that he bring along a girl.

My father had often visited my mother's home because her brother was one of his good friends. There had not been any romantic feelings between them, probably because my father was seven years older. Nevertheless, my father asked his friend's little sister if she would accompany him to the wedding.

My mother said yes, and several months later, they became engaged. My mother, whose family originated in Lithuania and was one of five siblings, remembers that her future in-laws organized a big gathering at a posh restaurant in Copenhagen to celebrate the engagement. Her father had died a few years before.

Despite the fact that Denmark was occupied by Nazi Germany, the everyday life of the Danish Jews was quiet and safe at that time. There were limits to what Danish citizens were allowed to do, but there was no difference between Jews and the rest of the Danish population. Jews were thoroughly integrated into Danish society; Christian and Jewish Danes were all "countrymen."

Because of a curfew after dark, the wedding took place at Domus Medica in Copenhagen, a place you could rent for special events, in the middle of the day. Chief Rabbi Max Friediger officiated. My mother was led to the chuppah by her mother and her brother, while my father was accompanied by his parents. About sixty guests, family and close friends, attended the ceremony—all dressed in their very best. (The Swedish members of the family could not participate because it was impossible to travel between Denmark and Sweden.) My mother wore a long white dress, sewn by a dressmaker, and carried a bouquet of white carnations. Her veil was a present from a friend who had recently married. My father wore tails and a top hat. Three *chazanim* (cantors), who were employed at the Synagogue of Copenhagen, sang at the ceremony.

The fish dinner was strictly kosher. One of my father's friends filmed the wedding, and before the party was over, he came back and showed the film to the guests. We still have it in black and white with no sound. The next day, the newlyweds took the train to a well-known hotel about fifty km from Copenhagen, where they spent a few nights. (When my parents celebrated their twenty-fifth wedding anniversary, they went back to the hotel with my wife and me and my two brothers.) They received many generous presents, including a silver cutlery set for twelve and furniture for an entire dining room.

But the quiet times did not last. On *Erev* Rosh Hashana that same year, my parents received a phone call from my grandmother. She somewhat confusedly told them that they should return anything that they had borrowed from anyone. On that day, the Jews of Denmark had been warned that an action against them would take place. They should not stay at home. My parents left their apartment while the goose was still in the oven. Their non-Jewish helper received a message that she could take anything she wanted without any questions.

The first couple of nights they were sheltered by Kurt, the friend whose wedding had initiated my parents' first date. They were told that the Swedish embassy was issuing passports. "We took a car to the passport office," my mother remembers. "When we got there, we were met with a terrible scene—a sea of people, weeping and in despair. Never in my life have I seen a similar tragedy." There were no passports at the embassy. It was a false rumor put into circulation by the Germans. "We hired a car and set off again. We did not know which moment all of us would be surrounded by the Gestapo. My father-in-law paid his entire fortune to a broker who said he would get us across to Sweden. But the fisherman who was supposed to take us turned out to be an impostor.

We managed to get some money back and tried again." The second time the crossing was thwarted when German patrols showed up at the port. The third time, as the family fled into the night, with help from friendly people, "wet and exhausted, we finally arrived in Sweden."

My parents lived in Sweden for a year and a half until the war was over. My father found work with an organization that took care of Danish refugees and saw to it that they had decent living conditions in the Swedish camps that had been set up for them. My mother worked with children and received a small monthly pension from Sweden.

Finally, in May 1945, they returned to Denmark, where they recovered all of their belongings. Their non-Jewish friends had taken good care of everything. The efforts of the Danes to save the seventy-five hundred Jews in their midst is world-famous. Approximately five hundred Jews were caught by the Nazis and sent to the Teresienstadt concentration camp. Of those, fifty-four mostly elderly perished in the camp, and only one single Danish Jew was transported to the gas chamber. The rest, like my parents, came home after the war and were welcomed back to Denmark.

ENGLAND

Rosalind Dobson

Rosalind's story reminds us that wedding celebrations of determined, resourceful, and optimistic couples and their families take place even during times of deprivation and uncertainty. Rosalind, who must have inherited her parents' can-do attitude, lives on the Isle of Man (between England and Ireland), as well as in Haifa, Israel. She is founder and chair of the Isle of Man Friends of Israel group. Her work history began at age nine as a salesperson in her parents' clothing shops and includes experience as a speech therapist, a publisher, a Weight Watchers lecturer, and a fire-eater's assistant.

During the Second World War, life was hard, especially for those from poor families. When my parents, Hilda Silverstein and Joe Kersh, decided to get married on November 17, 1942, they faced a number of difficulties. They had little money, and many goods were rationed or impossible to obtain at any price.

My father promised his fiancée that one day he would buy her a beautiful diamond ring and build her the house of her dreams. Meanwhile, he purchased an engagement ring, gold with a tiny diamond chip, at a second-hand shop for

£5 and a new wedding ring for £12. And, as he was a poorly paid army private, he talked the rabbi into setting a lower price to conduct the wedding.

Wedding attire was another issue. While my father was able to wear his army uniform, my mother's outfit presented a far more difficult challenge. At that time, few brides married in a long white gown, preferring a smart dress, which could be worn afterward. After a determined search, my mother eventually found some fabric in a dusty pink shade at the local open-air market, using some of her ration coupons to purchase it. Fortunately, she was a seamstress and able to make her own pattern, then fashion the dress at home after work. She also, bravely, made her own hat, covering it with the dress material—the first time she had ever attempted this. Dark wine leather shoes, which she already owned, a matching handbag made by one of her brothers, and a corsage of pink and white carnations completed the outfit—no bouquet, no synagogue choir, and no bridesmaids, as the budget wouldn't stretch to cover such expenses.

The bride traveled by taxi to the Montague Road Synagogue in London, a short distance from where she lived with her family. One of her brothers walked her down the aisle, as her father had passed away four years before. After a traditional Orthodox Ashkenazi ceremony lasting twenty minutes, the couple visited a local photography studio for a single wedding photo. Then they returned to my grandmother's home for a buffet reception.

In spite of the many restrictions, the family provided a fine spread for forty friends and family: homemade gefilte fish, fried fish, salads, small cakes, and candies, including an "unobtainable" box of fudge (evidently purchased by an aunt on the black market—no one asked about its provenance!). My grandmother supplied a baker with dried fruit and sugar from her grocery store. These hard-to-obtain ingredients enabled him to produce a simple one-tier wedding cake covered in plain white icing.

The reception over, *callah* (bride) and *hatan* (groom) donned their coats and caught a bus to the Strand Palace Hotel in London's West End, where they spent their three-day honeymoon. After that, my father went back to his army unit in Yorkshire while my mother returned to her childhood home. It was a year before my mother was able to join my father in Yorkshire to share their first home together in a small rented bedsitter.

Armed with nothing more than determination to succeed and the ethic of hard work, theirs was a successful union. They eventually opened prosperous businesses, and in the course of time, my mother received both her ring and her dream house. The marriage lasted for fifty-six years until my father's death in 1998.

FINLAND

Karmela Bélinki

The Helsinki Synagogue, where Karmela's parents were married, was inaugurated in 1906, a dozen years before Finland's small Jewish community gained full citizenship. It remains one of two synagogues in the country, the other in Turku, the city where her parents met during World War II, a complex period of Finnish history. Although Finland sided with Germany, it retained its democratic independence, fought only against the Soviet Union, and, as Karmela notes, did not persecute its Jewish population. Interestingly, in a country that adored open-air dancing in pavilions that dotted the country, it was the only one that banned dancing during the war. Later, dancing resumed and became the most popular way to meet a future spouse.

My parents met at the beginning of 1941 in Turku, called Åbo in Swedish. (Double names stem from the official bilingual status of Finland, both Finnish and Swedish.) My mother had lost her home in the bombardment of Turku-Åbo in the so-called Winter War of 1939 to 1940, a military conflict between Finland and the Soviet Union. Likewise, my father, who had been in the Finnish army, had to look for a new life as his hometown was lost to the Soviets after the armistice. So they were both starting from scratch when they met and were aware that a new war was on the horizon.

My father was mobilized again and war was once more a certainty when they became engaged in the summer of 1941. They wanted to get married as soon as possible but had to wait until late December because of the military situation, as well as Jewish and Christian holidays.

Although Finland was not occupied during World War II, and there was no persecution of Finnish Jews, there was a shortage of everything in wartime Finland. For her wedding, my mother wore a very pretty white silk dress—made of parachute fabric. My father got special permission to wear a civilian dark suit instead of his uniform. Obtaining a bridal bouquet in midwinter wartime Finland was nearly impossible, but my mother had a beautiful one of small roses and lily of the valley.

My parents were married in the synagogue and had a reception in the community hall. Food was also a big problem in wartime Finland, but somehow that was solved too. Thanks to community efforts, there were sandwiches, wine for the kiddush, a cake, and even real coffee, a special treat. There was no dancing, as it was prohibited in wartime.

Karmela's parents Itele and Sami on their engagement

My mother, who had graduated as an economist before the war, was happy to be married. But in pictures taken for the occasion, worry about the future is apparent in the couple's eyes. After two days of honeymoon in a resort in the central part of Finland, my father returned to the Eastern Front and my mother to her office job. It wasn't until 1945, when my father was demobilized, that my parents got their first home together.

Like so many other wartime couples, my parents got to know each other through their correspondence. They left several thousand letters that are now in my possession.

ISRAEL

Merav Levkowitz

The story of Merav's grandmother's first "fake marriage" would make a good plot for a movie, especially its coda at the end. Grandmother Ahuva was one of the lucky, foresighted, and/or Zionistic Jews who left Poland to emigrate unofficially with the rise of antisemitism in the 1930s. Her grandfather Mordecai's journey on foot from the Polish army to Romania, and then on to Israel in its birth years, is also the stuff of movie plots. Merav obviously descends from people with a lot of spunk. An editor and writer who grew up in Massachusetts, she returned to her grandparents' adopted homeland, where she met her husband on Tinder and married in Tel Aviv in 2017.

When I think of the words *marriage* and *wedding*, I think of poufy white dresses and big family gatherings with a band and lots of dancing. For my paternal grandmother, Ahuva (yes, we called her by her first name), the association was probably quite different.

Ahuva's first "marriage" in 1935 was a fictitious one. She was eighteen. Rather than being a family-filled affair, it was just a piece of paper that allowed her to leave her home—a false document of marriage to an acquaintance from her hometown. This paper marked the end of her life in Poland, an eternal separation from her family, and the beginning of a new life in the budding Zionist land. There was no honeymoon. Upon reaching the British Mandate of Palestine, Ahuva bid her "groom" farewell, never to see him again. (Several years before she died at age eighty-seven in 2004, she became obsessed with trying to find him. Internet searches weren't what they are now, and when my uncle finally found a phone number and Ahuva called, the man's family informed her that he had died the week prior.)

In the years following her big move, Ahuva lived with relatives in Tel Aviv, serving as the fetching young salesgirl at their bakery. Unhappy being just a pretty face and eager to contribute to her new homeland, she left them, rented a room alone in Rehovot, and found a job in the groves, picking Jaffa oranges. Then she worked several different jobs in Kibbutz Ginegar, in the Jezreel Valley. Though she liked the lifestyle, she saw little future there as the only unmarried female in a community of families. In 1941, on hearing about a grocery store that was looking for workers in Haifa, Ahuva picked up and moved once again, this time to the port city.

It was there, at the store, that she met Mordechai. Mordechai had been drafted into the Polish army on September 1, 1939, when World War II broke out. At the end of the month, he defected and walked from Tarnow, Poland, to Constanța, Romania, about eleven hundred miles! The story goes that he bribed his way onto a ship carrying cattle to Palestine. When the ship reached Haifa's port, he emerged, somehow wearing the uniform of one of the crew. We can only imagine the surprise on his sister's face when, in an era of no phones, not to mention email or WhatsApp, he appeared on her doorstep in the middle of the night in December 1939.

Mordechai joined his brother-in-law and became a partner in his Haifa grocery store. Ahuva showed up there in 1941, and the rest, as they say, is history. Except not—because over the course of the seven years that followed, Mordechai asked Ahuva, over and over again, to marry him. And she, over and over again, refused. A free spirit with more than a decade of independence, she wasn't ready to be tied down to a husband and a household just yet.

And speaking of independence, finally, in 1948, the night before he set off to fight in Israel's War of Independence, Mordechai knocked on Ahuva's door. "If I don't come back, everything I have is yours," he declared. Ahuva was forced to admit that she was thirty-one years old, and certainly not getting any younger, and that she did—eventually—want a family and children. When Mordechai returned from the war, they celebrated their marriage in Tel Aviv with a very simple wedding ceremony followed by a luncheon (no orchestra or dancing!) hosted by her bakery-owning Tel Aviv relatives and attended by the few other scattered family members on each side. Although the relatives had offered to put on a bigger wedding, lavishness wasn't Ahuva's style, nor was accepting such a big gift or celebrating so much in the shadow of the Holocaust.

And that's how Israel gained her independence, and our modern-day Jacob got his orange-picking Zionist bride.

NORWAY

Irene Levin

In her compelling personal story, Irene describes the wartime treatment of Jews under the Nazi collaborator Vidkun Quisling that culminated in the transportation and murder of about 50 percent of the Jewish population, her family among them. Her mother and aunt were among the approximately nine hundred Norwegian Jews who escaped over the border into neutral Sweden, helped by friends, neighbors, the underground, and their own resourcefulness. Today, the community is small but active, with synagogues in Oslo and in Trondheim. Irene, emerita professor of social sciences at Oslo University, is the author of the widely praised book in Norwegian, We Did Not Talk about Holocaust: Mother, I and the Silence *(Gyldendal publisher, 2020).*

"I remember how she cried when she was ironing her wedding dress," her sister recalled years later. The two sisters had fled from Norway to neighboring Sweden. The year was 1943, and the month was February. Norway had been occupied by Germany, while Sweden remained neutral. One sister was pregnant with her first child, while the other was about to get married. Both events are usually associated with joy. That was not the case for these two, however.

The reason for their distress was the arrest of their father three months before, the same day he was deported to Poland on the cargo ship Donau. At that time, they did not know that after his arrival in Stettin, Germany, a seaport on the Baltic Sea, he would be transported in a cattle car to Auschwitz. The bride ironing her wedding dress had never heard of Auschwitz. She only knew that the situation was not good. On the ship Donau were not only her father but also thirteen other close family members including her grandmother, aunts, uncles, and cousins. Worry overshadowed any possible feelings of joy.

The situation for the Norwegian Jews had gradually become worse as time went on after the German invasion on April 9, 1940. In the beginning, Jewish and non-Jewish Norwegians were treated more or less the same, if Jews a bit worse. If someone were arrested, he or she was usually released after a month or two unless politically active in resisting the German occupiers and their Norwegian collaborators. A few were executed, some were imprisoned in Norway, and others were sent to concentration camps in Germany.

October 26, 1942, represented a critical line of demarcation in the wartime history of Norway. On that day, an arrest order was announced for all Jewish men over the age of fifteen. They could no longer be in the streets, in their

Frida and Leon Leimann, Irene's aunt and uncle, on their wedding day in
Stockholm

homes, or at work without fear of arrest. Jewish women were required to show
up each day at the nearest police station. Bank accounts and property belonging
to Jews were confiscated.

The two sisters had done all they could to help their male family members.
Their father was placed in a hospital with their help. He pretended to be ill;
hospitals were considered safer than elsewhere. The head of the hospital knew
what was going on, but attempted to rescue Jews in this way.

But a month later, a new arrest and deportation order was announced. This
time it targeted *all* Jews, including women and children. The father of the two
sisters was among 529 Jews loaded and imprisoned aboard the ship Donau and
murdered in Auschwitz. In four deportations, almost eight hundred Norwegian

men, women, and children were killed—more than 50 percent of Norway's Jews, the highest percentage from a western European country after the Netherlands.

The two sisters managed to escape to Sweden in different groups using different routes. They knew how much their father had looked forward to the wedding and the birth of his first grandchild, hence their tears.

In order to marry in a Jewish ceremony, the bride and her fiancé, who had escaped separately, traveled to Stockholm by train from the small town where they had been sent as refugees. No one was present at the wedding except a rabbi and the cousin of the bride. After the ceremony was over and they were having dinner at a nearby restaurant, the bride received a telegram: Your sister has given birth to a girl! The date was February 11, 1943. The baby was me.

SWEDEN

Hédi Fried

Hédi's moving and intimate memoir about the heartbreaking meeting with her husband-to-be, their courtship, and their modest wedding brought tears to our eyes. An author and psychologist, an icon in her community and around the world, Hédi has been honored by Sweden, Romania, and Germany. She was named European of the Year in 1997 and won the prestigious August Prize for the best Swedish nonfiction book in 2017. Her story exemplifies the ability to renew life after surviving the worst of humanity's horrors. Equally, it shows the power of loving attachment to overcome "rational" obstacles to marriage.

I was born in 1924 in the small Romanian town of Sighet in Transylvania. I grew up in a middle-class Jewish family. When Hungarian troops took over Transylvania in 1940, I had to leave my school, where Jews were no longer allowed, one year before graduating, to transfer to a Jewish school in another town. Still, although there were restrictions, life went on much as before. In the evenings, my parents enjoyed playing rummy. One of the card players was a lawyer everybody called Premze. I hardly noticed him.

March 19, 1944, German troops entered Hungary. Two months later we were in Auschwitz. My parents were taken to the left, my sister, Livi, and I to the right. April 15, 1945, British troops liberated Bergen-Belsen where my sister and I had been taken and where we waited for death.

I was hoping that my father had survived. The day after the liberation, I started to roam the camp in search of him. Crossing formerly isolated areas through torn barbed wire, I saw men and women outside their barracks, lying in the mud, covered with lice. Walking on, I came across some men sitting around a fire, baking potatoes. One of those was Premze, the lawyer from Sighet. We recognized one another, and to my question he could only shake his head, saying that my father had never had a chance to enter Auschwitz. Then he told me that his younger brother, Josko, had died just a few days before the liberation. We sat there mourning, speechless, gazing into the fire. Before I left, he generously gave me some raw potatoes.

Time went on and a Swedish team arrived to collect survivors for recovery in Sweden. I arrived in Malmö with Livi and our cousin Zsuzsi. We were placed in a school for six weeks of quarantine. One day I was told that a visitor was asking for me. It was Premze, who was looking for an older cousin of mine. We exchanged a few words and he left. Our next meeting was a few months later on a street in Stockholm. He told me that he had just been released from a tuberculosis sanatorium and that he had a job at the office of the World Jewish Congress. We exchanged telephone numbers, said goodbye, and parted.

At that time, I was living with Marianne, a Swedish girl my age who took me in when I had nowhere to stay. When I told her about our meeting, she prompted me to invite Premze for a cup of tea. So the next Sunday, we were a pleasant threesome. Marianne was very impressed by this dashing young man. It was the first time, looking at him through her eyes, that I stopped thinking of him as an old man of my parents' generation.

This meeting was followed by several more. Suddenly, I found myself in love with this man eighteen years my senior. We had great fun together and lots to talk about—the past, the present, books, music, art, all that we had missed and had to catch up on. I felt that I had found the man I had always hoped to find, someone I could share my life with. We saw one another more and more often, and one day I understood that he shared my feelings.

But there were times when he seemed unreliable, when he did not call or did not show up for a date, but then later he would be as loving as before. At last, he told me that he had a problem with the difference in our ages, that I was too young, and that he felt wrong by tying me down. He urged me to find a younger boyfriend. But I did not enjoy the company of other men. We kept on this way for a couple of years. Finally, in the spring of 1948, we decided to part for a time. Then, if we still wanted to be together, we would marry.

At that time, one of London's Orthodox communities invited survivor girls to apply for Yiddish teacher education training, all expenses paid. So I left for England, knowing that I wanted to live my life with Premze, either as his wife or his mistress. It did not take many weeks before I received a letter: "Come back, let us get married." I explained the situation to the headmaster, bought a wedding dress of the latest fashion, and left.

Premze, whose name was actually Michael Fried, arranged the technicalities and logistics, securing the necessary papers while I discussed the upcoming wedding with my sister. We had hardly any money, so it had to be very simple. Michael did not want to be wed at the Great Synagogue of Stockholm, as this was a progressive one, had an organ, and much of the liturgy was in Swedish. We decided on a secular wedding at the town hall followed by a Jewish one. The Jewish wedding was to be held at the home of his landlady, Mrs. Kleinbord, with his friend, the Norwegian Rabbi A. I. Jacobsson, officiating. It was to take place the day of my twenty-fourth birthday, June 15, 1948. I could hardly wait.

Finally, the day arrived. I woke up early and dressed in my finery. Time passed slowly. I sat nervously, following the hands of the clock, willing them to move more quickly. At eleven o'clock, we were to meet at the entrance of the town hall. At last, it was time to leave. I had a last look in the mirror, feeling very elegant in my deep-blue two-piece Dior "New Look" dress. I put on the hat I borrowed from my friend Ella, the same hat every one of us wore when getting married. My shoes were not exactly the high-heeled ones the dress called for, but they were nice. Now I had everything: something old, something new, something borrowed, something blue. I went to the bus thinking that by now Michael would be waiting impatiently for me.

But when I arrived, Michael was not there. Time passed and there I was, waiting together with the witnesses—my sister and brother-in-law, and Michael's two colleagues. As we waited and waited, I became more and more nervous. Did he chicken out?

After some time, agitated and guilty, he hurried in, handing me a bunch of lilies of the valley. He had been searching for a flower shop selling roses. He absolutely wanted me to have roses at our wedding. I assured him that I loved the small lilies more than roses, and finally, we went into the Hall to be wed. After the short ceremony, we went back to Michael's place to prepare for the religious ceremony that would be performed later that afternoon.

We found the landlady, Mrs. Kleinbord, an elderly Swedish-Jewish woman, cooking and baking, not knowing how to sufficiently spoil her favorite lodger. By four o'clock, the few guests arrived—my sister Livi and her husband, Hans, my friend Marianne, and some colleagues of Michael's. We had a minyan plus a few women. Rabbi Jacobsson, a good friend of Michael and an emigree from Norway to Sweden, had great empathy with us. Four men held a tallit above us, and the ritual proceeded according to the rules. After a beautiful speech, Michael crushed the glass, and there we were—wed! Mrs. Kleinbord invited us to a sumptuous table, we emptied a couple of bottles of wine, we sang and danced, and were happy, though the past lingered about, not unnoticed. I thought that this happiness would last forever, that we would never lose each other.

The honeymoon lasted only a couple of days, as Michael was sent to a conference in Zürich and I could not join him since we had no money for my fare. He promised a belated honeymoon, and the following winter he arranged two weeks at a ski resort in the north of Sweden. There, we passed one of our most enjoyable times together, skiing during the sunny days and sitting by the fire in the evenings.

But Fate was not content with the tragedies in my life. It had to strike once more. In 1962, after fourteen years of happy marriage, Michael died, leaving me with three small children—Gabriel, age eleven, and Tomas and Kaj, age nine.

Still, Michael is present even today. I see him in our seven grandchildren and three great-grandchildren. Hitler wanted to exterminate my extended family of fifty-eight people. Today, counting my family and my sister's family, we have almost reached that figure.

SWEDEN

Livia Fränkel

The story by Hédi's sister, Livia, documents another love story, as her husband's initial attraction—love at first sight—evolved into a lifelong union. Both she and Hédi end their stories with the same thoughts: their multigenerational families testify to successful efforts to replace the number of family members killed in the Holocaust. Livia, a member of the Jewish community of about twenty thousand, frequently lectures in schools about the dangers of antisemitism and xenophobia, arguably on the rise in Sweden. She recently received the Illis Quorum award, the highest honor of the Swedish government, for her contributions to Swedish society.

I landed in Stockholm, Sweden, in the summer of 1945 after spending one year in concentration camps. I was seventeen years old. There were a lot of refugees in Stockholm, most of them Jewish, and the community was keen to arrange parties to bring the Jewish youth together. In September of that year, I went to one of those parties with a friend. It was an evening of dancing and music. I was wearing a red dress. Suddenly, a handsome young man came over to me and asked me for a dance. He was tall, blond, and had blue eyes—exactly my type.

It turned out that, like me, Hans was a refugee, escaping Hitler at age seventeen when his parents sent him to a Zionist school in Hamburg. In 1939 when the war broke out, the school moved to Copenhagen, Denmark. When the Germans were about to deport all the Danish Jews, they were saved by the underground movement that, together with the Swedish authorities, smuggled them all to Sweden within one week. This was how the Danish Jews were saved by the Swedes, a very important part of history.

According to what Hans told me later and confirmed by his friend, when he first laid eyes on me—before he asked me for that dance—he remarked to his friend, "Do you see that girl in red?"

"Yes," he answered, "what about her?"

"I will marry that girl!!"

When we met, Hans was twenty-four years old, studying engineering at the University of Stockholm. We spent a nice evening together, and he asked me if we could meet again. We started dating, and we fell in love. But I had met a Swedish boy whom I was dating as well. Remember, I was only seventeen and really did not know what I wanted. I broke up with Hans a couple of times, but he refused to accept it; he just kept calling. So our relationship was off and on.

Finally, a year later, he proposed and we became engaged on New Year's Eve 1946. I had just turned nineteen. Our marriage took place on June 15, 1947, in the Great Synagogue of Stockholm. When I was a little girl, I had always dreamed about my marriage in a beautiful, long white wedding dress. When the time actually came, I could not afford a white gown. I wore a new tweed dress. I also needed a hat, so I borrowed one from my good friend Ella who had worn it at her wedding the year before. I had no parents, so only my sister and a couple of friends from the camp attended our wedding. They were invited for dinner at a nice restaurant afterward, but since we were very poor, everybody had to pay their own bill.

We managed to find a small flat on the outskirts of Stockholm where our new life began. In May 1948, I gave birth to our son, Dan. In 1951, our daughter Judith was born, and in 1955, our daughter Lis. Hans and I had a happy life together for more than fifty years. When he was seventy-three, Hans came down with Alzheimers. He passed away in December 2000. Today, I have a large family: six grandchildren and nine great-grandchildren, all boys. This is my revenge. Hitler did not succeed in exterminating us!

THE NETHERLANDS

Shulamit Reinharz

Following the German occupation of the Netherlands and ultimate deportation to death camps, it has been estimated that twenty-five to thirty thousand Jews like Shula's parents, Ilse and Max, went into hiding. About two-thirds of those hidden Jews stayed alive with the help of Dutch Gentiles who risked their lives. Nevertheless,

Shulamit's parents Ilse and Max Rothschild

in contrast to other countries invaded by Germany, only a quarter of Dutch Jews sur-
vived the Holocaust. Some have attributed this to Dutch deference to authority and
others to increased Nazi facility to discover Jews. Ilse and Max subsequently were
able to emigrate to the United States, where Shula grew up to become a sociologist,
influential founder, and retired director of the Women's Studies Research Center at
Brandeis University, and coeditor of this volume.

One evening in early winter 1938, Ilse Strauss and Max Rothschild, two
eighteen-year-old German Jews, were enjoying themselves with their friends
at a Zionist youth camp. Suddenly, thugs from a nearby village stormed into
the camp wielding clubs and savagely striking everyone they found. It was
November 9, Kristallnacht, the Night of Broken Glass, the nationwide violent
precursor to the Nazi's "Final Solution." It would be almost seven years before
Ilse and Max would again experience the calm of that evening.

Fast forward four months to March 1939. Ilse and Max crossed the border
into the Netherlands where they were accepted as farmhands and domestic
workers on Dutch farms. Fourteen months later, the German army invaded
Holland, bringing with them Nazi laws and practices. By 1942, Ilse and Max
could no longer avoid government orders to appear for deportation. They made
the brave move to go into hiding—she in the north and he in the eastern Dutch
town of Almelo.

Underground existence took a heavy toll on Max's physical and emotional
life. He decided that he had to meet Ilse in Amsterdam so that they could go
into hiding together. Jews could not be seen in public, so Max removed his
yellow star and somehow managed to pass as a gentile and buy a train ticket
to Amsterdam. From the perspective of seven decades, it seems a miracle that
neither the Dutch police nor Nazi soldiers discovered he was a Jew.

From that moment on, Max and Ilse were never apart, finding refuge together in the homes of Righteous Gentiles who were willing to risk their lives
to save Jews. Many years later, when I asked them why they did not marry
during that time, they told me that neither wanted to be a widow or widower
when the war ended.

Finally, after five years under Nazi rule in the Netherlands, Max and Ilse
came out of hiding and were free to marry and begin their lives. Their first step
was to be married in a civil procedure.

Seventy-five years after their wedding day, I came across their civil marriage
document, written in Dutch. Following are excerpts of the document in italics,
to which I have added explanations:

Today, October 10, 1945, appeared before me, Official of the Civil Registry of Rotterdam, in City Hall, with the intent to enter into marriage:

Rothschild, Max Israel (the Nazi regime had given all Jewish men the middle name of Israel; his middle name was actually Michael), . . . *adult son of Rothschild, Karl, physician, whose place of residence is unknown* (Max had not yet discovered that his father had escaped Europe and was living in Massachusetts) *[and] Katzenstein, Thekla, deceased.*

Strauss, Ilse Sara (the Nazis gave all Jewish women the middle name Sara; her middle name was Herta), . . . *adult daughter of Strauss, Heinrich, attorney [and] Gern, Therese, without profession, whose places of residence are unknown.* (Ilse knew that her father had died in the Gurs concentration camp, and she was quite sure that her mother had died in Auschwitz.)

I have asked the groom and bride whether they take each other as husband and wife, and [whether they] will fulfill the duties that are incumbent upon the marital status. After these questions were answered positively by them, I have pronounced, in the name of the law, that they are bound in marriage to one another. The document was signed by two witnesses and the bride and groom.

On January 6, 1946, Max and Ilse finally found a rabbi who could marry them. They gathered at the home of a relative in Amsterdam, where they were married in accordance with Jewish law. On that joyful occasion tinged with sorrow, Max used his Hebrew name, Yehiel, which means "God shall live," and Ilse used Aliza, which means "the happy one." The next day, in broken English, they sent a Western Union telegram to Max's parents who had escaped to the United States: "Had pretty chuppah with (relatives) and other friends. Were in thoughts with you. Masseltow from everyone. Your happy, Max Ilse."

Max and Ilse were my parents—I was born in Amsterdam in June 1946, a time of great hope for this little baby and for the world.

—⟋⟍—

MARRIAGE ISSUES IN ISRAEL

ISRAEL IS THE HOME of nearly half of the world's Jewry. It is unique in many ways: It is the only Jewish state, and, for the most part, it does not separate church and state. Since the time of the British Mandate before the formal establishment of the state of Israel, matters of personal status, including conversion, marriage, and divorce (also alimony, child support, custody, and inheritance) have come under the jurisdiction of the Orthodox rabbinical court system. This judicial system is headed by Chief Rabbis of the Ashkenazic and Sephardic branches of Judaism, leaders whose judgments reflect strict interpretation of *halacha* (Jewish law), an arrangement that many secular Israelis see as infringement on personal choice and freedom. This is especially true in relation to marriage.

The stories in this chapter demonstrate the difficulties, barriers, and challenges that some potential Israeli brides confront. One out of five Israelis chose to marry outside of Israel in 2016.[1] Like Ruth Carmi, whose story is included here, many choose Cyprus as a wedding destination because it is a short plane trip away. Ruth and her husband are active in IRAC (The Israel Religious Action Center), an organization that has led the struggle for religious diversity in Israel. An increasing number of Israelis like Ruth object to the stringent rabbinical rules regarding Orthodox marriage rites and procedures that brides are forced to follow in order to legalize their marriages in Israel. Israeli citizens who marry in civil ceremonies in other countries, however, are allowed to register as married when they return to Israel. Therefore, that is the route chosen by thousands of couples.[2]

Other couples, like bride Yael Yechieli, who describes her wedding in this chapter, marry within Israel but outside of the sanctions of the Rabbinate, denying the authority of the Orthodox establishment to limit their choices in the conduct of their ceremonies and who should officiate. Given that their marriage may be the most important commitment they ever make, couples want their wedding to be true to who they are. A recent article in the Israeli newspaper *Haaretz* reported a study that showed an uptick in the number of Orthodox Israelis who are opting to marry outside the dictates of the Rabbinate.[3]

Another problem for potential Israeli brides concerns who is considered a Jew. To be married as a Jew in Israel, couples must present evidence to the Rabbinate, usually including the Jewish wedding certificate (ketubah) of their parents, and for immigrants to Israel, a document from a rabbi of their former community attesting to their Jewishness. The number of people that Israel's rabbinic courts deemed ineligible to marry on account of their not being Jewish doubled between 2011 and 2018.[4] For the most part, the Israeli Rabbinate recognizes as Jews only those who have been converted by Orthodox rabbis. (And even then, there may be some question of acceptance of conversions that took place in other countries.) People raised as Jews may not be considered "Jewish enough" if, for example, a mother's conversion in the United States was not an Orthodox one. In order to marry in Israel, many people who consider themselves Jews have had to undergo conversion.[5]

In 2014, Israel's Central Bureau of Statistics announced that marriage rates in Israel had dropped by 2 percent and the number of couples who married abroad increased by 5 percent.[6] Although these percentages are small, a report issued by the Cummings Foundation concluded, "This development has tremendous implications for Israeli society. [This] 'quiet revolution' . . . may eventually bring the collapse of the official Orthodox dominance in Israel in matters of personal status."[7]

At the same time, in Israel today as in the past, many couples—those who are religiously Orthodox and those who are not—marry according to traditional religious law without much hesitation. This volume contains several stories of weddings that took place in Israel without the emotional and philosophical conflict that marked the proceedings in the stories highlighted in this chapter.[8] Or, at least, the authors of those stories didn't tell us about it!

CYPRUS

Ruth Carmi

In 2018, about eight thousand marriages of Israeli citizens took place outside Israel according to the New Family advocacy group.[9] "Why?" you may ask. Ruth's story

provides an answer: the ultra-Orthodox rabbinate has strict control over mar-
riage in Israel. The rabbinic establishment requires an array of religious practices
and formalities that some liberal Jews like Ruth and Menny do not wish to follow.
Other wives-and-husbands-to-be, including certain converts, some immigrants, and
some divorced people, are unable to gain official sanction for marriage in Israel. For
couples like these, there is an option: marriages performed in civil ceremonies outside
Israel are recognized as valid when couples return to Israel. Therefore, Cyprus, a
short plane ride away with no waiting period, is often the venue of choice.

My husband Menny and I met at the beginning of 2006 at a friend's party in Jerusalem. I was a lawyer working for IRAC (Israel Religious Action Center), the legal arm of the Reform movement in Israel. We moved in together six months later. I didn't want to get married; I never thought it was necessary. But Menny wanted to, so we got married in a garden in Abu Ghosh by a Progressive rabbi, the head of the Reform movement in Israel, with 350 guests in attendance. I was twenty-seven, and Menny was twenty-six. I wore a vintage white dress without a veil, and Menny was without a kippah. We composed our own vows and exchanged rings under a chuppah.

We knew that the marriage would not be recognized by the state of Israel or by the Orthodox rabbinate, which strictly controls Jewish marriage in Israel. Brides must go to a class about family purity, submerge in a mikveh before the wedding, and bring documents to the rabbi including their parents' ketubah. According to Israeli law, our marriage was not legal, as we did not register with the rabbinate, it was not performed by an Orthodox rabbi, and we did not follow Orthodox marriage rites and procedures. Initially, my father was skeptical (my mother is second generation from Russia, and my father came from Hungary as a child) but both my parents are open-minded and, along with Menny's mother, accepted our decision.

This was fine until 2010 when I was awarded a scholarship from the New Israel Fund, based on my work in human rights, to attend American University in Washington, DC, for a postgraduate degree in international law. I had no trouble getting a student visa, but the situation was different for my husband: The United States did not consider us a married couple, as our marriage was not officially recognized in Israel. Therefore, he could not come with me as a dependent and would have to leave after three months. We had to act fast, as we were scheduled to leave for Washington in a month.

We decided to go to Cyprus for a civil ceremony. This would allow us to be considered a legitimately married couple in Israel and would satisfy the US embassy. Cyprus, along with the Czech Republic and certain places in the United States, does not require a waiting period before a wedding can take place. Therefore, it is the choice venue for many Israelis who are deemed ineligible to be married in an Orthodox ceremony or, like us, choose not to.

With so many Israelis desiring civil weddings in Cyprus, travel agents offer different packages depending on the level of amenities. Some include lavish meals and hotel rooms for couples and their guests. Menny and I wanted only the basic formality. We flew to Larnaca, a city on the south coast of the island. There, we boarded a bus with five other couples that took us to the city hall. Some people changed clothes, but we did not. We went into a room where a marriage officer said something to us that I don't remember. We exchanged rings and signed a paper. After we waited a number of hours, we returned home. The next day we went to the Ministry of the Interior in Jerusalem and registered as married. When we went back to the US embassy for Menny's visa, we had a hard time explaining what we had done, but in the end, he got the visa we required.

ISRAEL

Yael Yechieli

Yael is one of a growing number of Israelis who are unhappy with regulations by the controlling Orthodox rabbinate concerning who can marry and in what manner. Yael and her husband chose to modify their ceremony in ways that satisfied Jewish law (halacha) as prescribed by the rabbinate, while embracing their own principles—an unusual path. She mentions opposition to the "purchase" of the bride by the groom, an ancient foundation of the wedding ceremony now symbolized by giving the bride a ring. In the couples' reinterpretation of Psalm 137 ("If I Forget Thee, O Jerusalem"), the agunot Yael refers to are women who cannot marry again because their husbands refuse to give them a Jewish divorce (the get), an issue of great concern in Israel and elsewhere.

I was raised in a traditional family with five brothers and sisters, one of whom is a rabbi. Because I questioned some of the beliefs and practices at home, it took me a long time to find a partner and decide whether I wanted to marry him. In the meantime, I became involved in the Jewish Renewal movement in Israel and was particularly interested in Jewish life cycle events and rituals. I was among the founders of an organization called *Hovayah* (a name meaning God), and by the time of my own wedding, I had already worked quite a bit with couples who wanted to create their own rituals.

In addition, I had developed a strong and well-developed feminist consciousness. Although some of my friends chose to forgo a ceremony altogether, I very

Yael and her husband at their nontraditional wedding

much wanted a wedding ceremony. At the same time, I knew that I would have a very difficult time with parts of the traditional Jewish ritual. I was particularly unhappy about the fact that in the traditional Jewish wedding, there is no mutuality between the partners. The man is the one who *buys* the woman, and he is the only one who speaks and greets the bride. She has no voice.

To my great delight, my partner identified completely with my perspective and agreed to join me on the journey of creating our own wedding ceremony. We wanted to express who we are and the values that we believe in. These are the values on which we intended to build our partnership.

It was clear to us that we were not going to be married by the rabbinate. Our study of the rabbinate has shown it to be a corrupt institution in many ways. The prejudice of the official rabbis makes it impossible for certain people to be married here in Israel—same-sex couples, those who are not Jews according to Orthodox ruling, couples of differing faiths, and others. We did not want to strengthen the institution.

Our wedding planning was made even more interesting and challenging because I come from a religious family, while my partner comes from a secular, atheist family. It was clear that it was going to be difficult for my parents to accept what we wanted to do. It turned out to be even more difficult than I imagined. The fact that we were not going to be married by the rabbinate and that we wanted to change the traditional ritual was very difficult for them. The period prior to the wedding was extremely tense because of our clash of values.

After lots of tears and repeated conversations with my parents, they came to understand that we were not going to be married by the rabbinate, and they came to terms with it. I agreed, however, and with great difficulty, to be married using some of the traditional language, including *dat moshe ve'yisrael* ("the religion of Moses and the People of Israel"). I accepted the idea of being purchased, and my parents said they would participate in the wedding if a close family member who is a certified rabbi would give the OK to what we were doing. In other words, we had an Orthodox wedding but outside the jurisdiction of the rabbinate.

The position from which we began shaping the ceremony was that the ritual was ours and that we had total responsibility for and ownership of it. To get started, we broke the ceremony down into various parts. It was clear to me that many of the changes that I wanted to carry out were possible from a halachic point of view; the problem is not halacha but rather the social expectations of what a Jewish wedding is. Referring to some of the changes we wanted, the rabbi with whom we consulted said, "In thirty years this is all going to be accepted, but not today." I told him that in order for it to become accepted in thirty years, we need to blaze the path now!

A rabbi did not conduct the ceremony. Instead, we chose my oldest brother, a significant person for us, and a brother of my partner. In hindsight, I am sorry that two men conducted our wedding. Today I would have asked my two sisters-in-law to take part. A woman friend greeted the people who had assembled. Our male and female friends held up the chuppah; it was important to us that they take part. We did not make many changes in the traditional text of the ceremony itself because that is what we agreed upon with my parents. But wherever it was possible, we adjusted the wording according to our own conception.

Under the chuppah, I gave a ring to my partner. I did not wear a veil because I shudder at the idea that the bride is covered. Prior to the ketubah reading, we said personal words to each other. Men and women pronounced the seven blessings. Both of us recited the *shehechiyanu* prayer, as well as the psalm, "If I Forget Thee, O Jerusalem." My partner broke the glass. Today, after the fact, we would have broken two glasses.

While we studied the meaning of the breaking of the glass, we understood that this was our opportunity in the ceremony to talk about what was broken in our world. Therefore, we read the following words:

Which Jerusalem do we mourn?

The Jerusalem of the prophet Isaiah, who cries out

"What need have I of all your sacrifices?" says the Lord.

And Isaiah demands, "Wash yourselves clean, put your evil doings away from my sight.

Cease to do evil. Learn to do good. Devote yourselves to justice. Aid the wronged. Uphold the rights of the orphan. Defend the cause of the widow." (Isaiah, chapter 1: 11)

We want to celebrate the future Jerusalem, a city that is a symbol of justice, a city that carries the peace flag, a city within which a society resides that takes care of the weak, the convert, the orphan and the widow, and which takes responsibility for one another.

And on this holy occasion, we shed tears about all the *agunot* who are left without a *get*, and we pray for justice that will be carried out, and that the vision of the prophet Isaiah will soon become a reality.

"I will restore your magistrates as of old and your counselors as of yore. You shall be called 'City of Righteousness,' faithful city, Zion shall be saved in the Judgment, her repentant ones in the retribution" (Isaiah, 1: 26).

On this Jerusalem, it is said, "If I forget thee, O Jerusalem, may my right hand wither. May my tongue cling to its palate, if I do not remember thee, if I will not promote Jerusalem to the top of my happiness."

The wedding was very meaningful for us and for those who were gathered. We were married on Friday morning opposite the walls of Jerusalem. Prior to the ceremony, we practiced meditation in a room next to the hall, and we invited all the guests to participate. The music at the wedding was that of wind instruments; the guests were mostly the circle closest to us—our family and our friends. After the wedding, my parents were able to say that our wedding was special, meaningful, and beautiful.

Since the wedding, a few couples are consulting with us who want to marry in a similar way, who want to shape their own ceremony. They want to choose what will be said and which people will take part. In the last few years, we see changes in weddings among segments of the Israeli public. A growing number of weddings are taking place outside the rabbinate. More couples are choosing to design their own wedding ceremonies, and we are happy to be part of this process.

NOTES

INTRODUCTION

1. Barbara Vinick and Shulamit Reinharz, *Esther's Legacy: Celebrating Purim around the World*, a collaborative project of Hadassah International Research Institute on Jewish Women at Brandeis University (now HBI), and Hadassah, The Women's Zionist Organization of America, New York, 2002.

2. See https://kulanu.org/.

3. See https://www.brandeis.edu/hbi/.

4. See Shulamit Reinharz and Sergio Della Pergola, *Jewish Intermarriage around the World* (New Brunswick, NJ: Transaction, 2009).

1. MEETING

1. M. Rosenfeld, R. Thomas, and S. Hauser, "Disintermediating Your Friends: How Online Dating in the United States Displaces Other Ways of Meeting," *Proceedings of the National Academy of Sciences* 116, no. 36 (August 2019): 17753–58.

2. COURTSHIP

1. "The Shidduch: How Jews Date," Jewish Practice, Chabad, https://www .chabad.org/library/article_cdo/aid/3716771/jewish/The-Shidduch-How-Jews -Date.htm#You.

3. BETROTHAL

1. The 2004 Israeli film *A Little Bit Different* poignantly depicts the consequences of breaking an engagement. The only dates the matchmaker can arrange for an ultra-Orthodox young woman are sadly unacceptable.

2. For a detailed discussion of the history of the dowry from biblical times to the present, see "Dowry," Jewish Virtual Library, 2008, https://www.jewish virtuallibrary.org/dowry.

4. CONVERSION BEFORE MARRIAGE

1. Reinharz and Pergola, *Jewish Intermarriage around the World.*

2. Peter Medding et al., "Jewish Identity in Conversionary and Mixed Marriages," *American Jewish Year Book* 92 (1992): 3–76.

3. Kylie Lobell, "Stop Saying Women Convert to Judaism Just for Marriage," August 23, 2019, https://www.jta.org/2019/08/23/opinion/stop-saying-women -convert-to-judaism-just-for-marriage.

4. Medding et al., "Jewish Identity."

5. THE INVITATION

1. Gavriel Zinner, *The Laws and Customs of the Jewish Wedding* (Lakewood, NJ: CIS Publishers, 1993), 19.

6. BEFORE THE WEDDING: MIKVEH AND HENNA

1. The oldest mikveh is in Siracusa, Sicily, discovered when the foundation for a new hotel was being dug. See Jacqueline Alio, "Europe's Oldest Mikveh," *Best of Sicily Magazine,* 2012, http://www.bestofsicily.com/mag/art421.htm.

2. See Inbal E. Cucurel, "The Rabinnate versus Israeli (Jewish) Women: The Mikvah as a Contested Domain," *Nashim* no. 3 (2000): 164–90.

7. THE WEDDING VENUE

1. Michael Kaufman, *Love, Marriage and Family in Jewish Law and Tradition* (Northvale, NJ: Jason Aronson Publishers, 1992), 153–54.

2. Anita Diamant, *The Jewish Wedding Now* (New York: Scribner, 2017), 27.

8. THE KETUBAH

1. Diamant, *Jewish Wedding Now,* 44.

2. Ibid., 49–60.

9. THE WEDDING CEREMONY

1. "Chuppah History and Traditions," *Rabbi Barbara* (blog), July 10, 2012, https://rabbibarbara.com/2012/07/10/chuppah-history-and-traditions/.

2. Ghila Krajzman, "Photos Reveal the Hidden Side of Hasidic Weddings," Forward, August 5, 2020, https://forward.com/community/452067/photos-reveal -the-hidden-side-of-hasidic-weddings/.

3. Aryeh Kaplan, *Made in Heaven: A Jewish Wedding Guide* (New York: Moznaim, 1983), chapter 19.

4. Maurice Lamm, "Wine at the Jewish Wedding," Chabad, https://www.chabad.org/library/article_cdo/aid/481775/jewish/Wine-at-the-Jewish-Wedding.htm.

5. Diamant, *Jewish Wedding Now*, 143.

10. AFTER THE CEREMONY AND BEYOND

1. "Yichud Room," Chabad, https://www.chabad.org/library/article_cdo/aid/477338/jewish/Yichud-Room.htm.

11. ARRANGED AND FORCED MARRIAGES

1. The Wikipedia article on "Forced Marriage" includes an extensive bibliography and covers the countries where such marriages are more-or-less common.

2. An ancient exception was levirate marriage, where a wife was required to sleep with her deceased husband's brother if she had not produced an heir for her husband.

3. Even Ha'ezer, 42:1—a section of Jewish law that treats issues of marriage, divorce, and sexual conduct.

4. Sanhedrin 76a.

5. The popular Israeli television series *Shtisel* provided an eye-opening view of the shidduch system to millions in the United States and elsewhere.

6. According to scholar Esther Schely-Newman, "Marriage is the most significant event in the life of women in the Judeo-Muslim cultural world; unmarried women are socially invisible." See Schely-Newman, *Our Lives Are but Stories: Narratives of Tunisian-Israeli Women* (Detroit, MI: Wayne University Press, 2002), 52.

12. INTERMARRIAGE AND INTERETHNIC JEWISH MARRIAGE

1. Elon Gilad, "Intermarriage and the Jews: What Would the Early Israelites Say?," Ha'Aretz, June 4, 2014, https://www.haaretz.com/jewish/2014-06-04/ty-article/.premium/intermarriage-and-the-jews/0000017f-e6f5-dea7-adff-f7fff4900000.

2. Ibid., 4.

3. See, for example, Molly Katz, *Jewish as a Second Language: How to Worry, How to Interrupt, How to Say the Opposite of What you Mean* (New York: Workman, 2010).

4. Gilad, "Intermarriage," 5.

5. Zinner, *Laws & Customs of the Jewish Wedding*.

6. Reinharz and Pergola, *Jewish Intermarriage around the World*.

7. Alan Cooperman and Gregory A. Smith, "What Happens When Jews Intermarry?," Comparisons of Generations, Pew Research Center Fact Tank, November 12, 2013, http://pewrsr.ch/18p813h.

13. WARTIME AND POSTWAR WEDDINGS

1. For an academic history of Swedish politics in World War II and after, see Ryszard Michał Czarny, *Sweden: From Neutrality to International Solidarity* (London: Springer Nature, 2018).

2. For a fictional account of such marriages, see Ayelet Gundar-Goshen, *One Night, Markovitch*, trans. Sondra Silverston (London: Pushkin, 2015).

14. MARRIAGE ISSUES IN ISRAEL

1. Brian Blum, "This Normal Life: Wedding in Cyprus—The Modern Zionist Irony," *Jerusalem Post*, November 24, 2016, https://www.jpost.com/opinion/this-normal-life-wedding-in-cyprus-the-modern-zionist-irony-473569.

2. Another issue concerns same-sex marriage. Although such marriages are banned in Israel, the High Court of Justice ruled to recognize same-sex marriage performed in other countries, allowing such couples to live in Israel as married partners.

3. Judy Maltz, "More and More Orthodox Israelis Are Ditching the Rabbinate, Study Shows," *Haaretz*, December 4, 2019, https://www.haaretz.com/israel-news/2019-12-04/ty-article/.premium/nearly-50-rise-in-orthodox-israelis-marrying-outside-of-rabbinate-study-shows/0000017f-dec9-db22-a17f-fef928bc0000.

4. "The Number of People Deemed Not Jewish Enough to Marry in Israel Has Doubled Over 7 Years," *Jewish Telegraphic Agency*, June 21, 2018, https://www.jta.org/2018/06/21/israel/number-jews-rejected-rabbinical-courts-not-jewish-doubled-last-7-years.

5. Judaism is based on matrilineal descent, meaning that recognition of who is Jewish is traced through the mother's lineage. In traditional Jewish law, someone is a Jew if born to a Jewish mother. Reform Judaism recognizes the father's line as well.

6. Jeremy Sharon, "Marriages in Israel Down but Wedding Abroad on the Rise," *Jerusalem Post*, August 21, 2014, https://www.jpost.com/diaspora/marriages-in-israel-down-but-weddings-abroad-on-the-rise-371906.

7. Shulamit Reinharz, "The Freedom to Marry in Israel," *Jewish Advocate*, June 18, 2007.

8. See stories from Israel by S. Grinhaus, M. Levkowitz, and L. Nitzan, as well as stories of Israeli weddings that retained cultural elements of Afghanistan (D. Shemesh), Ethiopia (A. Winer-Avraham), and Yemen (T. Avizemer and D. Rabbo).

9. "Up to a Third of Israeli Nuptials Held Outside State Religious Bodies—Report," *Times of Israel*, February 5, 2019.

INDEX OF BRIDES BY COUNTRY

Page numbers appearing in italics refer to illustrations

BARBARA VINICK coedited *Esther's Legacy: Celebrating Purim around the World* and *Today I Am a Woman: Stories of Bat Mitzvah around the World* at the Hadassah-Brandeis Institute of Brandeis University. She is secretary of Kulanu, an organization that supports isolated and emerging Jewish communities worldwide.

SHULAMIT REINHARZ is Professor Emerita and occupant of the Jacob Potofsky Chair in Sociology at Brandeis University, where she founded the Hadassah-Brandeis Institute, the Women's Studies Research Center, and the Kniznik Gallery of Feminist Art. Her books include *American Jewish Women and the Zionist Enterprise, Jewish Intermarriage around the World, The JGirls' Guide,* and *Hiding in Holland, 1942–1945.*

FOR INDIANA UNIVERSITY PRESS

Tony Brewer *Artist and Book Designer*
Brian Carroll *Rights Manager*
Dan Crissman *Trade and Regional Acquisitions Editor*
Samantha Heffner *Trade Acquisitions Assistant*
Brenna Hosman *Production Coordinator*
Katie Huggins *Production Manager*
Darja Malcolm-Clarke *Project Manager/Editor*
Dan Pyle *Online Publishing Manager*
Stephen Williams *Marketing and Publicity Manager*
Jennifer L. Witzke *Senior Artist and Book Designer*